Grand Disillusion

Grand Disillusion

François Mitterrand and the French Left

JOSEPH P. MORRAY

Westport, Connecticut
London

Library of Congress Cataloging-in-Publication Data

Morray, J. P. (Joseph P.), 1916–
    Grand disillusion : François Mitterrand and the French left /
Joseph P. Morray.
        p.   cm.
    Includes bibliographical references and index.
    ISBN 0–275–95735–7 (alk. paper)
        1. Mitterrand, François, 1916–   —Political and social views.
    2. Presidents—France—Biography.   3. Socialism—France—
    History—20th century.   4. France—Politics and government—1981–
    I. Title.
    DC423.M672   1997
    944.08—dc20   96–32466

British Library Cataloguing in Publication Data is available.

Library of Congress Catalog Card Number: 96–32466
ISBN: 0–275–95735–7

First published in 1997

Praeger Publishers, 88 Post Road West, Westport, CT 06881
An imprint of Greenwood Publishing Group, Inc.

Printed in the United States of America

The paper used in this book complies with the
Permanent Paper Standard issued by the National
Information Standards Organization (Z39.48–1984).

10 9 8 7 6 5 4 3 2 1

To my grandsons
Alexander and Andrew

My inner France, the only country that every man, white, red or black, can choose as the fatherland of the mind.

—J. Amrouche

Nulla salus sine Gallis
No salvation without the French

Contents

Acknowledgments

Since 1948 my wife, Marjorie Morray, and I have been returning to France, sometimes for sojourns as long as two years. Research for this book began in the early 1980s, always with her support and indispensable help. She read the manuscript at every stage. My debt to her is enormous, not only in the development of this project but in the writing of my previous books.

Among the many people in France who gave me time, information, and advice, I would particularly like to thank Denis Brulet of Agence France Presse for his assistance in arranging interviews. In dealing with the history of the Communist Party of France I had the benefit of an exchange of views with Roger Martelli, historian attached to the Institute of Marxist Research in Paris. Many long and pleasant evenings with our friends, author Henri Alleg and his wife, Gilberte, contributed valuable insights.

Joseph T. Krause, associate professor in the department of foreign languages and literatures at Oregon State University, made valuable comments on an early version of the manuscript and thereafter contributed encouragement and suggestions. The same is true of Richard H. Wiebe, an expert on French culture after years of teaching at St. Mary's College of California. I would also like to pay tribute to the memory of Morris H. Lax, with whom I maintained an extensive correspondence about France until his death in 1993.

Grand Disillusion

Introduction

> Democracy by its very existence generates the need for a world subsequent to the bourgeoisie and to Capital, where a true human community can develop.
>
> —François Furet
> *Le passé d'une illusion (1995)*

The election of François Mitterrand in May 1981 to become the president of France sent thrills of excitement through millions of people in Western Europe and the United States. Mitterrand was first secretary of the French Socialist Party, a leading party in the Socialist International, which since the 1920s had been focused on the search for an electoral road to democratic socialism in advanced industrialized countries. A majority of French voters in free and lawful elections had now declared: The time has come to give this man and his Socialist Party the power to implement their program.

Mitterrand had shown that he could win the essential support of Communists in his campaign for votes without yielding to them on questions of policy. He had led a coalition of forces of the left to an impressive victory.

Indeed, there were strong grounds for believing that a turn of historic importance was in the making. Capitalism had been under attack in France by eminent and respected thinkers for well over a century. Socialism was considered by millions of educated French men and women to be the next and necessary stage in mankind's progress toward a more rational and just organization of society. The Socialist Party had always appealed to that widespread expectation of progress growing out of rational critiques of capitalism. Many of its leaders, among them first secretary Mitterrand, had defined their program as a necessary "rupture with capitalism." In a book published in 1969 Mitterrand had written that it was the vocation of the left to come to the aid of the oppressed and the deprived, victims of class society.[1]

At the same time, the Socialist Party and Mitterrand were known to advocate respect for French republican institutions. They were consistent critics of Lenin and Bolshevism. French Socialism would be "French" in the absolute priority given to rights and procedures defined by the French Constitution. Through his long career, Mitterrand had molded his image as the shrewd champion of this peaceful evolution, this continuation of the French Enlightenment into its next stage.

The French Socialist Party had certainly earned the confidence placed in it by the nation as a party of trustworthy respect for human rights. Even among those who doubted the wisdom of its economic and social policies, virtually all regarded the Socialist Party as devoted to the French tradition, 200 years old, rooted in the "Declaration of the Rights of Man and the Citizen." This revered French declaration had been elaborated by its authors with a constant effort, assisted by Thomas Jefferson and the Marquis de La Fayette, to emulate the declarations of rights enacted in Virginia and other American states of the eighteenth century. The Socialist Party yielded to none in its commitment to the principles set forth in that declaration and in the Bill of Rights adopted as the first ten amendments to the U.S. Constitution.

This justified confidence in the respect of the Socialist Party for human rights as they are understood in advanced industrial nations of the West was undoubtedly a major factor in the second thrill of excitement that passed through Western Europe and the United States when Socialists, soon after Mitterrand's election as president, won an absolute majority in the French National Assembly. Socialism, it seemed, was about to be introduced into an advanced democratic country with scrupulous respect for human rights. The Scandinavian precedent existed. If France opted to set out upon such a Socialist road, as seemed possible and even likely following the elections in 1981, it would serve as a laboratory for all the capitalist world, including the United States and Canada. It would accumulate experience especially pertinent for the peoples of Britain, France, Belgium, the Netherlands, Italy, Spain, and Portugal, countries with democratic socialist parties and a strong attachment to human rights.

To one who sympathized with Mitterrand and shared in the excitement of his election, it seemed relevant to the political science of the Western world to explore how his opportunity had emerged. Were there lessons here for Americans as well as Europeans? It also was important to study the sequel to the elections of 1981. How would this new French revolution develop? With this in mind my wife and I resided for a total of three years in France during the period 1983–1988. We were fairly fluent in French, having spent an earlier year in France while I did graduate work in international law at the University of Paris.

In many ways France is still a pioneer and tutor to the modern world. Rich in history, reflection, and self-consciousness, it seeks to find original solutions to political, social, and economic problems like those confronting all of Western Europe and the United States.

Deeply marked by a long-developed heritage of feudalism and scholasticism, by the Protestant Reformation and religious warfare, by an Enlightenment that led to the French Revolution in the eighteenth century, the French take pride in independence of thought. They do not look for models to imitate but feel themselves chosen by destiny and tested by history for a leading role in all fields. From their inclination and capacity to think anew they continue to show a creativity worthy of close study, because it may offer lessons of importance to ourselves and others. For example, French reflections on the rebellion by youth in May 1968, with an accompanying unprecedented general strike by workers, have been studied with interest throughout the world. That month of French turmoil is still seen as a milestone event in the history of the century. Perhaps, in the long run, similar or even greater importance can be claimed for the French experience in 1981 of electing Socialists to govern the nation. It too challenges analysis and interpretation.

With the overthrow of feudalism in the eighteenth century, the French bour- geoisie was able to embark on 200 years of colonial expansion and industrial de- velopment. France became a great imperial power in the golden age of capitalism. The social evils that accompanied this accumulation of private wealth and national power were depicted in the novels of Honoré de Balzac and Emile Zola, in the poetry of Charles Baudelaire, and in the essays of Walter Benjamin. These works won their way into a universal culture of the Western world. And during the middle years of the nineteenth century, France was the country that revealed to Karl Marx a new movement taking place in social and economic life. This process of change, this "real movement," refracted by the minds of Marx and Frederick Engels, en- tered history under the name of communism.

The class struggles in France in the period 1848 to 1852 provided Marx with material for penetrating political analysis, set down in essays that are still read with appreciation by observers of the scene developing nearly 150 years later.[2] It was in the Paris Commune of 1871 that Marx found new evidence that his discov- eries and theories fitted French reality, and he tried to give this short-lived episode in French history universal significance.[3] It became another chapter in his attempt to illuminate the moving scene of man's struggle to master his fate. Many French are agreed, neither grudgingly nor proudly but as a matter of fact, that France was the birthplace of communism. That would seem to give it a unique place in contemporary history. Now that the Cold War is over, we are freer than before to study the history of Socialism in France objectively, giving due attention to the role played by communists as well as Socialists.

The Socialist Party of France has a long history. Founded as the French Section of the Workers International and known as the SFIO for the first seven decades of this century, it was the party of four figures of historical importance: Jules Guesde, Jean Jaurès, Léon Blum and Guy Mollet. Whether the name of François Mitterrand is now to be added to that distinguished list is a question to be considered.

Because this book is written for readers beyond as well as within France, an attempt is made to convey some understanding of the unique cultural norms that made it possible for a candidate of the Socialist Party to be elected president of the Republic in 1981. Of special importance in this historical background is the career of Jean Jaurès, who was assassinated in 1914. The struggles of Jaurès, scholar, orator, and parliamentary deputy, on behalf of the Republic and Socialism are now cherished as an exemplary chapter in French history. Jaurès is still a presence in the French spirit, thanks to his courage in defending Alfred Dreyfus and Zola in the "Dreyfus Affair" and to his talents and passion in searching for an evolutionary path to greater justice.[4] A deeply rooted tradition of paying homage to Jaurès has contributed to the willingness of several generations of the French electorate to give votes to candidates of the Socialist Party.

We will also need some knowledge of the history of the French Communist Party, since its policies were a factor in the rise of Mitterrand to the presidency. In the twentieth century, France has continued to be a focal point where a world-historical drama moves through its tragedies into human consciousness. The French Communist Party, born in 1920 as the French Section of the Communist International, found itself confronted in the 1930s with a growing fascist menace, the rise of Hitler in Germany and the rebellion of Franco in Spain. The creation of the Popular Front in 1936 by French Socialists, Communists and members of the Radical Party had an impact on movements to resist fascism in all countries of the industrialized world. The history of the Popular Front, its successes, failures, demise, and rebirth, as interpreted in partisan polemics, are active ingredients in modern political culture. Socialists, Communists and Radicals drew on this heritage to create the Union of the Left in the 1970s.

France was one of the great colonial powers. In the twentieth century came the ordeal of the loss of that empire. A wealth of complexity continues today in France's relations with its former colonial dependencies.[5] Many have chosen to remain within a loose commonwealth known as the French Community. A few have retained status as departments of the French state, entitled to representation in the National Assembly in Paris. Others have declared political independence and now enjoy recognition of their sovereignty. In all these French-speaking overseas territories, whatever their political status, French men and women are working as teachers, advisers, engineers, doctors, and in some cases as investors and business agents for French or mixed companies.

The French today are tested by one of the great challenges of the age: How can the advances in science and production techniques now practiced in Europe and the United States be made useful to the peoples of the Third World? What relationships will emerge in the "new international economic order"? This will be a post-colonial order in which many of the newly sovereign governments bravely aspire to play an active role in promoting the economic development of their peoples. Mitterrand took a great interest in these questions. To him the relationship of France and Europe to the Third World was of fundamental importance. His influence as minister and president made French policy toward the Third World a more complex and therefore a more creative adjustment to these problems.

France suffered an agonizing crisis in the 1930s as the power of European fascism mounted and took the form of an aggressive German imperialism within striking distance of Paris and the heart of French industry. It is still a cause for sorrow that French will to resist the invading German armies proved so feeble. It is understandable only when perceived in the light of political strife within France itself. The deeply divided nation was then governed by parties that dreaded a German triumph in Europe less than a return to power of the French Popular Front.

Marshal Pétain, a national hero since World War I, gave voice and leadership to a movement that accepted the German occupation as an opportunity to purge the nation of its communists and their sometime allies. The humiliation of defeat by the invading Germans was commonly described as a deserved scourge for having given authority through a democratic process to the parties of the Popular Front. The Vichy government proclaimed a rebirth of the nation, a new revolution in which Germans, French, and Italians would be invincibly allied to defend the heritage of European civilization against the menace of communism.

Suffering can be a way to wisdom, as Sophocles taught. Because in 1940 a majority of the French accepted their defeat and followed the Vichy government into collaboration with the Nazis, prejudice took root in American and British opinion. A nation that had chosen to descend behind Pétain into such an abyss seemed to have forfeited any claim to respect from the world. But that is a very one-sided view of French character at this stage of history. As might be expected, some wisdom was born from this suffering. It is true that the nation failed its test in 1940. That failure has been impressed in the French psyche as a bitter and shameful memory. For half a century the French have continued to reflect on it; undoubtedly they learned lessons that confer a dimension and a depth on French political and intellectual life.

Experience has taught the United States that its fate is closely bound up with that of Europe. In two great wars, American soldiers fought for their own country and interests on European soil. And since its creation in the 1940s, an Atlantic alliance has kept a major part of U.S. military forces in Europe. These profound commitments, borne at some pain and expense, have changed the relationship of the United States to Europe in a fundamental way.

It is now virtually axiomatic that the defense of the United States requires the friendly support and cooperation of the Western European nations. As a military fact of life, a real community now exists, built on the practices of generals and admirals who share on a day-to-day basis the task of planning and training for war in Europe. At that military level there is constant give-and-take and a growing interpenetration. In a development that seems irreversible, North America and Western Europe are one "zone of the interior," to use a military term, and the North Atlantic is no longer a frontier dividing one military sovereignty from others. During the Cold War that frontier was moved to the dividing line between Eastern and Western Europe. No one can doubt that this change in "providing for the national defense" by incorporating Western Europe is of enormous consequence to the peoples of Western Europe and of the United States. To military planners the Atlantic alliance generated an irresistible movement toward consolidation. The end of the Cold War has not led to any significant retreat from the responsibilities expressed in the NATO Treaty.

Yet it is important to note that France stands out for its resistance to this consolidation. General Charles de Gaulle fully appreciated the threat to French independence from the practice of military unification through the North Atlantic Treaty Organization. He withdrew France from participation in the military, though not the political, organs of NATO in 1966 and ordered the departure from French soil of NATO military facilities, including an elaborate headquarters for the general staff of the Allied Central European Command at Fontainebleau. That large hole in NATO's military jurisdiction has been a perennial irritant to American secretaries of defense and a complicating factor in preparing to defend the Western European portion of the new, extended zone of the interior. In December 1995 President Chirac announced that France would return to participation in the military committees of NATO. But this rapprochement is being utilized by France to push for the development of a "European pillar" of defense that would aim to function with greater independence from the United States.

People in the United States are aware that the French are frequently at odds with Washington, but there is a tendency to treat these warning signs lightly, to brush off such annoyances as superficial, meaningless, and incomprehensible quirks. France has never regained the respect in Washington it lost in 1940. And in most U.S. commentary on the problems of the world, France's positions are given little weight or even attention.

In Europe French policies are accorded close attention even when they are resisted. Given the importance of French wealth, population, and production in the European community, it is inevitable that France will be a major force in the development of Europe, now engaged in an intense debate over integration. The end of the Mitterrand era offers the occasion to examine these common problems from a French perspective. This will be done here with a view to discovering insights of significance to all countries in the Atlantic Community.

NOTES

1. François Mitterrand, *Ma part de vérité* (Paris: Fayard, 1969), 153.

2. Karl Marx, *The Class Struggles in France*, with an introduction by Frederick Engels (New York: International Publishers, 1935); Marx, *The Eighteenth Brumaire of Louis Bonaparte* (Moscow: Foreign Languages Publishing House, 1954).

3. Karl Marx, *The Civil War in France*, with an introduction by Frederick Engels (New York: International Publishers, 1940).

4. Max Gallo, *Le Grand Jaurès* (Paris: Editions Robert Laffont, 1984).

5. Mort Rosenblum, *Mission to Civilize: The French Way* (San Diego: Harcourt Brace Jovanovich, 1986).

2

François Mitterrand

All great things have many reasons why they should not be undertaken.
—Jean Baptiste Colbert

EARLY LIFE

François Mitterrand was born in 1916 in the village of Jarnac in a region of west-central France, Charente, famous for its cognac wineries. His mother's father, Jule Lorrain, owned an extensive domain in the region. In the home of this grandfather young François lived for seven years with his brothers and sisters under the tutelage of local priests hired to lay the foundation of their education. The atmosphere was one of privilege. A staff of servants helped raise the children and maintain the house. Mitterrand later said he had been brought up "in another century" and that it cost him effort to adjust to his own.

François's mother, Yvonne Lorrain, was a pious woman who noted in her journal that she tried to lift her heart toward God four times each hour. She attended Mass daily. She was also attentive to the intellectual formation of her children and encouraged François in his love of reading. Naturally, Catholic writers figured largely in his youthful studies.

François's father, Joseph Mitterrand, was descended from an aristocratic family that had lost property and standing during the generations since the Revolution. His education had been in the humanities, including Latin and Greek, and he aspired to make a career for himself as a journalist. Instead, he had to earn a livelihood as an administrative employee with a railroad company. When François was three years old, Joseph resigned from the railroad to prepare to take over management of a vinegar plant owned by Jule Lorrain, his opulent father-in-law. The genes of this frustrated intellectual undoubtedly gave François a bent for the cultivation of the spoken and written word.

The political atmosphere in the home of this strongly Catholic family was conservative and traditionalist, yet republican. They would probably be described as Christian-Democrats in today's categories. In the 1930s Joseph Mitterrand came out strongly against the Popular Front, yet he also had a Catholic and aristocratic distaste for capitalism. In later life François wrote that his parents regarded hierarchies founded on the privileges of money as "the worst of disorders." [1]

After completing his primary study at home under the supervision of priests, François was placed in Saint Paul School of Angoulême for his secondary studies. There for eight years he lived and studied during the school year under the supervision of diocesan priests. He was known as a pious youth who took Communion every day. Twice a year he made a religious retreat under the guidance of a Jesuit priest. His philosophy professor noted his "profound and meditative life." These years gave him an appreciation of Catholic schools and religious rites that he carried into his later life.

After his studies at Angoulême, François Mitterrand took up residence in 1934 in Paris to continue his studies at the Sorbonne and in the Faculty of Law at the University of Paris. At a boarding house directed by the Marist religious order he formed friendships to which he attached high importance then and in his later political career. This was a group of students who took the name of their address in Paris during those university years, "104 rue de Vaugirard." As president, Mitterrand found occasion to honor most of them with the Legion of Honor.

The environment during his years of study in Paris continued to be one of privilege among companions from moderately wealthy Catholic families. François is remembered as one of the more devout among them. He attended Mass regularly each week. He was active in the Young Christian Student movement and above all in the works of charity organized by the Society of Saint Vincent de Paul. He spent his Saturdays visiting homes of the poor, seeing French life from angles he had never known.

THE WAR YEARS

In October 1938, when he was twenty-two years old and passionately in love with the daughter of a Catholic family much like his own, Mitterrand was drafted into the French army. The next six years as a soldier and former soldier changed the focus of his life and developed his character. He was wounded in battle, imprisoned by the Germans and lodged in camps with thousands of other prisoners of war. His fiancée broke off their engagement. Some of the events of those years gave Mitterrand, no longer a practicing Catholic, the ambition to enter politics.

During the "phony war" (*la drôle de guerre*), September 1939 to May 1940, Mitterrand was in the ranks of the army as a second-class private, sharing with others of his rank the feelings of aimlessness, loss of time and confusion as to what France hoped to gain by its declaration of war. His officers seemed no more motivated than the troops.

In the spring of 1940 Mitterrand was on the front in eastern France, not far from Verdun, when the Nazi attack began. He was hit in the shoulder by shrapnel from an exploding German artillery shell, a wound that earned him the *Croix de Guerre*. He was placed in a field hospital that was soon overrun by the advancing Germans, who made prisoners of the patients and packed them off to camps in Germany. In several of these Mitterrand spent the next eighteen months. He later said he had learned more from that experience than in all his previous years under tutors, teachers, and university professors.

Mitterrand was kept in "stalags," camps for soldiers from the ranks. Here he lived in intimate contact with persons of all classes, including blue-collar workers, members of labor unions, Communists and former Communists, Socialists, students, peasants, vagabonds, thieves, priests, and atheists. He was fascinated to discover human experiences so different from his own, and he formed friendships based frequently on exchanges of revealing, unvarnished life stories. "Tell me of your life," he would say. "I have some things to teach you, but you have even more for me." While teaching French to a recent Jewish immigrant, Bernard Finifter, he listened to the experiences and views of a man formed by a strong Jewish tradition in conditions of discrimination and persecution. He formed a friendship with Patrice Pelat, who had gone to work in the Renault factory at age fifteen and joined the Communist Party. Many of the relationships Mitterrand formed in the prison camps endured for years after the war, and as a broad-minded politician he frequently had the benefit of frank opinions of persons from a wide range of backgrounds who could all speak to him as old friends worthy of his trust. Thus did his captivity prove an asset to him in his later career.

From accounts provided by his friends during his years in the camps, it is clear he did not stand forth as a champion of left political currents.

The prevailing view in the camps toward Pétain was to regard him as a hero and to pay him respect as their "grandfather," their protector. Most important to the prisoners, it was generally felt that Pétain was trying through his acceptance of the armistice and the humiliating occupation to gain the release of prisoners from captivity and in the meantime to improve their treatment at the hands of the Germans.

Mitterrand seems to have shared this sympathetic attitude of his fellow prisoners toward Pétain. So far as is known, he expressed no dissent from the marshal's judgment, expressed in speeches and messages directed to the prisoners, that France was suffering expiation for faults of its own commission in the period leading up to the Popular Front. Mitterrand was even seen in those days (1940–43) as an advocate of the "national revolution" Pétain was promising to lead from Vichy: glorification of the family, respect for work, community spirit, love of country and region, return to the soil.[2]

Mitterrand found opportunities to exercise his talents as a writer by editing a camp journal, *l'Ephémère*. He conducted courses on Voltaire and Rousseau and on life in the Latin Quarter.[3]

It would have been possible to make the most of all this enforced leisure by simply writing and lecturing and carrying out his camp chores in the infirmary. Something in him refused such quiescence. Choosing as a trusted companion a priest, *l'abbé* Leclerc, Mitterrand began to lay plans for an escape to the Swiss frontier, 360 miles away. In March 1941, in early morning darkness, they made their escape from the camp. For twenty-one days they hiked at night through snow and mud, sleeping in the forest in the daytime, speaking to no one, with nothing to eat but a few biscuits and pieces of sugar each day.

In the last village before reaching the frontier they were discovered and taken into custody. The priest was nearly dead from exposure and exhaustion.

Mitterrand was then assigned to a more securely guarded camp. In November 1941, he attempted his second escape with two other prisoners. He managed to board a train and reach Metz, which had become German territory following the German defeat of France. Once again, he was apprehended and condemned to be shipped to a camp in Poland with others who had attempted escape. His situation was desperate, so he risked all. He climbed over a fence and ran for his life while shots whistled around him. He had learned the address in Metz of contacts who would help him reach French territory.

In France at the frontier he was received by French railway workers who were organized as a Resistance unit. Mitterrand was strongly impressed by their Communist camaraderie and their ability to get him safely into a railway maintenance car and away from the frontier. He was still in occupied territory and subject to rearrest by German authorities if discovered. Nevertheless he made his way to Jarnac for a Christmas Eve reunion with his astonished parents.

In periods of difficulty or defeat in later life, Mitterrand was frequently heard to say, "I only succeeded in my escape on the third try!" He had been born with a strong streak of obstinacy, and he was sure that was a virtue.

At the beginning of 1942 the evolution in French opinion that finally led to the repudiation and condemnation of Marshal Pétain at the end of the war was still in a very early stage. Mitterrand had just emerged from the German camps, where the old marshal was still revered, even by those who welcomed the news, always very sketchy, of the movement to continue the war led by General Charles de Gaulle in London. The widespread view among the French was that Pétain was not a collaborator with the German enemy, but a proven patriot who was doing his best to lead the nation toward a recovery from its defeat. Such respected writers as François Mauriac, André Gide, and Antoine de Saint-Exupéry had helped mold a public opinion of unquestioning support for the old hero of World War I after his recall to public service as president in the hour of defeat.

Through friends of his family, Mitterrand found an opening in a government agency established at Vichy on Pétain's initiative for servicing the needs of French prisoners of war. This was an opportunity to work on the project that had been taking shape in his mind, preparing for the integration of thousands of returning prisoners when the war ended.

Mitterrand's decision to accept the post and take up residence in Vichy as an employee of the Pétain government began a period of activity that was later described by his political enemies as a skeleton Mitterrand wanted to keep hidden in the closet. In fact the ambiguities that surrounded his work were essential to the activities themselves. Mitterrand, like Maurice Pinot, who headed the agency, the Commissariat for Prisoners of War, was soon taking part in a Vichy-based movement of resistance to the Germans. One of Mitterrand's first assignments was the preparation of false documents in large numbers for shipment to the camps in Germany. With money provided by the Vichy government, Mitterrand traveled to Montmaur in the Alps Mountains to organize returning prisoners of war into one of the first groups of *Maquis*.

During this period Mitterrand was closely associated with Gabriel Jeantet, a theoretician of Pétain's "national revolution." Jeantet was founder of l'Amicale de France, a group of loyal supporters of Pétain, and editor of its journal, *France, revue de l'Etat nouveau*. Mitterrand wrote several articles for this review, expounding a few of the themes emphasized by Pétain in his public speeches: denunciations of the "international of money," of the bourgeoisie, and of the party spirit in politics. In recognition of his work on Pétain's behalf, Mitterrand was awarded *la Francisque*, a decoration reserved for those who had performed "national and social actions" before the war and demonstrated an attachment to the person and works of Marshal Pétain. The historian Pierre Péan presents the testimony of several witnesses who saw Mitterrand wearing the decoration. He concludes that the award was made in the spring or early summer of 1943.[4]

Mitterrand's sympathy with and support for Pétain, which are undeniable, have to be seen in company with his immediate entry into activities supporting the Resistance, which is also undeniable.

The situation in Vichy changed during 1942. The Gaullist movement of Free French, based in London, was gathering strength. The United States had entered the war against Germany. In November the Germans tore up the armistice negotiated with Pétain and occupied all of France. Acquiescence by Vichy merged into collaborationism. The notorious Pierre Laval, whom many supporters of Pétain considered to be a traitor to France, became prime minister of the Vichy government in April 1942. The Commissariat of Prisoners of War, to which Mitterrand was then reporting, was subjected to a reorganization by appointees named by Laval.

In protest at the new direction of policy, which included the replacement of Maurice Pinot by André Masson, fourteen members of the Commissariat resigned in January 1943, among them Mitterrand. They suspected that returning prisoners were henceforth to be indoctrinated in the spirit of collaborationism. In February 1943, Mitterrand met with several of these dissidents in the Creuse region to create an independent movement to be known as the National Rally of Prisoners of War (RNPG).

This organization became the principal vehicle of Mitterrand and Pinot for engaging returned prisoners of war in the Resistance struggle against the Nazis. Mitterrand had taken the name Morland for his clandestine work, and he was soon in contact with Henri Frenay, founder of the movement *Combat*. Frenay had the confidence of General de Gaulle. As a favor to Mitterrand, Frenay tried to overcome de Gaulle's hostility toward Mitterrand, which sprang at that time from Mitterrand's reputation as a Pétainist. Later, de Gaulle would have other grounds for finding fault with Mitterrand.

Mitterrand saw his first task to be that of combating Laval, especially his recruitment of returning prisoners of war into collaborationism. At a meeting for prisoners in the Salle Wagram in Paris in July 1943, Mitterrand managed to gain entry without being recognized by Laval's henchmen. While Laval was speaking, Mitterrand shouted out a few well-chosen phrases to break the spell and put Laval on the defensive. This turned out to be the high point of the meeting, and when the identity of the interloper became known, Mitterrand's credentials for courage were established. It also put his organization, the RNPG, in a good position for recruiting members against competition from the Vichy agency led by Laval and Masson.

The Germans were soon looking for "Morland," and on several occasions Mitterrand barely escaped arrest. He traveled widely in France, working to increase the effectiveness of the returning prisoners by incorporating them into administrative and combat units of the Resistance.

De Gaulle's movement was gaining ground, and Mitterrand realized it was necessary to gain the general's support for the RNPG if it was to have any prospect of playing a political role in postwar France. Mitterrand managed to get to London in November 1943, and thence to Algeria, where finally, after several rebuffs, he was received by de Gaulle.

The first interview between these two men went badly. De Gaulle expressed little interest in the prisoners of war, thinking it was a problem that could wait. He also had a nephew, Michel Caillau, whom he favored over Mitterrand for the task of representing the prisoners while the war continued. He was not impressed by Mitterrand's vision of the prisoners as a choice force in the reconstruction of France after liberation. He also did not like to see several different organizations competing with each other for prisoner-recruits, and he gave the order to Caillau to take steps to fuse them. As for Mitterrand, the general was not even willing to help him return to France. He discussed sending him to Italy, and Mitterrand has said it was his impression that de Gaulle saw in such a course an expedient for getting rid of him permanently.

Mitterrand did nevertheless manage to get back to London, with the help of General Montgomery, and from there to France by motor launch, arriving in February 1944.

Little by little, with his superior energy, tenacity, and resourcefulness he beat out Caillau in the work of fusing several prisoner organizations into one, the National Movement of Prisoners of War and Deportees (MNPGD). With support from his admiring friend, Henri Frenay, who had become de Gaulle's minister for prisoners, Mitterrand was offered the post of general secretary for prisoners of war. This would be the No. 2 position in a postwar ministry, an opportunity Frenay thought the twenty-eight-year-old Mitterrand would surely accept. He was mistaken. Mitterrand did not want an administrative post, especially not one that tied him into the government of de Gaulle. Relations between the two since their first meeting had deteriorated.

Since returning to France in February 1944, Mitterrand had been linking his own work among prisoners with the general plans of the Resistance for an insurrection against the Germans and the Vichy government. In London he had met the Communist leader, Waldeck Rochet, in a cordial meeting that helped Mitterrand win the confidence of Communists. The two were in agreement on the importance of independence of action for the internal Resistance. It was clear to both that de Gaulle, on the other hand, wanted the liberation of France to be achieved by invading Allied armies, among them the forces of the Gaullist Free French. De Gaulle did not want to be met on French soil by authorities installed by a victorious popular insurrection and supported by armed partisans led in large part by Communists.

This was the final year of the 1938–44 period that wrought such profound changes in Mitterrand's goals and ambitions. His contacts with Communists in their joint struggles of the war years were a factor in those changes. He followed up on his meeting with Rochet by arranging a friendly fusion with another prisoner-of-war organization created and led by Communists. Preparations were intense to mount an insurrection at the earliest possible date. The experience of working with Communists undoubtedly changed his attitude toward them; on both sides a new respect took root. And they shared a bias in favor of the internal Resistance over obedience to orders arriving from de Gaulle and his generals.

One week before the general uprising in Paris, Mitterrand led a group of prisoners of war into the headquarters of the General Commissariat of Prisoners of War, the Vichy agency from which Mitterrand had resigned in January 1943. In the spirit of rising rebellion against Vichy and the Germans, Mitterrand broke into this nest of collaborationists and ordered them to pack. With support from the armed partisan unit that accompanied him, the operation made the General Commissariat one of the first corners of Paris to be liberated.

De Gaulle was not appreciative. When the general received Mitterrand a few weeks later in Paris for their second confrontation, it went no better than the first. The general's first words to him were, "You again!" It was apparently at that moment that Mitterrand decided not to accept the important administrative post offered him in the Frenay ministry.

Mitterrand's close cooperation with the Communists deepened the rift between him and the general. Mitterrand later described the spirit of de Gaulle's return to France:

On returning to Paris, the General followed a rule of shunting aside the leaders of the internal Resistance, judged by him to be unreliable for having loved and served their country beyond his control and without his permission. There was nothing so dangerous in his eyes as a patriotism that was not stamped with the Cross of Lorraine.[5]

Mitterrand had been elected president of the MNPGD (National Movement of Prisoners of War and Deportees), a post beyond de Gaulle's control. Its journal, l'Homme libre, allowed Mitterrand to influence the views of returning prisoners, a gathering wave of 1,800,000 men and women who needed orientation and tribunes devoted to their defense. Mitterrand wanted to make of them a pressure group, not only in their own interests, but also as a force of renewal in the political parties. L'Homme libre soon found itself in competition with the Communist press in voicing the grievances of returning prisoners, many of whom felt they were not wanted in their own country. A campaign of criticism of the Ministry for Prisoners, the Frenay ministry, for not doing enough on their behalf generated still more tension.

This tension led to a third confrontation between Mitterrand and de Gaulle and consecrated their mutual hostility. The Communists organized a march in the streets and an assembly to demand redress of prisoners' grievances. It drew a crowd of 50,000. In the front rank of marchers, arm in arm with the organizers, was François Mitterrand. In response to the question, "Do we want to hear from the minister, Henri Frenay?" the crowd shouted "No!" Instead, the leaders proposed to seek an interview with de Gaulle. A delegation including Mitterrand marched to his office in the Ministry of Defense. They were sent home and told to await a call from the general. This came three days later.

De Gaulle was enraged. He took Mitterrand to task for editorials that had appeared in *l'Homme libre*. He was heard to say: "Mitterrand? Why he's a Communist."[6] According to his memoirs, de Gaulle threatened the delegates with immediate arrest unless they gave him a commitment in writing that they would strive to bring prisoner agitation in the streets to an end. The following day Mitterrand launched an appeal for demonstrations to cease. He was opposed to any encouragement to insurrection. According to Mitterrand's account of this crisis, he had joined the march and the assembly in order to counsel moderation.

Frenay, who knew Mitterrand better than de Gaulle did, proposed him for the most coveted of decorations, Companion of the Liberation. His name, however, was stricken from the list, undoubtedly by de Gaulle himself. Mitterrand could take some consolation from the citation issued by General Koenig, French military governor of Paris, on March 1, 1945, "for outstanding energy and inflexible will in spite of the greatest dangers," to François Mitterrand alias "Morland," the Cross of War with silver star.[7]

LAUNCHING INTO POLITICS

At the end of the war, Mitterrand was no longer the evangelist for a religious approach to the problems of French society. In 1944 he had married a Socialist, Danielle Gouze, who had her own credentials as a political activist and a member of the Resistance. His experiences in the prisoners camps and in the organization of returning prisoners of war gave him grounds to believe he had the qualities of character and intelligence to lead men and women in political struggle. But where and how to begin and with what program was not yet clear.

After a few half-hearted attempts to stake out a livelihood at writing and publishing, Mitterrand decided in 1946 to try to win a seat in the new National Assembly created by the Constitution of the Fourth Republic. After failing in a first attempt in Paris, he cast about for a department that offered a fighting chance for a newcomer and found it in the Nièvre, a department in the Bourgogne region of central France between Bourges and Dijon.

He was totally unknown there except among the former prisoners of war and their families, who helped him organize a campaign. His positions were still sufficiently undefined to permit him to attract votes from the left and right. He had financial help from the Marquis de Roualle and from businessmen. He won the confidence of the Church hierarchy as a champion against the Communists. In his "profession of faith," a formal declaration of his platform for the benefit of voters, he called for freedom of education, for resistance to the Communist Party, and for defense of the rights of property against decisions of the legislature.[8]

There was little here to announce the arrival of the future leader of the Socialist Party and an architect-to-be of a Union of the Left with Communists. Because he was not identified with any of the major prewar parties, he was free to present himself as a spokesman for moderate rightists and centrists concerned above all with a defense of their traditions and their property against the Communists. Thus did he win his first seat and launch his career.

In the usual fashion of deputies who seek to consolidate their position and multiply their responsibilities and contacts, Mitterrand also managed to get himself elected general-counselor of a canton (Montsauche) and municipal-counselor of a city (Nevers). Henceforth he made this region, into which he had "parachuted" to seize a political opportunity, his base of operations. He gave its inhabitants his time and attention, and over the years he succeeded in making himself one of their own, a favorite son in which they could take pride because he was putting himself and them in the eyes of the nation.

In France's situation in 1946, the question of fitting the Communist Party into the political structure dominated all others. The party that won 28 percent of the vote in the national elections, more than any other single party, was positioned to compete legitimately for influence in the Assembly and posts in the government. But it did not have the support of a majority of the electorate and therefore could not claim the right to carry through its revolutionary program of establishing Socialism under a working-class dictatorship. Mitterrand came onto the scene at a moment when it was essential for him to take a stand on the prospect of a continued advance in the ability of the Communists to win votes, leading perhaps to their winning an absolute majority in the not too distant future.

There was no question where he chose to take his stand. He was determined to launch his political career as a champion of that two-thirds of the French public that wanted the Communists defeated at the polls. He succeeded in 1946 in establishing himself in such a role, and throughout his career he continued to convince the nation of his fundamental opposition to the establishment in France of a state in which Communists would hold decisive power.

In Mitterrand's first ministerial post, that of War Veterans, to which he was named in January 1947 by Socialist Paul Ramadier, he was compelled to confront the Communists over a strike at the ministry that had begun before his arrival. He was only thirty years old at the time, and he faced some seasoned and tough opponents who were determined to retain their control of the administration of veterans' affairs. Mitterrand established his authority by dismissing several department heads and generally forcing the Communists to back down.

Communists had been serving in the provisional French government as ministers since Liberation in 1944. This practice continued through the beginning of 1947 in the Ramadier government that had named Mitterrand minister. But for several months the gradual dissolution of the wartime alliance between the United States and the Soviet Union had begun to affect the political atmosphere in France. Churchill had made his "iron curtain" speech at Fulton, Missouri, in March 1946, and in the spring of 1947 the containment doctrine of President Harry Truman was receiving its first airing before the U.S. Congress. The presence of Communists in the French government caused grave concern in Washington.

There were important differences between Ramadier and his Communist ministers on economic and social questions. These were exploited to bring a vote in which the Communists refused Ramadier the support he demanded. He then had the pretext he needed to bring to an end three years of Communist participation in governments. Many Socialists expressed misgivings at this turn in events, which seemed a response to exigencies of the Cold War rather than a change in the balance of political forces in France. Mitterrand was among those ministers who gave full support to Ramadier's decision to remove the Communists.

Mitterrand's second ministerial post was that of secretary of state for information in the government of Radical André Marie. Once again he found himself at loggerheads with Communists. He was given the task of reducing their influence in the programming of national radio broadcasts. This led to heated debates in the National Assembly, with Mitterrand defending himself from attack by the Communists and justifying his policies of hindering their use of state radio for Communist propaganda. In one exchange a Communist deputy declared that the country had come to loathe Mitterrand.

These first years of his public career were marked by bitter strikes and high tension in the context of the Cold War, but Mitterrand established a reputation as a vigorous and resourceful defender of the social order against the strivings of Communists to rise to a position of dominance in the political struggle. This was the platform on which he won re-election to the National Assembly in 1951.

Shortly after entering the National Assembly Mitterrand joined a centrist grouping, the Democratic and Socialist Union of the Resistance (UDSR). This was the first time he had chosen to pin to himself a label which included the word "socialist." It was another sign, in addition to his marriage to a Socialist, that he was projecting a different identity from that of his prewar years. Founded by René Pleven shortly after Liberation, the UDSR was close to the Radical Party in orientation, emphasizing a vain hope that the old prewar cleavage between right and left could be conjured away by rallying "resistants," that is, participants in the wartime Resistance, to a broad center coalition. By the time Mitterrand joined it in 1947, the left-right boundaries were clearly crystallizing once again, with the UDSR somewhere in the middle, harboring both left-leaning Socialists and conservatives with Gaullist sympathies.

In 1952 the UDSR published a brochure stating that it intended to lead the fight against Communism on all fronts.[9]

Justifying his work for his constituents during his years as deputy and minister (with eleven portfolios) under the Fourth Republic, Mitterrand wrote in June 1958:

I have always fought communism. I can assert, with confirmation from the inhabitants of

Nevers, that I have forced it to retreat in this department. I will fight without any weakness to save France from the horrors of a collectivist dictatorship.[10]

These statements expressed his clearly defined commitment to avert the installation in France of a dictatorship of the proletariat. On this point he was never enigmatic. That left open the question of the attitude he would adopt toward the French Communist Party in the event that it revised its ideology by excising the dictatorship of the proletariat from its program and convincing him that the change was sincere.

Early in his career, Mitterrand specified that he stood for a constant effort to win popular support away from the Communists. He gave great importance to the fact that in 1945 and 1946, some five million French men and women voted for Communist candidates. He refused to look upon these voters as pariahs irrevocably lost and impervious to his own message. He began to formulate the thesis that the road to progress and prosperity required a long and patient struggle to win over these Communist voters to a more moderate, reformist strategy for dealing with the problems confronting the nation. This fundamental respect for the millions whose votes he wanted to change proved an invaluable asset in his contests with the leaders of the Communist Party over the next decades.

The evolution of the UDSR gave Mitterrand his first opportunity to emerge as the leader of a party. When de Gaulle called in 1947 for the creation of a new party, the Rally of the French People (RPF), many Gaullists deserted the UDSR to answer the call. Mitterrand shrewdly encouraged the Gaullists to depart in a kind of self-executing purge that left the UDSR smaller but more unified around a centrist ideology free to fight de Gaulle's incipient threat to the Fourth Republic. Mitterrand used his wide contacts among former prisoners of war to recruit into the UDSR new members who looked upon him as their guide and support.

When René Pleven became president of the Council of Ministers in 1950, he named Mitterrand minister of African affairs. In this role, Mitterrand had the task of strengthening the ties of the French empire with the sub-Saharan African nations. He cherished the cult of the empire, which was a part of his education and, except among the Communists, an unexamined tenet of French patriotism. Strong currents of anti-colonial sentiment were flowing in Africa, and to deal with them Mitterrand gave his support to several progressive African leaders then viewed as dangerously close to the Communist Party. Two of these were Félix Houphouët-Boigny of the Ivory Coast and Sékou Touré of Guinea. They were members of an inter-African group known as the Democratic African Rally (RDA) which was respected by black Africans as leaders for the emancipation of their peoples from colonial oppression. Mitterrand thought a liberal approach on the part of French authorities toward such movements was the best way to ensure that they would see a future for themselves inside a restructured French Community. He consulted and negotiated with them, even though some of the RDA deputies elected to the National Assembly in Paris were accepting voting alliances in the Assembly with the French Communist Party.

Mitterrand's support for the RDA was condemned by the more conservative parties, including the Gaullists, as dangerously naïve. The president of the council, Pleven, seemed embarrassed by the problems raised by his minister of African affairs. The party of the Christian Democrats, the MRP, joined the Gaullists in demanding the eviction of Mitterrand from his ministry. When Pleven acceded to this pressure he caused a crisis in the UDSR, the party of both Pleven and Mitterrand. It began to divide into factions, with Mitterrand emerging as the dominant figure in the left wing of the party.

Pleven favored an alliance of the UDSR with the Gaullists. Mitterrand was adamantly opposed to this and proposed instead to seek an alliance between the UDSR and the SFIO, the party of the French Socialists. He was clearly moving to the left. He also became a critic of Pleven's policies in Indochina, where the rebellion led by Ho Chi Minh was gaining ground against French colonial authorities. Pleven saw his own influence in the UDSR slipping away. At the party congress in 1953 he refused to run for re-election, leaving the field clear for Mitterrand's election as president. Mitterrand's experience in this battle to win control of the UDSR undoubtedly contributed to his preparation for the more important struggle years later to become first secretary of the Socialist Party.

AGONY OF THE FOURTH REPUBLIC

The decade of the 1950s saw Mitterrand at the center of some of France's most agonizing struggles: Indochina, Suez, and Algeria. These ordeals in the forced reorientation of a great colonial power underlined again and again his rejection of the Communist Party, the only major party to receive any comfort and vindication from the defeats for colonialism.

In January 1952, Mitterrand took the UDSR into the short-lived government of Edgar Faure. At the request of the president of the Council of Ministers, Mitterrand prepared a report on the state of relations with Morocco and Tunisia. In this he called for more understanding of the North Africans' desire for a greater voice in the conduct of their affairs, while placing himself solidly in opposition to the Communists' call for encouragement of the forces of independence. The problem was, Mitterrand explained, to find the policies that would ensure France's continued presence in North Africa. This was also the position of another liberal, Pierre Mendès France, who would be closely associated with Mitterrand during the next several years.

Because the French elites in Morocco, Tunis, and Algeria were resistant to any changes that would give the North African peoples greater sovereignty over their affairs, the liberals in Paris saw a need to confront and weaken this conservative opposition. Mitterrand had an opportunity to make the point forcefully in 1953, when a combination of French colonial officials and the pasha of Marrakesh, without consulting Paris, deposed Mohammed V from the Moroccan throne. When the president of the council, Joseph Laniel, seemed inclined to accept the *fait accompli*, Mitterrand resigned his post as minister. The episode confirmed Mitterrand's reputation as a determined reformer of the colonial relationship.

The war in Indochina was going badly for the French. In 1954 the disaster of

Diên Biên Phu sealed their defeat and posed the question of negotiating a withdrawal. Having resigned from the Laniel government, Mitterrand was free to shift his support to Pierre Mendès France, who favored withdrawal. This shift was decisive in bringing down the Laniel government and installing Mendès France. Mitterrand was rewarded with an important portfolio, minister of the interior. This made him responsible for French policy toward Algeria, since under the Constitution, Algeria was divided into three "interior departments of France" with the same status as departments of metropolitan France.

When Algerians in their struggle for independence suddenly launched an attack on French police posts on October 31, 1954, Minister of the Interior Mitterrand reacted vigorously to restore order and take steps to defend the police and the populace against such acts of "terrorism." Given the dogma that ruled French opinion, it is hard to see how he could have acted differently and remained in the government.

"L'Algérie, c'est la France. Algeria is not a colony, not a protectorate, not a possession; it is a part of France itself, just like the Nièvre and the other departments distributed about the hexagon of metropolitan France." This was the myth drilled into French children at home and in school. Mendès France accepted it completely, as did the SFIO and its General Secretary Guy Mollet. And so did the UDSR and its President François Mitterrand. Even the Communists took some time to support independence for Algeria, although the PCF did immediately criticize the government, and specifically the minister of the interior, for the measures of repression ordered in response to the developing rebellion.

Mitterrand's "reformist liberalism" in this instance took the form of an advocacy of "evolution within the law and more democracy for Algerians." A statute calling for a limited integration of Algerians into French political processes had been on the books since 1947 but it had never been implemented due to opposition from the European residents (mainly French) of Algeria. Mitterrand now called for its resurrection and application. This brought forth a tempest of invective against Mitterrand in the National Assembly from the French delegates representing the European population of Algeria.

Another of Mitterrand's proposals was to fuse the police forces of Algeria with those of metropolitan France, a matter within his jurisdiction. His aim here was to introduce gradually into Algeria a police force obedient to Paris rather than to the hard-line colonials. Even the centrist Radicals condemned this proposal as "irresponsible." In the ensuing debate brought on by Mitterrand's policies, the Assembly voted the fall of the government.

Following elections in January 1956, President Coty invited Socialist Guy Mollet to form a government. This time Mitterrand was named minister of justice. Mendès France became foreign minister and Alain Savary minister for Morocco and Tunisia. One of the first acts of this government was to confer upon the French military authorities in Algeria full powers over the administration of justice. Mitterrand countersigned this decree and thereby made himself partly responsible for the brutal period of torture of Algerian suspects at the hands of the French military.

Mitterrand agreed with Mollet on the primacy of "pacification," meaning repression of the rebellion rather than negotiation. As repression aggravated the rebellion, Mendès France protested the government's handling of the situation, to no avail. He then resigned as minister. A few months later Alain Savary resigned in protest over the military's violation of international law in intercepting a Moroccan plane bearing Ben Bella and other leaders of the Algerian National Liberation Front. Mitterrand, however, did not resign. Neither did he join in the public protests against the use of torture by the French military. This was a year that won him no glory.

Mitterrand was also an active participant in the fiasco of intervention in Egypt in response to President Nasser's nationalization of the Suez Canal. The canal was operated by a privately owned company of British and French investors. Nasser's assertion of Egypt's right of sovereignty over an enterprise conducted within its national territory was viewed in France as an intolerable humiliation by a dangerous upstart. Worse, Nasser's radio was giving encouragement to the Algerian rebels, and at least one Egyptian-flag vessel was intercepted off the Algerian coast with a shipment of Soviet-made weapons.

A rage of chauvinism seized the French, fanned by the press. Nasser was likened to Hitler in articles appearing in *Le Monde*, supposedly a voice of the moderate and enlightened left. The government, headed by Socialist Mollet, declared Nasser's conduct intolerable and ordered the secret preparation of a military intervention in cooperation with the British and Israeli governments. The Communists earned credit for good sense by opposing, despite the national mood, this attempt to reassert "the imperial destiny of an advanced Europe."

Mitterrand, however, gave Mollet his full support. He compared Nasser's nationalization of the canal to Hitler's annexation of Czechoslovakia and urged the government to act quickly. When the military landings began in November 1956, Mitterrand went before the Council of the Republic to justify them. He was one of the many who then had to drink from the bitter cup served up by the United States, the Soviet Union and the British Labor Party (which on this occasion showed itself a great deal more liberated from imperialist enthusiasm than did the French Socialists).

Under irresistible pressure from the two great powers the invading military forces were compelled to do an about-face and withdraw, not in ignominy, but with embarrassment to all those who had made the crucial political decisions. Perhaps the cold bath, while not appreciated at the time, awakened Mitterrand to the need to adjust his thinking to the reality of the worldwide revolution against the old colonial order. He might have done this earlier had he not been in the government as minister when the series of crises arose in the mid-1950s.

Mitterrand was strongly committed to the defense of the Fourth Republic against the menace of its overthrow growing out of the troubles in Algeria. By 1958 the French military command in Algiers and leaders of the colonial population were fearful that the government in Paris lacked the will to continue the colonial war. Among them, sedition against the Fourth Republic became a call of duty. This developing crisis, which brought de Gaulle back into power after twelve years of retirement at his chateau in Colombey, proved to be a crucial test for Mitterrand. It helped to prepare him and the French public for his rise in later years to dominance and a secure place in the history of his country.

The prestige of the Fourth Republic had fallen so low that France was without a government for a month in the spring of 1958. President Coty successively summoned five party leaders to offer them the office of prime minister, only to have his offer declined. Mitterrand would certainly have accepted had it been offered to him, but the president ruled this out. Finally, in late April 1958, Pierre Pflimlin, a Christian Democrat and mayor of Strasbourg, agreed to try to form a government. In Algeria, even he was suspect, and the colonial press warned its readers that he would surely consent to negotiations and a "diplomatic Diên Biên Phu." Some generals let it be known that the French army was at the end of its patience with Paris. In the newspaper, *l'Echo d'Alger*, Alain de Sérigny launched a stirring campaign in the direction of de Gaulle: "General, speak out!"

On May 13, 1958, the day on which the National Assembly was to vote on the investiture of Pflimlin, a crowd of French civilians seized by force the seat of government in Algiers. In a plain act of sedition a "government of *salut public*," headed by General Massu, was proclaimed. The cries for de Gaulle to step forward and again lead the country grew louder. The National Assembly went ahead and voted to approve the designation of Pflimlin. Mitterrand, though not named to become a minister, voted in favor. He made it clear that he was opposed to the gathering movement to recall de Gaulle to power.

De Gaulle published a declaration to say his answer would be yes: "I am ready to assume the powers of the Republic." A well-known Gaullist, Jacques Soustelle, traveled from Paris to Algiers to establish a symbolic liaison between de Gaulle and the seditious movement developing in Algeria. In a press conference de Gaulle declined to condemn the participation of the generals in the sedition.

On May 24, French military parachutists, expressing their solidarity with the seditious generals in Algeria, landed in Corsica, occupied government buildings and established a Corsican "government of *salut public*." Troops sent from Paris to resist the move allowed themselves to be disarmed and in fact agreed to support the parachutists, as did the local police. Rumors were rife throughout France that a military coup would shortly put an end to the government in Paris.

How did the Socialist deputies react to this menace to the Fourth Republic? On May 26, they voted 117 to 3 to oppose the nomination of de Gaulle, saying it would be a violation of legality. Nevertheless, Guy Mollet, still their nominal leader, was urging Pflimlin to step aside; on May 29 Mollet went in person to Colombey to consult with de Gaulle, returning to Paris to add his support to the growing movement in favor of de Gaulle.

Pflimlin concluded that the Fourth Republic was dead, and he had no heart to fight to preserve it. Though he still could have won a vote of confidence in the Assembly, he chose to resign on his own initiative and create the opportunity for President Coty to call on de Gaulle. This the president was more than ready to do. He even threatened to submit his own resignation as head of state if the Assembly refused to ratify de Gaulle's nomination as head of government.

On the day Pflimlin resigned, a giant demonstration organized by Communists, Socialists, and other groups of the left marched from the Place de la Bastille to the Place de la Nation. Mitterrand took part. The cry from all throats was an echo from the embattled Spanish Republic of 1936: Fascism shall not pass! The crowds were clear in their opposition to a military coup, less clear in their assessment of the return of de Gaulle to head a government. Salutes of devotion to the Fourth Republic were notably absent.

Mitterrand thereupon embarked on a role as the most intransigent and eloquent opponent of de Gaulle in a period of years that provided him many opportunities to criticize and challenge on principle the man who was to dominate the French government for the next decade. In this long polemic Mitterrand would solidly establish his image with the nation as a skillful moralist battling for republican principles.

On June 1, 1958, de Gaulle became president of the Council of Ministers. He asked the Assembly to vote him full powers for a period of six months, during which he would propose changes in the Constitution and put them to the nation in a referendum. Mitterrand voted no, saying that the general had taken power through a *coup de force* after being called for by an undisciplined army.[11]

Mitterrand had chosen to swim against the current of the times. For the first time in his political career, he became a part of the opposition. Most of the deputies who had belonged to the group he headed, the UDSR, supported de Gaulle. One who chose to stay with Mitterrand in opposition was Roland Dumas, loyalty in a dark hour that Mitterrand never forgot.

In the referendum-plebiscite on de Gaulle's constitutional changes, Mitterrand campaigned in his district against them. Except for the Communists, he was virtually alone. The national vote in favor of the changes was 79 percent.

In November 1958, Mitterrand had to run for election to the new National Assembly. He was defeated, losing to a little-known Gaullist.

A FIGHTER AGAINST DE GAULLE

Though he had been admitted to the bar in 1954, Mitterrand had never practiced law. Now it was necessary to earn a living, so at age forty-two, after having been minister of justice and minister of the interior, he had to learn his profession as an assistant to more experienced practitioners. Some of the judges before whom he appeared took pleasure from the occasional embarrassment of the illustrious debutante and commented from the bench on the ironies of his fate. But the lawyer, Irène Dayan, with whom Mitterrand formed a professional partnership and who worked hard to help him learn the procedures and formalities, came to the conclusion that her junior partner had outstanding talents for the practice of law. Soon he was winning cases on his own. One of these was his defense of a film company accused of producing a licentious movie based on the novel of Choderlos de Laclos, *Dangerous Liaisons*. He was able to draw on his wide reading of literature to enrich his performance as an advocate in court for artistic freedom from censorship.

But to Mitterrand, the return to political action, not the practice of law, was the principal goal. The main enemy to be engaged was of course de Gaulle and his band of "usurpers." Their regime he labeled "the conspiracy of May 13th," always emphasizing its origins in the seditious French military and colonials of Algiers. His plan for a comeback in national politics called for the creation of a non-Communist coalition of Socialists, democrats, republicans and liberals. The Communists, he insisted, were not the principal enemy in the situation created by de Gaulle's dominance: "The danger that menaces liberty and progress comes at present from another quarter. Sufficient to the day is the evil thereof." Every force that would help defeat the Gaullist coalition was to be welcomed.

Nevertheless, while fighting Gaullism with all available allies, including the Communists, it was also necessary, he wrote in 1959, to prevent the Communists from advancing to positions of dominance. This required building a "strongly structured" non-Communist left. The history of postwar regimes in Eastern Europe known as Peoples Democracies showed what would happen wherever this was lacking. Mitterrand's strategy for the long run, destined to leave a permanent and distinctive mark on European politics, was taking shape in his mind and in his formulations.[12]

Though Mitterrand was living and practicing law in Paris, he continued to make the department of the Nièvre his political base. In 1959 he successfully ran for two offices, that of mayor of a small town in his department, Chateau-Chinon, and a month later that of senator for the department. This latter office gave him status once again in the national Parliament, though still no seat in the more powerful National Assembly.

The SFIO, the Socialist party of the day, was at a low point following de Gaulle's triumph. There was a general feeling that the non-Communist left was definitely in need of restructuring, so Mitterrand's strategy was being born at the right moment. With what remained of the UDSR, Mitterrand joined in a new initiative called the Union of Democratic Forces (UFD). Its dominant figures were Pierre Mendès France and Socialists Daniel Mayer and Edouard Depreux. However, they lacked the will to build the group into a real political party, and Mitterrand had insufficient influence at that time to win control and use the group as an instrument of his own strategy.

The year 1959 inflicted on Mitterrand a trial that bruised his spirit but clarified the nature of his struggle and fortified his self-reliance. This was the scandal that grew out of his association with Robert Pesquet, a former deputy representing the Poujadist far right. Rumors circulated of plans to assassinate political figures who were the most outspoken critics of the seditious generals. Pesquet contrived to meet Mitterrand and inform him that the plot was a reality and that Mitterrand headed the list of targets. Pesquet claimed that he had for a time been a willing participant in the plans, but that he was filled with remorse and now wanted to save himself and Mitterrand. According to Mitterrand, Pesquet asked and Mitterrand promised not to give Pesquet's identity to the police. Perhaps because Mitterrand did not fully trust the police, he kept these warnings to himself.

After three meetings with Pesquet, in which the likely place and manner of the assassination attempt were described, Mitterrand noted while driving toward his home in Paris near midnight on October 16, 1959, that he was being followed. He tried to evade, then stopped and leaped from his car into the gardens surrounding the Paris Observatory. As he fled into the darkness, several shots from an automatic weapon riddled his car. Mitterrand then went to the police. Still he did not mention his conversations with Pesquet.

Pesquet called a press conference and announced that the assassination attempt had been staged by himself with the complicity of Mitterrand as a means of destabilizing the government.

When Mitterrand tried to discredit Pesquet by giving his account of their earlier meetings, he was met by skepticism, quite understandably, in the newspapers and Parliament. His failure, until forced by Pesquet's declarations, to come forward with information important to the investigation of a crime aroused suspicion. The premier, Michel Debré, a Gaullist, called for a criminal investigation of Mitterrand's role. In the Senate a motion was presented to lift Mitterrand's parliamentary immunity from prosecution. The motion was a direct attack on his honor and integrity. The Gaullists had a field day, and a majority of the Socialists and the center (e.g., Jean Lecanuet) also turned against him. The vote to suspend his immunity carried by 175 to 12. Only the Communists, a few Socialists (Gaston Defferre, Emile Aubert) and a few independent senators (Edgar Faure, Edgard Pisani, Pierre Marcilhacy) supported Mitterrand. The outcome of the vote was undoubtedly a grievous blow, and at the time many supposed he could never recover. But for Mitterrand, the experience proved to be a descent into hell from which he returned stronger than ever.

Mitterrand was formally charged with the crime of "outrage on the Court," substantially the same as obstruction of a criminal investigation. When Pesquet later came forward and cleared Mitterrand of any complicity, the prosecution lapsed without a trial. Mitterrand did not seek further vindication against Pesquet, perhaps because he concluded he was well out of an affair in which his own conduct had hardly been exemplary.

Mitterrand's explanation of this ordeal was that he had fallen into a trap. He had unwarily allowed himself to be taken in.[13] Most people came to accept this account, though for a long time his opponents in the heat of debate liked to use the code word "observatory" to throw him off balance by evoking anew the painful embarrassment and humiliation he had suffered.

A weaker person might well have concluded that his blunder foreclosed his ambition to rise to the highest positions of leadership. To Mitterrand the setback served to crystallize a renewed determination to prove to himself and to others that he had the qualities to lead the nation out of its fascination with de Gaulle. Throughout these years in the wilderness Mitterrand concentrated on opposing the general on every major issue, making himself the most intransigent critic of "the hero of June 18, 1940." Mitterrand stood for the proposition that the de Gaulle of 1958 was a dangerous dictator, a violator of the legality of republicanism, a vainglorious general who was abusing his prestige as founder of the Free French movement to reduce the French to the status of subjects in a virtual monarchy. He summed up his attack in a pamphlet published in 1964, *The Permanent Coup d'Etat*.

The death blows administered to the Fourth Republic by de Gaulle, ratified by overwhelming votes in popular plebiscites, left the Socialist (SFIO) and Radical parties weakened as political contenders. In the legislative elections of 1962, the SFIO received only 11 percent of the vote. In Paris and most major cities, new political clubs sprang up, most of them searching for ways to renew and strengthen the non-Communist left and prepare its strategy for the future. Mitterrand gave these new clubs close attention and sought occasions to attend their meetings and express his views. These small groups had to serve him in lieu of a national forum, since he was not welcome as a speaker at the congresses of either the SFIO or the Radical Party. When he made enquiries through his friend Charles Hernu as to whether he might be accepted as a member of a new Socialist Party, the PSU, being launched by Pierre Mendès France, Michel Rocard, Gilles Martinet, Jean Poperen, Edouard Depreux, and Pierre Bérégovoy, he was told that not one of these notables would vote for his admission.

That he nevertheless had the capacity for a comeback from the depths was suggested by his electoral success in his home department of the Nièvre. At the height of de Gaulle's popularity, in the 1962 referendum that ratified the general's proposal to make the presidency an office elected by direct popular vote, Mitterrand campaigned in vain against it. Yet one month later after another determined campaign he was elected to return to the National Assembly as a deputy, a much better vantage point for his campaign against de Gaulle than his seat in the Senate. He was emerging as a formidable adversary, a candidate for the unofficial role of "counter president."

AN AMBITION TAKES HOLD

The new Constitution and the referendum establishing the direct election of the president meant that political campaigning would be dominated by the contest for that newly powerful office, which would be independent of votes in the National Assembly, with a term of seven years and the possibility of running for re-election. Mitterrand concluded that with these changes in the Constitution, even though he had opposed them, the only course for him was to prepare to become a candidate for the presidency.[14]

With Louis Mermaz and a few other personal friends who had stood by him, he helped form the League for Republican Combat. This small group then fused with the Jacobin Club led by Charles Hernu to become the Center of Institutional Action (CAI). In 1963 Mitterrand was named president of CAI. Hernu said that its purpose was to organize the democratic and Socialist left.[15] After further recruitment and mergers, the CAI became the Convention of Republican Institutions (CIR). This was to become an important group over the next several years, because it was dominated by Mitterrand and his closest friends as one of their principal instruments of action. It will be referred to many times in the account of Mitterrand's activities of the 1960s.

Georges Brutelle, a leader in the SFIO, was at this same moment looking for ways to revive and enlarge the influence of his party. He organized seminars and study groups to address the question of how to renew and revive the left. On the invitation of Brutelle, Mitterrand began to attend these gatherings, where he surprised the other participants by professing an attachment to the ideals of Socialism. He expressed himself in 1963:

I say to our organized socialist friends: There is no divergence among us. When it is a question of choosing friends, enemies, the battlefield, the future for our country, I believe truly that socialism is the only response to our Gaullist experience. That is my position on principle.[16]

Guy Mollet was still the leader of the SFIO, and he needed allies in the endless competition among the different currents of his party. He made it clear that he was not averse to Mitterrand's approach to the party and his proclaiming himself a new champion of Socialism. Further, in his courtship of Mollet and the SFIO, Mitterrand could make use of some of his past actions as minister in the old Fourth Republic, especially the loyalty he had given Mollet, then the embattled prime minister, in the trials of 1956 over Suez and Algeria.

An important difference between Mitterrand and the SFIO, including the Mollet current, was their view on relations with the Communists. Mitterrand brought a bold new line, fitted to the new challenge of presidential elections. He wrote in December 1963 that the Communist Party was contributing to the struggle against de Gaulle: "Four to five million voters who are of the people, workers, vote communist. To neglect their participation and their votes would be culpable or simply stupid."[17]

Here was a clear statement rooted in electoral pragmatism. Mitterrand was still primarily engaged in his struggle against de Gaulle. In that struggle, which over the years had molded for Mitterrand a unique position in French politics, he found himself in a de facto alliance with the Communist Party. The Communists, too, had consistently opposed de Gaulle since his return to the political scene from retirement in 1958. The Communists regularly denounced de Gaulle on grounds of class struggle. He was depicted as the loyal servant of the bourgeoisie, obedient to the spirit of the nineteenth century, hostile to the rise of the working class to an independent and aggressive activity in political life.

Though Mitterrand did not employ the concept of class struggle in his speeches and writings, he did join the Communists in denouncing the bourgeoisie as a privileged, greedy sector of society protected by Gaullism. To Mitterrand, the "wealthy bourgeoisie" was another useful epithet in belaboring that social evil, money, against which he had been inveighing since his early Christian days.

This de facto alliance against de Gaulle did not arouse suspicions that Mitterrand was secretly a sympathizer with Communist goals. Far from it. There was too much evidence in Mitterrand's life and career to make any such suspicion credible. He had been publicly at odds with Communists on numerous issues, notably on France's attempt to suppress the Algerian independence movement. As minister of the interior in the Mollet government, Mitterrand had regularly denounced the Communists for their opposition to government policy on this and other issues.

In more philosophical discussions, in books, speeches, and articles, Mitterrand had defined himself as one who found the Communist program for France contrary to his deepest principles and beliefs. He was as vehement as any public figure in his denunciations of Soviet and Communist policies in Eastern Europe.

The French Communist Party was evolving behind the leadership of Waldeck Rochet toward an emphasis on electoral struggle, independence from the Soviet Union, utilization of the institutions established by de Gaulle, and Eurocommunism as a means to promote reforms and strengthen its position by forming an alliance with the SFIO. In a later chapter this evolution will be explored in some detail.

Gaston Defferre, the mayor of Marseilles, emerged as a leading spokesman for a strong anti-Communist stand by the SFIO. His announcement of his intention to run for the presidency in 1965 seemed to pre-empt the field and exclude Mitterrand from endorsement by the SFIO. Fate shaped events differently from Defferre's hope. His strategy called for an alliance of the SFIO with the Christian-Democrats, who shared with him an aversion to any contact with the Communists. He hoped to be the creator and champion of a Socialist-centrist coalition that would run against de Gaulle and the Communists.

Bowing to necessity, Mitterrand indicated he would support Defferre, whose standing in the SFIO gave him a strong claim to be the candidate of the Socialists. But while declaring his support, Mitterrand also indicated that he had reservations. In June 1964, when the Defferre candidacy was still building, Mitterrand stated before the Convention of Republican Institutions that, despite some misgivings, he judged it necessary to support Deferre, because he was a Socialist and the choice of his party.[18]

Defferre's attempt to forge an alliance with centrist groups failed, and he decided to abandon his candidacy rather than seek support from the Communists. Mitterrand was rewarded for his dutiful support. The moment was ripe for the advancement of a candidate whom both Socialists and Communists could endorse.

Fortunately for Mitterrand, the other logical candidate from the left-of-center sector, Pierre Mendès France, chose not to run. He did not wish to give countenance to de Gaulle's contested constitution by seeking the presidential office it established. Maurice Faure and Daniel Mayer, who each could claim a right to enter the lists against de Gaulle as a candidate of the left, also declined the challenge. No one expected any opponent of de Gaulle to receive more than 20 percent to 25 percent of the vote, and few would court such a political disgrace. Fate thus cleared the way for Mitterrand.

The Communist Party leadership communicated to Mitterrand that it would support his candidacy. This was crucial to Mitterrand's strategy and made the election a testing ground for his bold initiative. Having asked for and received the endorsement of Mendès France, Maurice Faure, Daniel Mayer, Gaston Defferre, and the head of the SFIO, Guy Mollet, Mitterrand delivered the declaration of his candidacy to the press on September 8, 1965. It was a model of moderate republicanism, the statement of a sober, safe, and responsible opposition to the general.[19]

The name chosen by Mitterrand to identify the electoral alliance supporting his campaign was the Democratic and Socialist Federation of the Left (FGDS). This was how he was identified on the ballot, a last-minute campaigning opportunity to sway votes in the voting booth. It is significant that he judged the French electorate to be ready for an appeal in the name of democratic socialism. He was also trying to clarify his place in the political spectrum as an aspiring leader of the left, a term broad enough to embrace Socialists, Communists and progressives of many different stripes. He had campaigned for office many times as a centrist against Communists and Socialists in his department of the Nièvre. Now as he embarked on his first nationwide campaign, he ceased to identify himself as a centrist. He was deliberately striving to imprint on the national consciousness an image of himself as a man of the left, at home with Socialists as long as they were "democratic."

Leftist intellectuals were skeptical. Editorialists in *Le Monde* and in *France Observateur*, leading journals to the left of center, coldly greeted the Mitterrand announcement with calls for Mendès France to become a candidate. Professor Maurice Duverger in *Le Monde* said it was necessary to find a candidate with a personality to inspire confidence. Jean Daniel in *France Observateur* thought Mendès France would have a better capability to unite the opposition against de Gaulle. But these appeals did not move Mendès France, who made good on the endorsement he had promised Mitterrand by responding to Daniel on October 28th in a letter to *France Observateur*: "Mitterrand is the best one to unite the ensemble of democratic and socialist votes. I do not see how one can continue to hesitate. I will vote for him and ask those who have confidence in me to vote for him."

There was little reason to suppose that the militants of the SFIO would campaign vigorously for Mitterrand, who was not one of their own. In the search for a nationwide corps of campaign workers, Mitterrand relied mainly on the personal loyalties developed during his years as a prisoner of war in German camps and as general secretary of the National Movement of Prisoners of War and Deportees during and following the German occupation.

Mitterrand turned his lack of formal party affiliation to good account. He was free to make his campaign as the champion of a broad sector he designated as the "left." The word evoked a sense of opposition to de Gaulle on the basis of a vaguely suggested solidarity against the privileges of the wealthier classes. It was broad enough and vague enough to embrace everyone who resented the inequalities of opportunity in French life. His campaign tapped the dormant springs of working-class enthusiasm, the memories of the Popular Front from the period of the 1930s. This suited the strategy of the Communist Party, which guided its adherents and sympathizers, after soul-searching debate in the central committee, toward support for Mitterrand.

Yet Mitterrand did not mention the Popular Front or echo the language of Communists. He capitalized on his past to reassure those who above all wanted to keep the Communists in check. By omitting attacks on the Communists, another departure from his earlier campaigns for election in the Nièvre, he fostered a sense of unity in a broad popular sector that included the Communists. This campaign launched Mitterrand in his chosen role as the leader of a voting bloc that he had the skill to draw together by addressing his appeal to the left. In his cultivated phrases, "left" was a respectable and reassuring word, and yet at the same time a promising word. It could embrace all the diverse hopes of a discontented society that longed for reforms without anguish, for change without shock. It promised progress in material and social life without specifying how this was to be achieved or even what was to be sought. When looked at closely, the concept of the left leaves unanswered the question: Left of what? It is a word that hints at class consciousness as a positive force to be called into play, but the hint remains to be developed. In 1965, the concept was as ambiguous as it was suggestive, which made it a useful rallying cry in building momentum for an election.

Mitterrand made the presidential campaign the beginning of an effort that looked beyond the attempt to unseat de Gaulle in the short run. It became the occasion to mobilize the contentious parties of the left through de facto cooperation toward a shared goal without requiring any wrenching commitment to a more formalized declaration of unity like that of the Popular Front. Mitterrand made the real weakness in his prospects of winning, which all recognized, a point of departure for building a new coalition for the future. This was to be his strategy for a struggle of long duration.

By way of program Mitterrand conciliated every group in the embryonic coalition by adopting something from each. From the SFIO he took an ardent defense of both European unity and the Atlantic alliance, along with a sweeping condemnation of de Gaulle's economic and social policies. From the Radical Party, he reiterated emphasis on individual liberties, and from Gaston Defferre, nationalization of banks. From the Communist Party, he borrowed nationalization of some industries and opposition to allowing trusts and cartels to dominate Europe. There was no reason to suspect Mitterrand of insincerity in defending these positions. Some of them he had already supported before becoming a candidate, and all of them seemed to fit together well enough to form a coherent image.

Most important, no one could question his confrontation of the general on the issue of personal power as a violation of a revered republican tradition. In addition to his systematic opposition to de Gaulle in the Senate and the National Assembly, he had recently issued a pamphlet condemning Gaullism as "a permanent *coup d'état*," depicting de Gaulle as another "little Napoleon," like Napoleon III, who had also used a national referendum to confirm his destruction of the Second Republic in 1852. Three others with similar opposition to de Gaulle were Mendès France, Roland Dumas, and Charles Hernu; they were conspicuously rallying around Mitterrand as their champion in challenging the general. So were the Communists, who since 1958 had also been unrelenting in their criticism of de Gaulle and his Constitution.

That Mitterrand was creating a truly new force in French politics appeared in a surprising addition to his program: support for greater sexual freedom for women, specifically for the practice of contraception. He had freed himself from his Catholic tutors. That was a bold and risky advance at a time when the feminist movement provoked such strong antipathy that it could doom any candidate associated with it. Mitterrand brought the issue into the mainstream of French politics, thereby moderating its emotional charge and absorbing it as a feature, along with numerous others, in a program of reform on behalf of human liberty.

The six weeks of his campaign produced a steady gain in momentum. Mitterrand strove successfully, with some lyricism, to make the left a pole of popular emotion. At Lyon he linked it to French generosity, to love between peoples, to hope even in conditions of misery.[20]

The climax of the campaign came in Toulouse, where standing before an enthusiastic crowd of 35,000 people, Mitterrand stirred their emotions with the salute, "Citoyennes et citoyens," words that subtly evoked the French Revolution. Those who wished could find in his use of this phrase a suggestion of willingness to go further down the road toward a new revolution than the candidate could declare outright. Was it pure electoral demagogy or a lifting of the veil on his intentions?

De Gaulle was still the heavy favorite to win on Election Day in December 1965. Numerous candidates of the center and right were certain to receive some votes. The still doubtful question was whether the general would receive an absolute majority of the votes cast in the first round of voting. If Mitterrand received only 25 percent as predicted, de Gaulle would be declared winner without the need for a second round.

When the votes were counted and Mitterrand was found to have received 32 percent, the country took it as a sure sign that a new force had come on the scene. In the second round two weeks later, Mitterrand's vote had climbed to 45 percent.

It was obvious that Mitterrand owed his success in part to disciplined support from Communist voters. The campaign of 1965, in which a candidate supported by the Communist Party made such a good showing, influenced the party to move further and faster toward cooperation, for electoral purposes, with Socialists and Radicals who had also given their support to Mitterrand. Such a Union of the Left, however, was still opposed by Guy Mollet and most of the SFIO and the Radical Party.

OVERREACHING IN 1968

As a result of his surprisingly effective campaign, Mitterrand had acquired status as the principal leader of the left, even though the group he headed, the Convention of Republican Institutions, had no deputies in the Assembly other than himself.

His first project following the presidential election was to fuse the SFIO, the Radical Party, and the Convention (CIR) into a federation with authority to select a unified list of candidates for the legislative elections of 1967. Since the Communists were excluded from this fusion, it was accepted by the SFIO and the Radicals. It kept the name used during the campaign, the Democratic and Socialist Federation of the Left (FGDS).

Mitterrand also proposed the creation of a "shadow government" modeled on those named in Britain by the party out of power. He won approval from his federation partners and soon acquired a new title as "Contre-président" with authority to designate a cabinet of ministers who would provide a concrete alternative government competing for votes from the electorate. These shadow ministers were drawn from the non-Communist left. Mitterrand announced that he and his coalition were prepared with a program to assume the full responsibilities of government. Some were amused, others infuriated by his cool presumption.

But this federation was not yet a Union of the Left, because the Communists were still not included. Mitterrand in 1966 was trying to persuade the FGDS to begin formal talks with the Communist Party in preparation for the 1967 elections. Messages were passed between Mitterrand and Waldeck Rochet, general secretary of the PCF, indicating their agreement that the time had come for such an effort at cooperation. The two of them met formally in December 1966, heading their respective delegations, and reached agreement on "désistement" in the second round of elections to the legislature. This meant they promised each other that the candidate of the left for an Assembly seat who won the most votes in the first round would be aided by the withdrawal of the other left candidates so as not to divide the left vote in the final round.

Gaston Defferre, who still wanted to see an alliance between Socialists and the center (for example, the group around Jean Lecanuet), complained that Mitterrand was using the tactic of the *fait accompli* to have his way. Mitterrand's position on these contrasting types of alliance was that one did not exclude the other. He was not yet ready to insist that the SFIO decide in favor of a Union of the Left at the cost of alienating the center. During the campaign for the legislative elections, Mitterrand frequently expressed warm praise for Lecanuet, even though Lecanuet had made it clear and continued to do so that there could be no question of his cooperating with the Communists in any way.

The strategy of "désistement" helped increase the number of FGDS deputies to the Assembly from ninety-one to 116. The most striking gains were made by Mitterrand's CIR, which increased its representation from one (Mitterrand himself) to seventeen. The Gaullist coalition held on to a majority in the Assembly, but it had been reduced to one vote, assuming that Lecanuet and the center would continue to vote as an opposition to the rightist government.

At the end of 1967 Mitterrand and the FGDS seemed to have solid grounds for optimism. But in May 1968 the dramatic revolt of students at French universities suddenly changed the political picture and sent Mitterrand once again to the sidelines after a bold initiative that failed.

The student revolt grew out of boredom with the Gaullist regime and with the moderate, traditional, and orderly strategies of the opposition parties to win power for themselves. The Vietnam War had stirred campus agitation in France no less than in the United States. There were real grievances of the students against university administration, connected with the great growth in the student body in the previous decade. To everyone's surprise, on May 10, 1968, thousands of students took to the streets in Paris, waving banners condemning the government, the system, consumerism, the bourgeoisie, the French Communist Party, the administrations of the universities, President Johnson and the United States. "Make love, not war!" "Power to the people!" "Power to the imagination!" Maoists, Trotskyists and anarchists were conspicuous in the excited scenes of frolic covered by the press and television. Barricades went up; cars were overturned and burned. The government reacted with force, giving the Communist Party the issue of police repression on which it could focus its own protests.

The Communist leader of the General Labor Confederation, Georges Séguy, called for a manifestation in Paris on May 13th in opposition to the government, declaring the solidarity of his union against the use of force by the police. The other big labor union, the French Demcratic Confederation of Labor (CFDT), joined in this call. Millions were in the streets, most of them chanting such anti-Gaullist slogans as "Ten years are enough!" Workers accepted the order to cease work and occupy their factories. Condemnation of the government developed into the largest strike in French history. Workers had their own grievances and demands that had nothing to do with student discontent. The events of May 1968 had these two separate aspects. Together they were a formidable threat to the stability of the regime.

De Gaulle tried unsuccessfully to restore order with a television address on May 24 and the promise of a referendum. He then flew secretly to Baden-Baden to consult with the commander of French military forces in Germany as to how to deal with the crisis. He was seriously shaken by events in Paris and considered resigning, according to the commander who received him. He did not return to Paris until May 28.

On May 28 Mitterrand stepped into the limelight with a proposal that proved to be a costly mistake. At a press conference he envisaged the defeat of de Gaulle in the "plebiscite" that the general was proposing in the form of a referendum. In that case Mitterrand proposed that Mendès France assume the leadership of a provisional government pending the outcome of an election of a new president to replace de Gaulle. Mitterrand immediately added, before anyone asked, that he himself would be a candidate in that presidential election. With this proposal he laid himself open to the charge of too eagerly trying to exploit the crisis to serve his personal ambition. His nomination of Mendès France to head the provisional government seemed a transparent device to take this potential rival out of the running for the presidency.

De Gaulle undermined Mitterrand by canceling the referendum, calling instead for dissolution of the Assembly and new legislative elections. A huge Paris street demonstration on May 30 in support of de Gaulle, marked by much mockery of "Président Mitterrand," showed that a backlash against student anarchy and workers' strikes was working to the general's benefit.

In the ensuing elections it was clear that de Gaulle had won the battle. The federation headed by Mitterrand, the FGDS, dropped from 118 to fifty-seven seats in the Assembly. Mitterrand retained his seat after being forced into a runoff vote. His closest supporters, those in the Convention, were all defeated. The new Gaullist government, headed by Couve de Murville, who replaced Pompidou as prime minister, had an increased majority in the new Assembly. Mitterrand's esteem had plummeted. The Communist Party, however, had weathered this storm without serious losses and retained thirty seats.

Close association with Mitterrand seemed to have become a political handicap;

the cement of interest that had previously bound the FGDS together began to dissolve. There were maneuvers to replace Mitterrand as the president of the FGDS, to oust him from the federation's voting group in the Assembly, and to abandon the federation. Mitterrand decided not to fight for this organization that now seemed too loose and undisciplined to serve as an effective vehicle for a long struggle. He announced his resignation as president of the FGDS.

During this period Mitterrand moved to clarify his identification with socialism, thereby preparing his campaign to play a dominant role in the renewal of the SFIO. In one statement he said he believed in the socialization of investment, production and exchange. This, he said, would create an important publicly owned sector capable of pulling the whole economy.[21]

He was still the unchallenged leader of the group of his friends assembled in the CIR. Its document on these questions published in 1968 engaged the responsibility of Mitterrand:

Because they are consistent democrats, socialists believe that real democracy cannot exist in a capitalist society. It is in this sense that the Socialist Party is a revolutionary party. Socialism makes its objective the common good and not private profit. The progressive socialization of the means of investment, of production and exchange is its indispensable base. Economic democracy is, in effect, the distinctive characteristic of socialism. Socialist transformation cannot be the product and sum of reforms correcting the effects of capitalism. It is not a question of adjusting a system but of replacing it with another.[22]

That these were also Mitterrand's views was made clear in an article he wrote for *l'Express* a few years later (1971), commenting on the evolution of his ideas during this period. It had become evident to him, he wrote, that socialism was the only response to the problems of today's world. That meant putting an end to the present system in which money is king. He continued:

Socialism means that a people collectively takes charge of its own destiny. It is in itself revolutionary because it is a rupture with the established social and economic order. But there is not the slightest chance of success without creating a large party. Having understood that, I drew the consequences.[23]

Mitterrand had many times indicated his ambition to win the highest office in France through the ballot box. Was his conversion to Socialism based simply on an electoral calculation? He claimed to be sincere in the views he then began to publish as his own beliefs, reached from study and experience. What seems most important and worth stressing in examining his life and career is the state of public opinion in France.

If Mitterrand was indeed ambitious, it is interesting that he saw in the Socialist Party a prospective winner in the electoral struggle. Coming from the center as he did, he could have evolved in either direction. If his choice was indeed rooted in calculation, it was an indication that Socialism, in his judgment, was on the way to winning acceptance with a majority of the French people. If the event proved him to have been accurate in that assessment, it would be an extremely important revelation as to the likely future course of French history. Have the French people in their majority, evolving in conditions of freedom, come to accept as desirable a change from capitalism to Socialism? Mitterrand's subsequent career will be a series of tests that shed light not only on his character and views, but on the state of opinion in France.

Mitterrand offered to the SFIO a strategy that made use of the evolution of the French Communist Party away from an attachment to Leninist Bolshevism and toward an emphasis on electoral struggle. Since 1962, the party had been trying to win the SFIO's assent to the generation of a "common program" of government that could serve as the basis of an electoral alliance aimed at defeating the parties of the right and the center. In adjusting to the new Constitution, which gave great importance to the office of a president elected by direct popular vote, Mitterrand saw in such a Union of the Left around a common program a promising vehicle for his own ambition. One of the great ironies of the period is that the decline of the Communist Party (as the Socialists ascended to power) began in earnest with its finding in Mitterrand a Socialist who was receptive to its initiative.

The Soviet Union's use of tanks to end the "Prague Spring" in August 1968 seemed to make any kind of agreement between Communists and Socialists out of the question for the time being. Still, it is significant that the French Communist Party denounced the Soviet intervention and criticized the Soviet leadership. The party was moving to change its image as subservient to the Soviet Union. At a central committee meeting in Champigny in December 1968 under the leadership of Waldeck Rochet, a manifesto was issued stressing the aim of a peaceful transition to Socialism. The manifesto emphasized the strategy of joining with the SFIO around a "common program," the strategy of union, with the goals of establishing an "advanced democracy" and winning the support of a majority for the transition to Socialism.

Mitterrand did not attempt to run in the 1969 presidential election. His star was in eclipse. De Gaulle precipitated the election after 53 percent of the electorate voted in a national referendum against his proposals for a reform of the Senate and the regions. Since he had called on the public to vote in favor of his plan as an expression of confidence in his leadership, he responded to the defeat by resigning and retiring from public life.

The Gaullists nominated Georges Pompidou, the longest-serving prime minister under de Gaulle (1962–68), as their candidate. With Mitterrand out of the picture and the SFIO moving toward the center in its search for allies, the Communists ran their own candidate, Jacques Duclos.

Despite the unfavorable climate, the Communist campaign focused on the need of the parties of the left—SFIO, Radicals, and Communists—to come together on a "common program." In the first round Duclos won 22 percent of the vote. The candidate of the SFIO, Gaston Defferre, who was strongly supported by Pierre Mendès France and centrists, received only 5 percent. This humiliation confirmed the opinion of many Socialists that a renewal of their party was absolutely necessary. It helped clear the path for the reorganization that brought Mitterrand into the party at its highest level.

No party of the left had enough votes to qualify for the second round. In that round Pompidou defeated Alain Poher to become president for a seven-year term. Here too the division between Communists and Socialists worked to the advantage of the Gaullists. Socialists called on their supporters to vote for Poher; the Communists said it was a question of Tweedledum and Tweedledee (in French, *bonnet blanc* and *blanc bonnet*) and called for an abstention from voting.

One month later, at its Congress in July 1969, the SFIO changed its name to Socialist Party. Guy Mollet resigned as party leader. The question was: Who would succeed him? Mollet's wish on this question would carry great weight, probably enough to determine the outcome. Prior to the Congress, Pierre Mauroy had been Mollet's candidate to replace him as leader with the new title of first secretary. But at the Congress Mollet inexplicably shifted his support to Alain Savary, a change that left Mauroy embittered. This switch had important consequences in the maneuvering within the party in preparation for the next congress at Epinay in 1971.

In 1969, Mitterrand was still not a member of the Socialist Party; in the National Assembly he described himself as "unaffiliated." He had, however, begun his campaign for a fusion of his group, the CIR, and other socialist-oriented groups into the new Socialist Party and for his election as first secretary. He was not yet formally a member, but he was already a candidate for the top position. Mollet scoffed at this presumption; Mauroy helped bring it to pass.

NOTES

1. François Mitterrand, *Ma part de vérité* (Paris: Fayard, 1969), quoted in Catherine Nay, *Le noir et le rouge* (Paris: Bernard Grasset, 1984), 29.

2. Since the publication of the book by Pierre Péan, *Une jeunesse française, François Mitterrand 1934–1947* (Paris: Fayard, 1994), there is no longer any doubt that Mitterrand was a supporter of Pétain during the period 1940–43.

3. Nay, *Le noir et le rouge*, 94.

4. Péan, *Une jeunesse française*, 294. In memoirs written after his retirement and published posthumously, Mitterrand admitted he had accepted *la Francisque*, saying he had committed an error of judgment. François Mitterrand, *Mémoires interrompus* (Paris: Editions Odile Jacob, 1996), quoted in *Le Monde* (Paris) April 23, 1996.

5. Mitterrand, *Ma part de vérité*, 23.

6. Nay, *Le noir et le rouge*, 129, quoting René Pleven.

7. Translation of part of text reproduced in the Appendix of Nay, *Le noir et le rouge*.

8. Nay, *Le noir et le rouge*, 149.

9. Ibid., 156.

10. Ibid., 158.

11. Ibid., 244.

12. Ibid., 249–50.

13. Danielle Mitterrand, interviewed by Christine Okrent in *L'Express* (Paris), February 29–March 6, 1996. See also Danielle Mitterrand, *En toutes libertés* (Paris: Editions Ramsay, 1996), 99–105.

14. Mitterrand, *Ma part de vérité*, 47.

15. Nay, *Le noir et le rouge*, 273.

16. Ibid., 275.

17. *Le Courrier de la Nièvre* (Nevers, France), December 10, 1963, quoted in Nay, *Le noir et le rouge*, 276.

18. Nay, *Le noir et le rouge*, 277.

19. Ibid., 283.

20. Ibid., 288.

21. Ibid., 311.

22. Ibid., 311.

23. *L'Express* (Paris), June 21, 1971, quoted in Nay, *Le noir et le rouge*, 315.

3

The Congress of Epinay

The 1971 congress of the newly renamed Socialist Party opened on June 11 in the town of Epinay. No one seems to have realized as it began that the potential existed for a profound shake-up. It was widely assumed that Guy Mollet and his allies would continue in control of the party.

In accordance with the usual custom, each faction in the party had prepared and circulated a motion expressing its views of the strategy the party should follow until the next congress. At Epinay there were five such motions, identified by a letter, but usually referred to by the names of the principal leader or leaders supporting the motion. At the outset, a vote was taken to determine the support in the congress for each motion. The count showed the following distribution:

Mollet-Savary	33.5%
Mauroy-Defferre	28.5%
Mitterrand	15.8%
Poperen	11.9%
CERES (Chevènement)	8.5%

Since no faction had a majority, the outcome of the congress depended on alliances negotiated by the leaders of the factions and on the willingness of the delegates to follow their leaders in carrying out the alliances negotiated when crucial questions were put to the vote.

This congress, almost unnoticed when it opened, proved to be one of the decisive events in the history of the left in France. It shed light on the functioning of the Socialist Party and on the character and skills of François Mitterrand.

Gaston Defferre represented the far "right" in this Socialist assembly. He was allied with the more centrist Pierre Mauroy, because these two Socialist notables represented important federations of the Socialist Party and both were interested in preserving control over their regional patronage. Above all, they wanted the party to improve its ability to win votes, which had declined in recent years under the leadership of Mollet. Because the faction formed by their alliance was relatively well-disciplined behind these two powerful regional leaders (Defferre in the Bouches-du-Rhône and Mauroy in the north), the play for their 28.5 percent of the delegates' votes would be intense. Mitterrand had to win their support to stand a chance of emerging with a majority. Undoubtedly, Mauroy's pique with Mollet (over having been abandoned at the previous congress in 1969 as candidate for first secretary against Savary) played a part in the outcome.

Mitterrand's big problem in winning support from Defferre lay in the question of the creation of a Union of the Left with the Communists, which Mitterrand advocated and Defferre had always adamantly opposed.

But Mauroy agreed with Mitterrand that the strategy of a Union of the Left (*Union de la Gauche*) was now ripe for a trial. Furthermore, as fate would have it, Mauroy happily found in this question a convenient ground for criticizing Mollet, whom he wanted to see defeated. Mollet was advocating ideological talks with the Communist Party as a precondition of forming the Union of the Left. Mauroy argued that if these talks on ideology proved successful, they might go too far and open the door to a merger of the two parties into one. Mollet could not answer this candidly with the cynical assurance that such talks would lead nowhere and were really designed to preclude such a Union of the Left. In these Mauroy-Mollet polemics the idea of insisting on preliminary agreements on ideology lost favor, leaving the road clear for a Union of the Left.

Thanks to this warm support from Mauroy on Union of the Left, Mitterrand had a good chance of joining with the Defferre-Mauroy faction to try for control of the congress.

But even if Mitterrand succeeded with Defferre and Mauroy, together their factions, barring any defections, added up to only 44.3 percent of the voting delegates. It would be necessary to win support from one of the two "leftist" factions, Poperen's or CERES (Center for Socialist Studies and Research). Jean Poperen, like Mollet, was suspicious of Mitterrand, who was after all still a newcomer to Socialism, an immigrant from bourgeois parties in the center of the political spectrum. Mitterrand concentrated his efforts on the two principal CERES leaders, Jean-Pierre Chevènement and Didier Motchane. They were strongly in favor of the strategy of a Union of the Left with the Communists, which Mitterrand had made his platform.

To marry CERES and Defferre in the same alliance, the task Mitterrand undertook, seemed impossible. With great skill he lobbied in the caucuses of both factions. He had come to occupy a position in the center between them. He brought forth an argument that proved appealing: The Socialist Party would become the dominant party on the left, that is, it would overtake and surpass the Communist Party in elections. That would make it safe to join with the Communists in an electoral coalition (the Union of the Left) that stood a good chance of winning control of the government away from the rightist parties that had monopolized it since de Gaulle established the Fifth Republic.

This argument was absolutely essential in overcoming resistance among Socialists to the Mitterrand strategy. They had always dreaded being used by the Communists as allies in bringing the Communists to power. If the relation of forces between Communists and Socialists could be reversed, a Union of the Left at election time would be a way of defeating the right and putting the Socialists in power, strong enough on balance to hold the Communists in check. This was the promising picture Mitterrand presented to the delegates at Epinay.

To make it clear that his strategy posed as a first indispensable step the taking away of votes from the Communists, he said that "it is not normal" that five million or more people voted for the Communists. The constant effort of the Socialists, he said, must be directed at changing the beliefs of those voters who think the Communists defend their interests. Mitterrand thus spelled out his view that two goals of the Socialist Party were to be regarded as inseparable: (1) the conquest of hegemony among the parties of the left, so that the Communists were left in a position of subordination to the Socialists in any alliance formed between them, and (2) the conquest of state power, that is, the presidency and control of the Parliament, by Socialists.

The followers of Defferre and Mauroy responded in their caucuses with enthusiasm to this Machiavellian justification of an alliance with the devil. They approved the consent given by their "notables" to a "motion of synthesis" with the Mitterrand theses. Thus Mitterrand won support from the right wing of the Socialist Party.

With the more leftist Socialists of CERES, he stressed another side of his strategy, the explicit rejection of reformism in favor of the promise of revolution. This was exactly the language used by CERES, and Mitterrand made it his own. This also demonstrated a first step in implementing the strategy of taking votes away from the Communists. They had been winning votes by promising revolution. Now the Socialists would vie with them in the exploitation of a word that evoked memories of the past and hopes fixed on a future revolution. Mitterrand said he wanted to accomplish a rupture of the French people with their true enemy, "monopoly." That was only possible, he said, with help from the Communists. It was therefore necessary in preparing such a revolution to create a Union of the Left.

Mitterrand tried to appeal to the leftist followers of Poperen with expressions of support for the idea of anchoring the Socialist Party in a "class front" against the bourgeoisie. Poperen was not convinced by such expressions from a longtime fellow-traveler with bourgeois Radicals. To him they smacked of opportunism in Mitterrand's search for votes. He decided to continue with Mollet and Savary, who still could not believe this newly arrived "Socialist" was about to capture their party.

Concerning the matter of a preliminary dialogue with the Communists on ideological questions, Mitterrand joined with Mauroy in opposing such a step because it was not necessary to the creation of a Union of the Left. In its stead Mitterrand proposed immediate discussions with the Communists on a "common program" of government to serve as a platform in future electoral campaigns. For those who had really come to believe in the strategy of a Union of the Left, this proposal had the practical advantage of putting the Socialists in accord immediately with the Communists on procedure.

Mitterrand succeeded in making it clear to all that he had a real strategy that promised to serve the interests of the Socialist Party. Why should it matter that, at the same time, he was obviously striving to implement his own ambition to become the elected president of the Republic? Socialists were coming to appreciate what Mitterrand had already discovered: In the new political order established by a Constitution that provided for direct election of a president, the power of a personality to win votes in an electoral contest would become the dominant factor in future French politics. Mitterrand wanted to use the Socialist Party as an instrument to serve his own ambition. If he succeeded, the Socialist Party would rise to power with him. Experience had shown that Mitterrand had a rare ability, exceeding that of any other Socialist, to win votes on Election Day. With help from the Socialist Party, he stood a chance of launching both himself and the party into a trajectory leading to power.

The Congress of Epinay marked the change of the Socialist Party from a party of the Fourth Republic, with its focus on maneuvers in an all-powerful parliamentary Assembly, to a party of the Fifth Republic, concentrating on helping a skillful and promising aspirant to win the presidency in a direct election. Mitterrand's performance at Epinay contributed enormously to that historic change of focus.

He had the benefit at the congress of his close friends of the Convention of Republican Institutions, who knew he would reward their loyalty when it was within his power. Among these were Georges Dayan, Pierre Joxe, Roland Dumas, Claude Estier, and Charles Hernu. They too played important roles, perhaps crucial and indispensable, in shaping the results of Epinay.

The three factions, CIR, CERES, and the Defferre-Mauroy alliance, agreed to join in a "motion of synthesis" for presentation to the congress in plenary session. Opposed to them with another motion were the factions of Mollet-Savary and Poperen. It was impossible to foresee the number of defections and abstentions. The final vote was so close that the margin of victory for the factions supporting Mitterrand was smaller than the number of abstentions and "refusals to vote." The will of that small group to stand aside and let the palace fall was a factor determining the outcome. Too late, Mollet and Savary discovered the force of the Mitterrand appeal; to him and his allies they lost control of the party.

Mauroy could probably have been named first secretary by the new Directing Committee had he wanted it. He chose to remain free to concentrate on consolidating his position in the Socialist fief of Lille, the party's capital in the northern region. Mauroy stepped aside and made Mitterrand's triumph at the battle of Epinay complete. Mitterrand, the promising candidate that many in the party had already chosen to carry its colors in future presidential elections, would henceforth have the title of first secretary of the Socialist Party. That proved an invaluable asset to him in the internal battles with other Socialist factions that lay ahead.

4

The Communist Party of France

> The whole problem is this: the old is dying and the new has not yet been born.
>
> —Antonio Gramsci

THE CONGRESS OF TOURS

All the previous history of French Socialism was background to the birth of the Communist Party of France in 1920. The party was born of a scission among French Socialists produced by the revolution in Russia in 1917 and the founding of the Communist International, the Third International, also known as the Leninist International, in 1919.

If we could put ourselves into the mind of a French Socialist in 1919, we would inevitably feel some of the excitement radiating from the Bolsheviks' seizure of power in Russia. Lenin was proclaiming a new birth of the Paris Commune of 1871. He challenged the French to see him as a European carrying forward the struggle launched by their common French and German ancestors. He described the events in Russia as the opening of a new period of revolution in all of Europe, including France. He said that the survival of this exciting new leap forward into a social order based on Marxism now depended on the response from the Socialist parties of Western Europe.

In judging the actions of French Socialists in 1919 and 1920, we should keep in mind the powerful appeal of Marxist internationalism, with its roots in France as the birthplace of Communism. Lenin seemed to agree with Marx on the crucial importance of Western Europe to the fate of capitalism. Could it be that a new chapter in the history of Western Europe was opening with the overthrow of the old order in Russia?

It came as a surprise to European Socialists that the overthrow of capitalism had begun in a backward country like Russia. Conditions in Western Europe were very different from those in Russia. Marx had assumed that the working class in the industrialized countries would accomplish the transition to Socialism on the basis of the world's most highly developed and productive economies. That is why Lenin looked to support from the European working class as absolutely essential to the success of the Bolsheviks' revolution. And this support, he predicted, would develop into a Europe-wide revolution led by Marxists for the overthrow of capitalism in the ruling countries of the world market. To defend the revolution in Russia and to encourage its timely eruption in Europe (that meant sooner rather than later), Lenin insisted on the creation of a new International.

With the establishment of this Leninist International, French Socialists were compelled to take a position on his call for an extraordinary level of solidarity with the Bolsheviks. If Lenin had not been so focused on Western Europe as the decisive theater in the new revolution beginning on Russian soil, the attitude of French Socialists would probably have been more reserved. For what was the relevance of these events taking place in far away and backward Russia to the problems of working people in France? In the circumstances it was hard to give a cool-headed answer to that question. To many Socialists it seemed Philistine, even craven, to doubt that Lenin was correct in stressing that the time was ripe for a Europe-wide revolution and that the Bolsheviks had begun it. What the Paris Commune had hoped to trigger in Europe was now the aim of a second inspiring leap into the future, a new attempt "to take heaven by storm."

At a congress of French Socialists in Strasbourg in February 1920 a decision was taken to send delegates to the second congress of the new International, to be held in Moscow. Here would be discussed the conditions a party would have to accept to gain admission to the new International. These conditions, which came to be known as "the 21 conditions," can be summarized in the following seven:

1. The necessity of a dictatorship of the proletariat must be continuously inculcated in workers and members by party organs.
2. All reformists and centrists must be excluded from posts of leadership.
3. An organization must be established to work for the party in clandestine conditions, in anticipation that bourgeois law and police repression would be turned against Communist revolutionaries.
4. The party must maintain close supervisory control over its representatives elected to parliaments, to make sure they carry on a truly revolutionary program and propaganda of agitation.
5. The party must function on the basis of democratic centralism, in which an iron discipline appropriate to a condition of civil war would ensure the effective authority of the central directorate.
6. All decisions of a congress of the Communist International or its executive organ are to be obligatory for member parties. However, the International will take into account the differing circumstances of the different parties and make decisions binding on all only where practicable.
7. Anyone rejecting these conditions was to be expelled from party membership.

The spirit of these conditions was that civil war was inevitable; prepare for it, and repudiate reformism.

Following the decisions at Strasbourg, French Socialists ultimately chose as their representatives (with the status of observers) to the second congress of the new International two leaders known to be uncommitted on the questions of accepting these conditions and applying for membership of a French party in the International. They were Ludovic-Oscar Frossard, general-secretary of the SFIO; and Marcel Cachin, editor of the party newspaper, *L'Humanité*.

The course of debate during the next several months was strongly influenced by these two representatives of the French party, who returned from their mission expressing enthusiasm for the Leninist thesis set forth in the twenty-one conditions. They became its advocates in the ensuing debates across France in the sections of the SFIO.[1] The strategy had worked in Russia. The Bolsheviks were consolidating their authority and winning the civil war. No one could doubt that a real revolution had taken place, that Marxists were in power with the active support of masses of working people and the goal of building a socialist order.

News of these historical achievements reached France at a time when the confidence of the SFIO in its approach to French problems was at a low point, due to a series of defeats in strikes following the war.

By the time the congress of the SFIO assembled at Tours in December 1920, a large majority of the sections and federations of the SFIO had declared themselves in favor of the Third International and the twenty-one conditions.

But there was a sizable opposition, some of whom supported Léon Blum in resisting pressure from Moscow to break with the reformist tradition of the Second International. These were called the "resistants."

A third group, known as the "centrists" and headed by Jean Longuet, acknowledged the validity of the Bolshevik model but with a reticence similar to that of Karl Kautsky in Germany. The centrists wanted the party to keep itself open to all three currents, with proportional representation in the leading party organs. They sought to avoid the split in the SFIO made inevitable by adherence to the severe conditions demanded by the new International. The centrists also proclaimed the teaching of Jean Jaurès, the SFIO martyr who was assassinated on the eve of World War I, to be still the best guide for French Socialists. The repudiation by the Tours Congress of the centrists and, by implication, of Jaurès, is a measure of the capacity of the Bolshevik leadership in Moscow to influence the course of events in that period among Socialists in France.

The Communist International, knowing that the prestige of the martyred Jaurès gave his champion Longuet an emotional leverage in favor of a centrist compromise, sent Clara Zetkin to insist on the need to purge Longuet and the centrists along with Blum and the "resistants." A telegram signed by Zinoviev, president of the Communist International, pressed the delegates to adopt without equivocation the same hard-line resolution. Whether these two last-minute interventions were crucial to the outcome at Tours can never be known for sure. The final vote to accept the twenty-one conditions and thus repudiate Blum and Longuet was not greatly different from the tally of votes taken in the sections and federations during the weeks before the Tours Congress convened. The potency of the Bolshevik revolution had swept aside reverence for Jaurès and trivialized French pride of place in a world movement.

It was an extraordinary moment, a clear expression of the feeling among most French Socialists that a worldwide revolution had begun, that it would soon overthrow the capitalist regimes in Europe, and that Paris would join and perhaps even surpass Moscow as a radiant model to the new world in birth.

It is from the Congress of Tours that the Communist Party of France dates its founding. The decades since 1920 have not realized the high expectations that surrounded its birth. When one considers just a few of the tremendous world events that could not have been foreseen by the delegates at Tours in 1920—the rise of Hitler and Nazi Germany, the rise of Stalin after Lenin's death, World War II and the arrival of U.S. forces in Europe, the dissolution of the Communist International in 1943, the invention of nuclear weapons, the Cold War, the collapse of Communist regimes in Eastern Europe and the Soviet Union itself—it is inevitable that most French Socialists and even some French Communists should come to question whether the strategy adopted at Tours really fitted the conditions of struggle of a French working class.

LOUIS ARAGON

Louis Aragon was born in Paris in 1897. He had just passed his baccalaureate examination at age seventeen when World War I began in 1914. He had begun the study of medicine when he was mobilized and sent for military medical training at Val-de-Grace Hospital in Paris in 1917. In 1918 he was sent to the front with a medical corps in northeastern France and experienced some of the cruel fighting of the war. After being shelled, buried by debris and reported dead, he survived to receive the *Croix de Guerre*.

His months at Val-de-Grace proved to be a turning point in his life, because there he began a friendship with another young mobilized resident-doctor, André Breton. The two shared a passion for the avant-garde poet, Guillaume Apollinaire, and for a little-remembered French poet of the nineteenth century, Isidore Ducasse, who wrote under the name "le Comte de Lautréamont." In their duty hours the two young doctor-recruits were treating the mangled victims of the war. The observation of these horrors, supplemented and illuminated by their readings aloud from the works of the rebellious genius, Lautréamont, produced in them a state of mind that ultimately set its mark on France and Western culture.

The two friends became active participants in the Dada movement, which aimed at destruction of all inherited cultural values, itself a striking expression of the postwar mood, *Plus jamais ça!* ("Never again!"). Revolution was in the air, made urgent by the widespread revulsion at the killing of so many of Europe's young in the war. It was out of this experience that the movement of surrealism in the 1920s suddenly became a powerful and self-conscious force, displacing Dada. Breton was its principal promoter and theoretician. It profoundly affected the literature, painting, and music of a generation of artistic creators. Some of the better-known luminaries who publicly supported the movement were Pablo Picasso, Paul Eluard, Max Ernst, Paul Masson, and Man-Ray. A volume of Louis Aragon's poems published in 1925, *Le mouvement perpétuel* (Perpetual Motion), is now a classic of literary surrealism. One of the poems is dedicated to André Breton.[2]

One of the heroes and models of the movement was Charlie Chaplin. A play by Apollinaire, *Mamelles de Tiresias* (Breasts of Tiresias), was lauded as a French expression of the Chaplin approach to life. In a review of its opening Aragon offered it as a key to the new age:

That is theater, the theater of this epoch. To amuse us was the sole aim of the playwright, who is a creator of illusions and wants us not to despair. Pessimism is out of date. He reveals to us the lesson of the war and moralizes while amusing us.[3]

This young poet and philosopher Aragon was seized by a passion for the infinite. He could not give a satisfactory account of this inspiration through thought alone. Certain mysteries thrilled him, and this shiver of excitement [*ce frisson*] became a signal commanding his obedience, like the demon of Socrates.

He came to the conclusion that his frequent states of excitement from consciousness of infinity was due to a "vertigo of the modern." He gave vent to this excitement with a book about strolling through the streets of Paris, *Le paysan de Paris* (The Peasant of Paris).[4] It marked him as a writer of extraordinary talent with visual imagery and literary allusions. It is regarded by some critics as one of the masterpieces of twentieth-century French literature.[5] Aragon could wander through everyday places and surprise the reader by conferring significance on ordinary objects. Breton called him the "detector of the unexpected."[6]

These two brilliant young rebels, immersed as critics and creators in the exciting novelties of the literary and artistic world (Apollinaire, Eluard, Jarry, cubism, Picasso, Braque, surrealism, collage) expressed nothing but scorn for the call of the political. Aragon stated:

If you find me closed to the political spirit, or rather, violently hostile to that dishonoring pragmatic attitude...the reason is, do not doubt it, that I have always placed, that I place the spirit of revolt well beyond all politics.[7]

The decade of the 1920s worked a change in Aragon with respect to the importance of the political. Breton attributed the beginning of the change to Aragon's close study for the first time of the classics of Marxism. He found in Marx's concepts of alienation and dialectical materialism compelling reasons to re-examine his philosophical idealism (i.e., his belief that spirit was the origin of change). He was also captivated by the extremism of the Bolshevik revolution. The Bolsheviks and the surrealists were being condemned in similar terms of outrage and indignation by the same voices of tradition and authority. In a spirit of bravado and solidarity with fellow pariahs, Aragon and Breton applied for membership in the French Communist Party in 1927. The party was skeptical of their sincerity and, with good reason, of their sense of discipline. Could these two anarchistic rebels, fierce champions of individualism, subject themselves to the interests of the proletarian revolution? Formal approval of their applications was delayed for five years. Aragon and Breton took no offense at this lengthy coolness toward them, because they were the first to admit they had hitherto been scornful of all political movements, including the revolution in Russia.

Aragon was troubled by one aspect of his own favorite revolution, the surrealist revolution. In 1929, in the magazine of the surrealist movement, *La Révolution Surréaliste*, Aragon deplored the fact that social snobs were embracing surrealism as chic. Indignant, Aragon felt frustrated by the paradox that made of surrealism a luxury precisely because it was revolutionary. He came to the conclusion that individualism was proving itself ineffective in social life and that in the troubled Europe of 1930 it was essential to fight against alienation and despair by committing one's work to the class struggle. This was a change, and it brought on the beginning of a rupture with Breton.

Fortunately, Aragon did not repudiate or abandon the insights he had accumulated in the decade of the 1920s regarding surrealist painting. In 1930 he published *La peinture au défi* (Painting That Defies) with twenty-three reproductions. It was a valuable contribution to the understanding and appreciation of the works of Braque, Dali, Derain, Duchamp, Ernst, Lissitsky, Gris, Magritte, Man-Ray, Miró, Picabia, Picasso, Rodtchenko, and Tanguy.[8] It was the first theoretical exposition of the discovery by Picasso and Braque of the power of collage. The surprising and moving encounters of unrelated objects in the collages of Max Ernst were explored. Throughout his life Aragon upheld the view that surrealism had proved its ability to open the doors of artistic creativity by exploring dreams and the unconscious.

Near the end of 1929 Breton tried to summarize, update, purify, and revitalize his movement with his *Second Manifesto of Surrealism*. It condemned by name those intellectuals who were failing to live by the principles of the movement. This form of terrorism by the pen naturally provoked ire, especially from those excommunicated. Breton denounced the narrowness of political action, specifically that of the Communist Party of France. He wanted the dialectical method of Marx (which he seemed still to approve as one of his "principles" of research and action) to be applied with a focus beyond and outside the social and political:

How can it be admitted that the dialectical method applies solely to the resolution of social problems? I truly do not see, whatever certain narrow-minded revolutionaries may say, why we should abstain from raising the problems of love, of dreams, of madness, of art and of religion.[9]

To underline his independence from any authority claimed for Stalin and the Communist Party of the Soviet Union in the development of revolutionary thought, Breton cited favorably a work of Léon Trotsky, whom Stalin had just succeeded in expelling from the U.S.S.R.

Aragon's turn to dialectical materialism meant it was necessary for him to come to terms with the Bolsheviks and the Soviet Union. At the end of 1930 he traveled to Moscow and Kharkov to attend an international conference of revolutionary writers. Aragon began his participation at the conference as a defender of the revolutionary character of surrealism, aiming to win recognition for it from representatives of the Communist Party of the Soviet Union. It was soon made clear to him that Breton was judged in Moscow to be a Trotskyist, an idealist, a Freudian, and a pseudo-revolutionary. Breton's *Second Manifesto of Surrealism*, Aragon was told, could not be reconciled with dialectical materialism and had to be condemned by anyone aspiring to receive favorable recognition from cultural organs of the Communist Party of the Soviet Union (CPSU). Aragon was probably fully aware of the impossibility of reconciling some of Breton's positions with the Moscow line. Forced to choose between the revolutionary surrealism of Breton and the proletarian revolution of the Bolsheviks, Aragon went over to the Bolsheviks just as Stalin was consolidating his dominating position in the party.

The extremism that Aragon had been indulging since his days and nights with Lautréamont, Dada, and surrealism was now let loose on new themes and targets. As was his habit, he threw caution to the winds. He called for revolutionary terror: "Fire on Léon Blum, fire on Boncour." Such violent phrases from his poem, "Front rouge," published in 1931 in a review in the Soviet Union, became the basis of a prosecution against him in France for inciting military personnel to disobedience and for incitement to murder with anarchistic aims.[10]

Artists and writers rallied to his defense in what became a *cause célèbre*. At the heart of this drama was the developing rupture between Breton and Aragon. Breton came to the defense of his friend, arguing the case on the grounds of absolute freedom of expression for the poet, who was not to be held responsible for what came from his pen. Poets write from the inspiration of their unconscious over which they have no control, he argued. Aragon had written nothing more than a "poem of circumstance." Breton belittled its political message, judging it rather by the literary standards set forth in his own surrealist manifestos. By these he found the poem a retrogression from Aragon's earlier writings, because it was a return to the exterior world. Still, it had to be defended in the spirit of liberty for revolutionary poets like Nerval, Baudelaire, Rimbaud, and Lautréamont.

Aragon refused Breton's support in such terms. For Aragon it was the responsibility of every writer to judge his own work in terms of the class it served. The appropriation of "revolutionary" surrealism by upper-class snobs showed its irrelevance or even negative relevance to the class struggle. As for him, Aragon said, "Comrades, to each his own way. At the risk of passing for a demagogue or a charlatan, I say to you that I defend poetry when I defend the Soviet Union."[11]

The ardor with which Aragon threw himself into the defense of the Soviet Union and the priority he attributed to the struggle for a proletarian revolution brought an end to his partnership with Breton. One feature of Aragon's new stance was an absolute public loyalty to the French Communist Party. This was heresy to Breton, since it subjected the poet to political authority. Many critics, among them André Gide, expressed regret that Aragon's artistic creativity, so fertile in his first decade of work, would henceforth be inhibited by political considerations. Aragon had made a choice that offended against a principle highly valued by cultural aesthetes: No one should inhibit the freedom of the artistic creator. In the nineteenth century this principle had been fought for and vindicated against the bourgeoisie. Now Aragon was knowingly and deliberately subordinating it to the interests of the proletariat.

Others found signs of an admirable self-reliance in Aragon's willingness to break with Breton, who ruled his circle with the power to make and break reputations with a stroke of his pen. It is rather remarkable that Aragon, a worshiper of Rimbaud and Lautréamont, after having drunk so deeply of the wine of artistic freedom, should have chosen to become a member of the Communist Party in the era of Stalin and made himself its champion.

The definitive rupture between Aragon and Breton was precipitated by a text, *Rêveries*, published in Breton's review. It was written by Salvador Dali, well known for his surrealist paintings. The Freudian, pornographic text featured an eleven-year-old girl, Dulita. A commission of control of the Communist Party summoned Aragon and three other party members associated with surrealism to express a severe condemnation of the text, saying: "You only try to complicate the simple, healthy relationship between man and woman." Aragon recounted this rebuke to Breton, who, amused and delighted, wanted to incorporate it in his essay *Misère de la poésie* (The Poverty of Poetry), about to be published. Aragon objected on the ground it had been a proceeding internal to the party. When Breton persisted, Aragon warned that it would make their rupture inevitable. That was in fact the outcome.

In commenting on the episode Breton protested against the attempt to prohibit poets from drawing on the sexual domain, where the collisions of human life are richest. He hoped it would be the honor of surrealists to have infringed such a prohibition, "which in spirit is so remarkably petit-bourgeois."[12]

Certainly Aragon would not have disagreed with the content of that declaration. He himself had asserted and practiced the freedom to write on erotic themes. Nevertheless, he refused to condemn his new party for not being as avant-garde as the surrealists. He was betting on its ability to change over time in the direction demanded by Breton. Thus began the long drama of Aragon's role as a member of the Communist Party. On March 10, 1932, *L'Humanité* published the following note: "Our comrade Aragon advises us that he has absolutely nothing to do with the appearance of a brochure entitled *Misère de la poésie* and signed André Breton."

Breton was not willing to make the same bet on the future of the party as Aragon. He wanted to retain his freedom to denounce it for its conservatism and narrow-mindedness.

What quickly became clear is that Aragon found new inspiration in the struggle he had joined. Those who had foreseen that the springs of his creativity would cease to flow were proved wrong. He became a journalist at *L'Humanité*. Without Breton's influence to restrain him, he produced his first novel in a realistic genre, *Les cloches de Bâle* (The Bells of Basle). One of the heroines is Clara Zetkin, a liberated woman. The background of his new life is reflected in the denunciation of police practices and the description of strikes and of their suppression. It is a novel of social struggle still gripping to the reader of today.

Every account of Aragon's life and work pays high tribute to the importance of Elsa Triolet. She was born Elsa Kagan to a family of Jewish intellectuals in Moscow, and in the years before the October Revolution she was a student of architecture. She met Mayakovski and became interested in avant-garde poetry. Elsa's sister, Lili, became the companion of Mayakovski, who introduced them to other leading intellectuals on the Moscow scene. Elsa married an officer in the French Navy on duty in Moscow. With her new name and papers as Elsa Triolet she escaped the chaos of revolutionary Russia in 1918 and traveled to Paris to join her husband. He took her to Tahiti where it was his hope to escape from the world. Within a few years the two began separate lives, though they saw each other occasionally on friendly terms.

Elsa was determined to be a writer. While living near her sister in Berlin and writing Russian prose, she received encouragement from Maxim Gorky, who assured her she had great talent. Triolet returned to Paris, where she worked as a correspondent for a Russian review. Mayakovski and Lili helped her and arranged her return to Russia in 1925, where she produced her second book. In 1926 she was back in Paris, serving as a link between the literary avant-garde of the two countries. She read Aragon's *Le paysan de Paris* and began looking for an opportunity to meet the author. While working on her third book, *Camouflage*, published in 1928, she drew on her own life as a Jew in the Russia of pogroms, as a lucid observer of revolutionary events in Soviet Russia in the 1920s, and as an independent woman living alone in exile from her country of birth. Gorky's confidence in her talents as a writer was vindicated; the reader is struck by her intelligence, courage, and vitality—"enough life for ten," in the words of Pierre Daix.

Mayakovski arrived in Paris in the autumn of 1928. Aragon wanted to meet him, the most famous of the Russian revolutionary poets, with a strong appeal to all French lovers of Apollinaire. This gave Triolet the chance she had been waiting for. As a friend of Mayakovski, she arranged for the two poets to meet and made it her opportunity to meet the author of *Le paysan de Paris*. Triolet was thirty-two years old, Aragon a year younger when they met on November 6, 1928. It must have been destined. Aragon has said that meeting Triolet saved him from suicide. She became a new anchor in the years of his disillusionment with surrealism and his growing rift with Breton.

Aragon had to be persuaded to give up his bohemian life before Triolet consented to join her future to his. Within six months they were living together, and Triolet, while continuing her work as a writer, became the beloved of a poet who made her famous forever by pouring out his passion for her in book after book of love poetry sung to her name. Their union continued until her death in 1970.

In 1932–1933 they were living in Moscow, where Triolet was an invaluable aide and guide in exploring and interpreting. Aragon made the acquaintance of all the leading Soviet intellectuals and thereafter served as their champion in France. In his enthusiasm for the revolution, despite all the daily hardships he observed first-hand, he found a world that was fraternal to him. He later wrote about this period in his poem *Le roman inachevé* (The Unfinished Novel). He referred to the piled-up heaps between walls never repainted, to the "atrocious tonsillitis of corridors," to the bugs, to the cries, the bad tempers, and the lack of everything where a pin is a treasure. Every evening in the tramways he saw the fatigue where fury and brutality were joined. Nevertheless, he wrote, he felt for the first time the gaze of human eyes. He felt a trembling from words pronounced by unknown persons along his path, as if he had received the physical revelation of the deaf person who one day learns what music is.[13]

After his return to France with Triolet in 1933, Aragon put himself at the service of the party. In 1935 he was one of the organizers of a World Congress of Writers for the Defense of Culture. It brought together humanist writers (Malraux, Gide, Roger Martin du Gard, Aldous Huxley, Ilya Ehrenbourg, Boris Pasternak) and others more frankly committed to support for the Communist Party of the Soviet Union (among them Aragon and Bertolt Brecht). André Breton was convinced that some of Stalin's policies deserved the severest condemnation by European intellectuals and wanted the chance to say so at the congress. It so happened that Ilya Ehrenbourg, a delegate from the Soviet Union, had recently published a book in France containing a severe repudiation of surrealism. The paths of Breton and Ehrenbourg chanced to cross, and the two exchanged sharp words, creating an embarrassment for the organizers. In the end Breton consented to stay away from the congress, allowing his speech to be read to the assemblage by Paul Eluard. This took place at a late hour and passed largely unnoticed. Aragon could doubtless have done better by his old friend if he had wanted to.

Aragon had passed into the camp of socialist realism. Under the strong influence of Stalin, this concept was singled out by the Soviet Writers Guild in 1934 as particularly apt for proletarian culture. It was established as the Soviet response to the idealism, anarchism, and extreme individualism in movements like Dada and surrealism, which were alleged to be symptomatic of bourgeois decadence. Aragon and Breton had always conceived Dada and surrealism as anti-bourgeois in spirit, and indeed Aragon in the Congress at Kharkov had strongly defended Breton and insisted on the revolutionary character of surrealism. On entering wholeheartedly into his new Stalinist world, Aragon did not, then or later, explicitly repudiate these earlier views. But he did become a champion in the West of socialist realism, putting aside the question of whether it could be reconciled with surrealism.

He accepted the Soviet proclamation of socialist realism as the artistic theory best suiting the needs of the rising proletarian class. He equated it with revolutionary romanticism. In it are joined, he said, the Emile Zola of *Germinal* and the Victor Hugo of *Châtiments*. That synthesis was made possible by the collapse of capitalism and the victory of Socialism over one-sixth of the globe.[14]

It is possible to interpret such statements in support of socialist realism as a new and still faithful expression of the revolutionary spirit that had moved him to support Breton in the promotion of surrealism. Breton gave them a different interpretation. To him, freedom for an avant-garde could not exist under Communism as practiced in the Soviet Union. Aragon was moving in the wrong direction, Breton believed, by putting himself at the service of the French Communist Party. Aragon responded by expressing his confidence that the PCF would some day hail the poetry of Apollinaire, Rimbaud, and Lautréamont, as he and Breton continued to do. Other avant-garde artists, like Picasso and the poet Paul Eluard, agreed with Aragon.

In 1936 Aragon's novel, *Les beaux quartiers*, (Upper-class Quarters), written in the spirit of socialist realism and portraying the class character of French society in the years leading to World War I, was awarded the Prix Renaudet. With his literary successes in the market of commercial publishers, Aragon contributed during the period of the Popular Front (1936–38) to the rising prestige of the Communist Party.

At the end of 1938 Triolet published her first book in French, *Bonsoir Thérèse*. This was highly praised by a young writer and philosopher, Jean-Paul Sartre. She began to be recognized for her own talents as a teller of stories. With a new self-confidence as a writer in France, she decided to marry Aragon. Thus when war broke out, as they expected might well happen, their papers would be in order as husband and wife. Aragon was ecstatic.

In 1939 he was editor of a Communist newspaper, *Ce Soir*. Like other French Communists, he condemned the Munich agreement and called on the French and British governments to join with the Soviet Union in an alliance that would deter Hitler. He interpreted Munich as evidence of a desire in Paris and London to see Hitler march to the east against the U.S.S.R. When news arrived on August 22, 1939, of the Nazi-Soviet pact, Aragon, in that moment of surprise and confusion among French Communists, wrote an editorial which had to be rooted in his own instincts. He did not condemn the pact, seeing in it a respite from threatened aggression for the Soviet Union and therefore justified in the circumstances. (He did not know of the secret protocols on Poland, the Baltic region, and Bessarabia.) Aragon seized immediately the new importance of French independence of action, of French patriotism, of a spirit of resistance. The editorial appeared in the last edition of *Ce Soir* before the government closed it down. In it he affirmed that the fight against Hitlerism ought to be carried on without mercy. Referring to France's obligations to defend Poland if aggression took place, he hoped all the French would do their duty as patriots for the re-establishment of international law.[15]

Within ten days of this prescient call to arms from Aragon's pen, Germany had attacked Poland, France had declared war on Germany, and (on September 3, 1939) Aragon had been mobilized into military service.

This brought the pain of his first separation from Triolet. It was easy to find the time to write consoling love poetry during the first few months of his mobilization, the period of the "phony war" (September 1939 to May 1940).

Joined to these poems of love for Elsa were his songs of love for his wounded country. Jean Paulhan perceived in these an extraordinary combination of lyrical gifts and sincerity of feeling. He arranged publication in the review *NRF* with support from the commercial publisher Gallimard. This meant that Triolet would have some needed financial resources. And it meant that the country would have in its dark hours the poetry of a genius who was living with his countrymen the tragedy of the defeat of France in June 1940 and the German occupation for four years. There is no doubt that this combination made Aragon the much-beloved "poet of the Resistance." Through his ability to give expression to the nobility and grandeur as well as the pain of the struggle in France against the occupying power, he helped restore morale and create the consciousness of a glory to be remembered. He helped to win for the Resistance a position of high honor in French tradition.

Aragon was evacuated with his military unit at Dunkirk on June 1, 1940. He returned to France with a light motorized division, which fought the Germans until the Armistice. For his actions during this period Aragon received the *Croix de Guerre* and *Médaille Militaire*. Thus at age forty-three he had fought honorably for France in both world wars.

After the Armistice he was demobilized. He and Triolet were reunited and took up residence in Nice. They were soon engaged in organizing intellectuals in some forty-two departments of France to facilitate their work and maintain communication despite the German occupation. With the aid of Jean Paulhan, this led to the creation of a review, *Les Lettres françaises*, and a National Committee of Writers. Aragon sought to write with allusions that would pass the German censors and yet serve as inspiration to patriotic resistance when read by the French. During the dark period 1940–44, Aragon felt himself directly engaged with his pen in a historical struggle worthy of a great people.

One of his themes during this period was the painting of Henri Matisse, who was neither a surrealist nor a Communist. He was a painter of which all French men and women could be defiantly proud in the face of the Nazi occupier. Aragon wrote an article titled "Matisse or Greatness, Matisse in France," published in the January 1942 issue of *Poésie 42*. In it he wrote of "unalterable possessions," of "incomparable motives for pride" in French painting. Nothing awakens that sentiment as do the works of Henri Matisse, he wrote, which are its fulfillment and summit.[16]

That was a powerful essay because it was true. It reawakened a resolution born of pride in every French reader and therefore aided the Resistance. Yet it passed the German censors to reach a wide audience. With his prodigious knowledge of French painting, literature, and history, Aragon employed hundreds of such tricks to communicate encouragement widely yet intimately.

This may well have been the most stimulating and satisfying period of Aragon's long life. Claude Roy made the acquaintance of Aragon and Triolet in Nice in 1942. In 1969 he wrote:

Aragon and Elsa have never been happier and freeer than in those years of grief and troubles. The words of Aragon rose with a violence and an ease that reverberated from one end of France to the other. He had the total but distant support of a Party that no longer wished, was no longer able, to bridle the "intellectuals." The Thorezian project [i.e., of Maurice Thorez] of a Communist Party truly French, national in its roots and international in its head, proved its chances of realization in the Resistance.[17]

During the occupation and the rule of France by Germany and the Vichy regime, the Communist Party gave Aragon great freedom of action. With the end of the occupation and the return of the Communist Party to a legal existence, the question of his status in the party was once again opened. He was named to return to his old post as editor of *Ce Soir*, a sign that he had support in the party leadership. There was still suspicion in the minds of many party members that he was too independent, too much loved and appreciated for his literary gifts, too much at home in the world of avant-garde artists. Nevertheless, in 1950 he was elected as a temporary member (that is, probationary) of the Central Committee of the PCF. It took four years for him to be named a permanent member. In 1953 he was named director of *Les Lettres françaises*, a literary journal under the control of the party. The death of Stalin a few months later brought on an episode that illuminated Aragon's precarious status in the party.

When the news of Stalin's death arrived, Aragon asked Picasso to create a portrait that would be on the cover of *Les Lettres françaises*. Picasso chose to make a freely drawn portrait adapted from a photograph of Stalin as a young man. On his own initiative, Aragon approved its use as planned. When the review appeared on the newsstands, there were many expressions of indignation from hardline worshipers of Stalin; this portrait was lacking in respect for the hallowed dead. On orders from a delegation of the party headed by François Billoux, Aragon was required to publish in the next issue of the review a selection of letters condemning his approval of the Picasso portrait.

Aragon published his self-criticism in the issue of April 9, 1953, without stinting his praise for the portrait by Picasso. But he concluded:

It is grave that, habituated all my life to look at a drawing by Picasso in function of its being a work of Picasso, I forgot the reader, who would look at it without paying attention to the strokes, to the technique. That was my error. I have paid for it dearly.[18]

The party humiliated Aragon in this episode. Triolet saw his suffering and feared for his life. It appeared that Breton had been right about the PCF and Aragon wrong in his bet that he could win respect for his views on avant-garde art. Then the episode took a surprising turn. Maurice Thorez, the general secretary of the party, who had been absent when the decision was made to rebuke Aragon, sent a telegram condemning the action that had been taken against Aragon. With this sign of support Aragon decided to remain in the party.

In the spring of 1954, at the PCF Congress of Ivry, Aragon's views on artistic creation were publicized and circulated by the party. He was in a position to exercise some influence, which would steadily rise over the next ten years, the years of de-Stalinization. They were years of painful political drama for Aragon, and they caused him to re-evaluate the Soviet Union. This in turn contributed a great deal to the changes that ultimately reoriented the PCF. The ordeal of the artist and human produced some marvelous poetry, which entered into the political drama of the country and the party.

In the months following the Khrushchev report denouncing Stalin at the 20th Congress of the CPSU (February 1956, published in France in June), Aragon was composing his long autobiographical poem, *Le roman inachevé* (The Unfinished

Novel). In some stanzas on Moscow ("Moscow Night") he hinted quite openly at his pain and shock. This was the first such public expression from a member of the Central Committee. He acknowledged that he had loved the flame to the point of becoming its fuel. It is easy after the fact, he wrote, to conclude against the burned hand in seeing its burn. Well, then, he was in the ditch; he had lost his life and his shoes, he wrote. He was counting his wounds. People were smiling at his devotion, smiling for the good of their souls. So, he would not arrive at the end of the night. What does that matter if at the end the night dissolves? In the darkest of grief he heard the cock crow, he carried victory in the heart of his disaster. He carried, he wrote, the sun in his darkness.[19]

In Budapest in October 1956 the entry of Soviet tanks to crush an uprising made blood flow. Jean-Paul Sartre protested as did Picasso. Aragon was president of the National Writers Guild, where there was a division of opinion. Aragon's personal decision was to support the position of his party, which called the intervention justified. But in the review he directed, *Les Lettres françaises*, he published communiqués from persecuted intellectuals in Hungary and expressed solidarity with them. He helped win the commutation of two death sentences against Hungarian writers.

His next literary creation, a novel titled *La semaine sainte* (Holy Week) (1958), proved to be a tremendous success with critics and the public.[20] While writing it, he had freed himself from any engagement to promote the party or the principles of socialist realism. The setting is France during Holy Week 1815, as King Louis XVIII is fleeing north from Paris to escape from Napoleon, who has suddenly returned from his first exile. The hero of the novel is Géricault, a French artist and friend of the great David d'Angers, painter of the French Revolution. Aragon later said that he modeled his Géricault on James Dean, a young American movie actor gifted with human qualities of goodness, force, and intelligence. The moral of the story is that the diversity of the French nation is a treasure and that no one has the all-serving key to history. The vision of all the participants is too short when judged from the perspective of later generations. This is a judgment on himself for having placed so much faith in Stalin.

He continued to serve as a member of the Central Committee of the PCF. In 1960–61 on the invitation of a commercial publisher, he participated with André Malraux in a volume titled *Histoire parallèle de l'URSS et des Etats-Unis* (Parallel History of the USSR and the USA). Aragon wrote the section on the Soviet Union, relying for most of his information on Soviet sources. These were opened sufficiently to researchers to allow him to confirm the charges of errors and crimes made in Khrushchev's campaign against Stalin. Aragon's comment suggested that other Soviet leaders must have been collaborators with Stalin in these crimes. There had been, he wrote, a "framework of complicities," though this did not diminish Stalin's responsibility.[21]

Emerging here for the first time was an assertion by this French Communist leader of an independent right to pass judgment in a public forum on the conduct and policies of Soviet leaders. The trial of Bukharin and Rykov in 1938 had not yet been challenged publicly in the Soviet Union. Nevertheless, Aragon scathingly wrote: "The question posed by the trial of March 1938 [that of Bukharin and Rykov] is not: what are the false elements in this trial? Rather it is: what are the true elements in it?"

Aragon continued as editor of *Les Lettres françaises*, subject to control by the party. He used this publication to draw the PCF leadership, which was still dominated by views and habits formed in the Stalin era, toward a more critical and independent conscience. Many times he or Triolet or both were condemned by *L'Humanité* or in speeches of delegates at party congresses for their writings critical of the Soviet Union. But Aragon knew he had the support of Roger Garaudy, a member of the Political Bureau, and he believed he also had the sympathy of Maurice Thorez. Garaudy, a philosopher who put a premium on original thinking, wrote a defense of Aragon in 1961.[22] Fortified by his notable success in linking Communism with French independence of action during the period of the Resistance, Aragon again listened to his own instincts in betting that he could strengthen the party's self-respect as well as its respect by the public by fearlessly showing critical judgment, whatever the reaction in Moscow.

As editor of his review, he pushed to the limits his independence of decision to give open support to intellectuals in Prague and Poland. Thus during the years leading to 1968 he played an important role in encouraging the development of the Prague Spring.

He and Triolet traveled to Prague in 1965. There Aragon delivered a speech in which he urged the Czech party to show a greater openness to the new currents flowing in the circles of European intellectuals. A year later Aragon asserted the importance of independence of artists and intellectuals from party control by protesting publicly against the condemnation of Andrei Siniavski and Yuri Daniel in the Soviet Union.

In the spring of 1966, at the meeting of the Central Committee of the PCF at Argenteuil, Aragon had the satisfaction of seeing his amendment to a party proposition on artistic freedom adopted. In its final form this stated that the right of creators to conduct research must not be limited. The party would sustain the contributions of creators to human progress in the free deployment of their imagination, their taste, and their originality. Artistic creation could not be conceived without research, without currents, without a diversity of schools, and without confrontation among them.[23]

This was a strong French contribution to a debate over artistic and intellectual freedom then taking place in Eastern Europe.

THE UNION OF THE LEFT

In this meeting of the central committee of the PCF at Argenteuil in March 1966 (Maurice Thorez had died in 1964) General Secretary Waldeck Rochet confirmed the orientation he wanted to give his troops:

We think that the parties of the left, and above all the Socialist Party and the Communist Party, should immediately reach an accord on a common program. Since the concept of the "unique party" has been abandoned for that of a "plurality of parties," it is obvious that no single party will be in power; all parties working for the construction of socialism will be in power. We consider that the only way to hasten the advent of socialism in France is to be found in close cooperation between the Communist Party and the Socialist Party and, more generally, in the collaboration among all the political and social forces interested in the construction of socialism and the development of socialist democracy.[24]

Some Communists, out of their attachment to Leninist tradition, condemned Rochet and his strategy of the French road to socialism as revisionist and reformist, a kind of "French exceptionalism." Rochet replied that, on the contrary, his was "the way to be a revolutionary in France in our time."

Rochet's succession to the top office after serving for several years as principal aide to Thorez seemed to indicate the party was steady on course with no important reorientation in prospect. It now appears, looking back on the period of his mandate, that the party was starting down a new road under the compulsions of French electoral conditions. It would be several years yet before the full implications of the Rochet initiatives would become clear. By then a new ideology had taken root through practice become habit. Theoretical justifications would be undertaken only after the fact.

During the 1960s the PCF took its first steps in putting some distance between itself and the Communist Party of the Soviet Union. It expressed publicly its concern over the removal of Khrushchev as general secretary of the Soviet Party in 1964. And in 1966 it protested, as we have noted, through statements made by Louis Aragon, the trials of Soviet dissidents Siniavsky and Daniel.

The clearest expression of this new independence from Moscow came when five countries of the Warsaw Pact, led by the Soviet Union, intervened militarily in Czechoslovakia on August 19, 1968. Rochet had warned the Soviet leadership not to expect support from the PCF for such an action. He and most of his colleagues in the French politburo believed the Prague Spring was not a danger to the Socialist order in Czechoslovakia. On the contrary, it promised to strengthen popular acceptance by making changes in the direction of more democracy and a more "human face." This would help the Communist Party in France. To the French Communist leaders it was important to establish the freedom of Communist parties, including those of Eastern Europe, to deal with their problems in their own way, especially when, as in the case of Czechoslovakia, there did not seem to be much danger of counter-revolution emerging from the reforms proposed by the Czech party. On several occasions during the months prior to the August intervention, emissaries from the PCF had offered their good offices in mediating between Czechs and Soviets.[25]

The crisis, when it came, was viewed as an unwelcome challenge for the PCF, forcing a break in the tradition of solid support for Moscow since 1920. Rochet and the politburo, through the pages of L'Humanité, took the plunge into public condemnation of the Soviet-initiated action. In this they were opposed by Jeannette Vermeersch, the widow of Maurice Thorez, a clear sign that an older order was being put aside with an unprecedented manifestation of independence from Moscow. Still, the case was treated as exceptional and clearly did not signify any break by the PCF from its overall loyalty to the Soviet camp.

In the turbulent national crisis of May 1968, begun by students, the general strike of French workers for political goals eventually played an important role. Millions of workers laid down their tools, stopped their machines, and occupied their enterprises for several weeks. In the ensuing negotiations among government, employers, and labor unions over union demands, agreements were reached that led to increases in wages and salaries and increased freedom for the unions to act on workers' behalf, with formal recognition on the shop floor. The scope and intensity of these workers' struggles might well have caused the Communist Party of France to reconsider and revise the emphasis that Rochet was placing on elections as the principal means of advance into Socialism. That did not take place.

On the contrary, despite a setback at the polls (a decline of 2 percent) in the first electoral test following the May 1968 confrontations, the Central Committee of the PCF issued at a meeting in December 1968 at Champigny a manifesto committing the party to a loyal focus on democratic elections as the strategy to be employed in replacing capitalism with Socialism.[26] At the heart of this strategy was a "Union of the Left" around a common program. This would produce electoral victories to create an advanced democracy and thereby open the road for a peaceful change to Socialism. The explicit promise was to save the country the pains of civil war by generating through "union" a majority sufficiently strong to dissuade reactionary forces from taking up arms to preserve their old privileges as the peaceful democratic revolution realized itself in Socialism.

Coming at the end of 1968, a year with unmistakable expressions of widespread discontent, the Champigny manifesto was a significant document in the history of the party, of France and even of Western Europe. It meant that Bolshevism itself (not just the Stalinist variant) was being cast aside under the pressure of experience in "French conditions." It expressed an acceptance of the necessity to compete for support from philistine voters in the pursuit of the vaguely envisioned goal inherited from Jean Jaurès, of socialism *aux couleurs de la France* (with French characteristics). The need for unity with the SFIO had already been recognized in the formal abandonment by the PCF of the Bolshevik concept of *le parti unique* (the single party). The Communists, slipping in the polls from election to election and not seeing any real possibility of winning an electoral majority on their own, made the fundamental decision at this time to find a way to incorporate themselves into an electoral alliance that stood a chance of winning political power. This way, they told themselves, lies Socialism.

The leadership of the PCF undoubtedly was tempted into the strategy of a union of the left by its strength relative to the Socialists. After the envisioned victory of the Union at the polls, the Communists could expect to hold sway in a new government. In the presidential election in 1969 after de Gaulle's resignation (with Mitterrand forced to watch from the sidelines), the Communists ran Jacques Duclos as their candidate, since in the circumstances there was no possibility of a Union candidacy. He won 21.5 percent of the vote in the first round compared with 5 percent for the Socialist candidate, Gaston Defferre.

The Communists saw this spread between the results of the two candidates, rivals for votes of the left, as a further indication that they could keep their advantage over the Socialists into the distant future. History proved them wrong in that assessment. Overconfidence in their rivalry with Socialists was a factor in the determination of the Communists in the early 1970s to concentrate their efforts on achieving a Union of the Left. At just this moment (1971), Mitterrand was joining the renewed Socialist Party to became its principal leader (see Chapter 3). This would make a Union of the Left possible but, as we shall see, with different results for the PCF from those they foresaw in proposing it.

The Gaullist, Georges Pompidou, was elected president in the second round of the 1969 election. Neither the candidate of the Communists nor of the Socialists had enough votes to run in the second round, another argument for seeking unity of the left in the future.

Rochet was forced into retirement by illness in 1970. Georges Marchais became acting general secretary of the PCF, and when Rochet's disability proved permanent, Marchais was named to succeed him. The moment was right to impress public opinion with the ability of the PCF to change course and prepare for electoral battles on new terms, strengthened by alliances formed on the basis of a common program. This was the tenor of the first major document issued by the party under Marchais's leadership (1971). It was titled *Changer de cap*, (Change of Course).

NOTES

1. "If Frossard, in private, describes himself as reticent regarding what he has seen in Moscow, Cachin returns converted and his proselytism will act with decisive weight in the tilting of French socialism toward communism, carried out during the Congress of Tours." Stéphane Courtois and Marc Lazar, *Histoire du Parti communiste français* (Paris: Presses Universitaires de France, 1995), 52.

2. Louis Aragon, *Le mouvement perpétuel*, preceded by *Feu de joie* (Paris: Editions Gallimard, 1970).

3. *Sic* (Paris), March 1918, quoted in André Gavillet, *La littérature au défi: Aragon surrealiste* (Neuchatel, Switzerland: Editions de la Baconnière, 1957), 49.

4. Louis Aragon, *Le paysan de Paris* (Paris: Gallimard, 1926); an English translation by Frederick Brown was published with the title *Nightwalker* (Englewood Cliffs, N.J.: Prentice-Hall, 1970).

5. Lucille F. Becker, *Louis Aragon* (New York: Twayne Publishers, 1971), 113.

6. Gavillet, *La littérature au défi*, 170.

7. Ibid., 218.

8. Louis Aragon, *La peinture au défi* (Paris: Librairie J. Corti, 1930).

9. André Breton, *Second manifeste du surrealisme* (1930), in André Breton, *Manifestes du surrealisme* (Paris: Gallimard, Collection Folio/Essais, undated), 89.

10. Pierre Daix, *Aragon* (Paris: Flammarion, 1994), 317.

11. Ibid., 337.

12. Ibid., 320.

13. Louis Aragon, *Le roman inachevé* (Paris: Gallimard, 1956); republished (Paris: NRF, Gallimard, 1966), 186–87.

14.   Quoted in Daix, *Aragon*, 341.

15.   Daix, *Aragon*, 366.

16.   Ibid., 393.

17.   Claude Roy, *Moi je* (Paris: Gallimard, 1969), 444–46.

18.   Daix, *Aragon*, 461.

19.   Aragon, *Le roman inachevé*, 233–34.

20.   Louis Aragon, *La semaine sainte* (Paris: Gallimard, 1958).

21.   Daix, *Aragon*, 488.

22.   Roger Garaudy, *L'Itinéraire d'Aragon (du surrealisme au monde réel)* (Paris: Gallimard, 1961).

23.   Daix, *Aragon*, 516.

24.   Roger Martelli, *Communisme français: Histoire sincère du PCF 1920–1984* (Paris: Messidor, Editions Sociales, 1984), 188.

25.   Ibid., 198.

26.   Ibid., 199–202.

5

How Mitterrand Won the Presidency

Oh villain! Thou wilt be condemned into everlasting redemption for this.

—William Shakespeare
Much Ado About Nothing

At the Congress of the renewed Socialist Party at Epinay in 1971, Mitterrand had emerged victorious, thanks to some astute alliances with regional notables such as Gaston Defferre and Pierre Mauroy and with the left currents in the party represented by Jean Poperen and Jean-Pierre Chevènement (CERES). Mitterrand had made it clear that he regarded the formation of an electoral bloc with the Communists as a promising strategy in the battle to win power away from the rightist parties, which still dominated the Parliament and held the office of president in the person of Georges Pompidou, elected in 1969. As the new first secretary of the Socialist Party, Mitterrand began the delicate maneuvering within the party to promote agreement on a common program to be presented to the PCF as the basis for their alliance in a Union of the Left.

To reassure Socialists who feared that negotiations with the PCF would put them in a subordinate position, Mitterrand used his good relations with the Radical Party of the Left (MRG) to bring them into the Union as an additional counterweight to the Communists. Some 80 percent of the MRG deputies were favorable to this overture and were represented in the subsequent negotiations by Robert Fabre. The leadership of the PCF, elated that the Socialists were finally being brought around by their new first secretary to acceptance of the electoral Union, agreed to inclusion of the Radicals. This was a clear indication that all, including the Communists, recognized the necessity of drafting a modest, reformist, social-democratic program on which these partners of convenience could campaign without compromising anyone's abhorrence of Bolshevism.

The Communists had decided to court a wider national audience by burying their distinctive revolutionary message within the Union. This might, they thought, be a road to power by using the electoral process in collaboration with others. On the basis of elections since 1945, the Communists in 1972 still saw themselves as the strongest of the parties of the left. If the Union was able to win a majority in Parliament, it was likely the Communists would be in a position to demand key positions in the government, including the office of prime minister. That promised to open a wholly new epoch with unlimited possibilities for the Communists.

Among the Socialists the CERES current was closest to the Communists and was the strongest in its support for cooperating with them in an electoral Union. Mitterrand, who had received the crucial support of CERES at Epinay, naturally gave it a dominant role in carrying forward the drafting of a common program and negotiating it with the PCF. Jean-Pierre Chevènement, a principal leader in CERES, was named to the Secretariat of the Socialist Party (PS) with special responsibility to prepare the Socialist position on a common program. This was Mitterrand's way of maximizing the chances of successful negotiations. Few other Socialist leaders shared the conviction of Mitterrand and Chevènement that the common program and a Union of the Left would ultimately place the Socialists in power. It did not worry Chevènement that the Communists would be sharing in that conquest of the powers of government. Mitterrand foresaw that the common program was a way of bringing an end to Communist hegemony of the Left, a way of strengthening the Socialists at the expense of both the right and the Communists.

To disarm opponents to negotiations within the PS, Mitterrand and Chevènement asked the PCF for formal guarantees on three issues: (1) respect of the PCF for the results of elections; (2) willingness to respect and implement the principle of *alternance*, meaning that the Communists, like others, would surrender power if voted out of office; and (3) independence of all parties from foreign control, specifically of the PCF from Moscow. In the course of negotiations the PCF representatives gave guarantees on all three of these matters.

These demands incidentally helped the new leader of the PCF, Georges Marchais, move his party from a proudly cherished tradition of Bolshevism toward positions soon to be proclaimed in documents of the PCF as essential features of the French road to socialism. The PCF option, under Marchais's leadership, for a common program and a Union of the Left was one feature of a broad re-examination of theory and reorientation of strategy. This evolution was examined in Chapter 4.

In the ensuing negotiations over the common program, Chevènement and the PCF favored an undertaking to nationalize the automobile industry (thus adding Peugeot and Citroen to the already nationalized Renault works), the Hachette publishing house, and Thompson, a leading firm in the electronics industry. Mitterrand resisted these proposals on the ground it would be too much for the Radicals to swallow. Accord was reached on an imprecise formula that promised nationalization of major banks and some industrial enterprises. In the steel industry the government would undertake to acquire ownership of a majority share interest through market purchases.

Since there was a will to end these discussions in a public announcement of agreement, neither Mitterrand, Chevènement, nor the PCF insisted on specificity. To satisfy the PS, a goal of *autogestion* (self-management by workers) was jointly proclaimed, because the leaders of the Socialist-leaning labor union, the CFDT, was using it as a recruiting and mobilizing slogan. (Later the PCF also adopted this word to define a part of its program). In foreign policy, lip service was paid to the Atlantic Alliance. There was also agreement on a commitment to abandon reliance on France's strategic nuclear weapons.

The most striking consequence of the common program was the following paradox: It was proposed and sought by the PCF and achieved only because Mitterrand was able to overcome opposition in the Socialist Party. Yet during the period of the duration of the agreement on a common program (1972–77) the Socialist Party steadily gained in strength while the Communists were losing. Mitterrand was able to profit from the common program by drawing to himself the votes of Communists. Yet in the same period he reassured centrists opposed to any collaboration with Communists and won their votes by conspicuously distancing himself from the common program.

Underlying the common program, in fact, was an implacable hostility between its two promoters, the PCF and Mitterrand. Both hoped they could outwit the other in a contest for the most benefit from appearing to reach agreement. In the end the PCF clearly did not win at this game. It is not certain, however, that Mitterrand gained much, if anything, with this Machiavellian twist in his rise to power. Its most permanent result was to reinforce the PCF's hatred of Mitterrand and Mitterrand's satisfaction at its declining influence.

The presidential election of 1974, made necessary by the death in office of Georges Pompidou, came while the PCF was still triumphantly waving the banner of the common program. Immediately, even before the Socialist Party had decided whom to endorse as a candidate, the PCF called on Mitterrand to run and promised its support. The PS was in accord and named him the candidate of the Socialist Party at a special congress called for the purpose.

Mitterrand declared his candidacy but soon indicated he would not run on a platform of the common program. He would try to emulate de Gaulle in running as a candidate independent of the parties that had declared their support for him. It was a way of wooing centrist voters by assuring them he was not an ordinary Socialist ideologue and certainly not beholden to the Communist Party. He also excluded Chevènement and other representatives of the CERES faction from his campaign team because they, too, frightened centrist voters.

The principal references to the common program during the 1974 campaign came from Mitterrand's opponents, Valéry Giscard d'Estaing and Jacques Chaban-Delmas. They used it to warn voters of the dangers in voting for this candidate of the "socio-communist" Union of the Left. The PCF tried to counter this campaign by declaring that it would expect to receive only a third of the portfolios in a Mitterrand Cabinet and not the post of prime minister.

Most commentators, especially the Socialists, expressed surprise at this modesty in Communist expectations. It underlined the commitment of the Communists to participate in a subordinate role in a social-democratic government with reformist, not revolutionary, pretensions. It also gave added poignancy to the dilemma they had created for themselves in fostering pursuit of a role in government through a common program. As Mitterrand had insisted, a condition of electoral success on the basis of a common program was that the Socialist Party replace the Communist Party as the dominant party of the left. Otherwise, a Union of the Left could never win the centrist votes essential to majority support. By effacing themselves to help Mitterrand win, the Communists were showing that they agreed with that analysis. Yet the Communists wanted to raise the numbers in their own electorate. Victory in their rivalry with the Socialist Party continued to be an orienting ambition.

Mitterrand had the highest vote of the three candidates in the first round of the 1974 election, with 43 percent. That was a substantial improvement over his first round score in 1965 (32 percent) and much better than that of the Socialist candidate, Deferre, in 1969 (5 percent). Under Mitterrand's leadership, the left was clearly gaining. In the second round of voting, the margin of his loss to the single candidate of the right, Giscard d'Estaing, was less than 2 percent.

Later in 1974, in the course of by-elections to fill vacant seats in the Parliament, the Communists saw evidence that the common program was working against their interests. In five of six elections the Socialist candidate received more votes than the Communist in the first round. And in the Savoie, where the Communist came in ahead of the Socialist in the first round, it was clear from the count after the final round that many votes that had gone in the first round to the Socialist were not then transferred to the Communist, who ended by losing to the candidate of the right. Discipline in the practice of *désistement* (voting in the second round for the left candidate who had done best in the first round) was lacking in the Socialist Party. The better-disciplined Communists, on the other hand, were helping put Socialists into the Parliament. There were some complaints regarding this imbalance from the politburo, leading to speculation that the PCF might formally renounce the Union of the Left. However, given the years of effort the PCF leadership had invested in its pursuit and promotion, that was not acceptable. Loyalty to the Union of the Left and the common program had been proclaimed Communist virtues. This would continue to be the fundamental line right through the important Twenty-Second PCF Congress in 1976.

MICHEL ROCARD

To continue this narrative of Mitterrand's rise to the presidency, it is appropriate to give a fuller account of another important character: Michel Rocard. Born and raised in a Catholic family and educated in a Catholic school, Rocard showed a spirit of rebellion by converting to Protestantism and taking the name of Michel Servet. This was the French name of a theologian, better known as Michael Servetus, burned by Calvin in 1553. He is regarded as one of the progenitors of Unitarianism. There is in Rocard a lively appreciation of the rich heritage of religious polemics produced by the Reformation and the wars of religion. His salute to the martyred Servetus expressed an overriding attachment to independence of thought and commitment on moral and political questions. He was greatly influenced by his study of Proudhon, who reached conclusions favoring socialism on the basis of considerations of morality, humanity and justice. The importance Rocard attached to religion as a foundation of personal morality and social solidarity kept him from paying much attention to the teachings of Karl Marx.

While still a student, Rocard joined the SFIO in 1949 and in 1955 became national secretary of the socialist youth movement attached to the SFIO. He demonstrated his willingness to defy his own party (Mollet was premier) by opposing the "Algerian War," that is, the French effort in Algeria to put down the movement for independence. His differences with the SFIO during Mollet's ascendancy led him to take part in the creation of a "renewed" party, calling itself the Unified Socialist Party (PSU), critical of the SFIO on colonial issues and on the SFIO's traditional tendency to rely on the state for the promotion of social progress.

The PSU, for many years led and dominated by Rocard, was never a promoter of bourgeois liberalism in the economic sense. But it fostered a spirit of libertarian openness to rebels around the new causes of the 1960s: feminism, ecology, "freedom of imagination," anti-authoritarianism, pacifism, Trotskyism. The PSU was not at all repelled by the anarchist spirit prevailing in these movements, and it supported their anti-Communism. Much more than the SFIO or the PCF, the PSU immediately shared in the enthusiasm of the student rebels who took to the streets in May 1968. The PSU was considered to be a factor in the "new left." Its membership grew rapidly from 9,000 to 15,000 in 1968 following the *carnivalesque* May political crisis. Thus Rocard's political career had the aura of libertarian leftism. In contrast with Mitterrand, he did not come to the Socialist Party of the 1970s from the right or from the centrist sector, the Radicals. He began his career in the SFIO and left it to form a party that claimed to be more modern, more adapted to the concerns of a new generation, more in tune with technocratic changes and no less devoted to socialist goals.

In the presidential election of 1969, the PSU refused to join the SFIO in support of a single Socialist candidate. Instead, it named Rocard to run as its candidate. He received national attention and conducted a dynamic campaign. He won 3.7 percent of the votes cast, considered promising since he was competing with candidates of both the SFIO and the PCF. A few months later he was elected to the national Parliament from Yvelines, defeating a Gaullist luminary, Couve de Murville.

Rocard was not present at the Congress of Epinay in 1971, where Mitterrand made his play for the leadership of the Socialist Party and won. Rocard scoffed at the claim that the Party had been "renewed." He continued to see in the PSU the real hope of a socialist future for France. He rejected the idea of a common program with the Communists, a difference over strategy with Mitterrand that made him attractive to many Socialists. A campaign began to bring Rocard and his faction back into the "old house" of the new Socialist Party.

The parliamentary elections of 1973 were a disappointment to Rocard. The vote for the PSU candidates showed no gain over past elections, and Rocard lost his seat in the National Assembly. He resigned as first secretary of the PSU and let it be known he was disillusioned with his previous role as a socialist knight on his own.

When Mitterrand ran as an independent candidate for the presidency in 1974 rather than as the candidate of the Socialist Party, he invited Rocard to join his campaign staff and Rocard accepted. Despite their differences a rapprochement had begun. This complemented and illuminated Mitterrand's playing down the common program during the 1974 campaign. With the Communists fully committed to his support in the long-range strategy to win the Elysée Palace from the right, Mitterrand began to focus on the task he saw as vital to victory, strengthening the Socialist Party to give it hegemony in the Union of the Left.

Pierre Mauroy, the mayor of Lille and Socialist notable of northern France, played a key role in opening the doors of the Socialist Party to Rocard and his faction and urging them to enter and advocate their ideas from within. In this initiative Mauroy was opposed by Chevènement of the CERES faction, who feared a change in the balance of power within the Socialist Party, leading perhaps toward an abandonment of the common program and a serious internal crisis. Mitterrand was not moved by these warnings from Chevènement and supported Mauroy's call for a "Socialist Assize" (*des assises du socialisme*). This was held in October 1974 with the purpose of bringing together numerous socialist currents, like that of Rocard's PSU, leaders of the CFDT labor union (Edmond Maire, the general secretary, close to Rocard), and members of various political clubs including Exchanges and Projects, founded by Jacques Delors, hitherto best known as a counselor to Jacques Chaban-Delmas. Mitterrand wanted to strengthen the Socialist Party by recruiting in all directions, especially in the center of the political spectrum. This was more important to him than maintaining a stable majority for the common program.

In his speech at the Assize, Rocard declared the common program outdated and too oriented on centralized state authority. Still, this difference did not prevent him from responding favorably to the courtship of Mitterrand and Mauroy. He began the process of rejoining the Socialist Party, accompanied by many of his faction. The Assize approved a text titled "For Socialism" (*Pour le socialisme*). It left in doubt future relations with the Communist Party, which had not been invited to attend the Assize. The text did not, however, repudiate the common program. It declared the common will of participants in the Assize to cooperate with each other in coming together in one organization, thereby working for a union of forces of the left "in the perspective of *autogestion*." This emphasis showed the willingness of the Socialist Party to adopt some of the slogans dear to Rocard and Edmond Maire.

Chevènement and the CERES faction inveighed against this introduction into the Socialist house of new elements opposed to the strategy of the common program. Mitterrand had come to power in the party at the Congress of Epinay with the help of CERES. Nevertheless, Mitterrand was now ready to offend CERES by keeping its representatives off the party's executive committee. This was another signal to the Communist Party that the orientation of the Socialist Party was changing and that the Union of the Left was taking on a new character.

Over the next two and a half years, Mitterrand worked astutely to placate CERES by supporting some of its calls for more discipline in forcing on reluctant local Socialist Party organizations the obligation of preparing joint lists of candidates with the Communist Party and living by the rules of the common program and *désistement*. This reassured the Communists and enabled Mitterrand and the Socialist Party to maintain an image of champions of unity on the left. Unity appealed to workers, and for that reason no party to the Union of the Left wanted to lay itself open to the charge of betraying and wounding the Union.

During this period (1975–76), the revolution in Portugal put a new strain on the French Union of the Left. The Portuguese Communist Party under General Secretary Alvaro Cunhal was playing a dominant role through its ability to stage strikes and street demonstrations in support of factions in the military government that had overthrown the colonial dictatorship. The Communists were opposed by Mario Soares and a Portuguese Socialist Party affiliated with the Socialist International. In France, as anyone could have predicted, the PCF gave its support to Cunhal and the Portuguese Communists, while the PS expressed its preference for Soares and fellow Socialists of the Socialist International. There were many parallels here to the 1930s and the historic Popular Front, which was subjected to great strain by differences between French Communists and Socialists over how to deal with the situation created by the civil war in Spain.

In an article published in *Le Nouvel Observateur* on Mitterrand's departure from the presidency in May 1995, Mario Soares gave an account of the support he received from Mitterrand during the civil strife in Portugal following the "Carnation Revolution" in 1974:

Mitterrand, while remaining faithful to the strategy of Union of the Left that he had defined, never hesitated to give his active solidarity to the Portuguese Socialist Party, grasping with great lucidity what was at stake in Portugal as in Europe and in Africa. He spoke to French Socialist voters who were less conscious or less sensitive to this problem, opening their eyes to the totalitarian turn then being taken by the Portuguese revolution. He even warned Brezhnev, in Moscow, of the dangers to détente if Portugal should become the "Cuba of Europe," as some wished. In that line, his help and his frank solidarity were precious to the Portuguese Socialist Party.[1]

Mitterrand undoubtedly used these years to build the strength of the Socialist Party and establish the condition he judged to be vital to his own election in 1981, which he called *rééquilibrage*. This meant that the Socialist Party should acquire "hegemony" on the left by surpassing the Communist Party in the ability to win votes in elections. The goal was achieved for the first time in the cantonal elections of March 1976, when 502 Socialists were elected (against 308 in the previous cantonal election) with 26.5 percent of the votes, compared to 22.8 percent for the Communists. This was a rude blow to Georges Marchais, who had recently led the PCF through its Twenty-Second Congress confirming the dedication of the party to the common program, democracy and "socialisme aux couleurs de la France."

Most of the gains in this growing Socialist Party vote were attributable to its opening toward the Rocard faction, toward the Catholic-oriented sectors of the labor movement (Edmond Maire and the CFDT), and toward the centrist sectors symbolized by Jacques Delors and Jacques Attali. Efforts at recruitment in these centrist sectors became more productive as the Mitterrand strategy of Socialist hegemony on the left became more evident and better understood. It was easier now for confirmed anti-Communists to vote for the Socialist Party and even join it. Confidence rose that Mitterrand and his faction were strong enough and shrewd enough to keep the Communists in check. This made it more difficult for candidates of the right to draw votes away from Socialists by playing on fears of Communism.

This movement of the Socialist Party toward the center in its campaign to increase its vote was the cause of frequent polemics within the Socialist Party. The CERES faction, supported by Poperen and his left-wing followers, accused the Mitterrandists of abandoning the strategy of the common program. These complaints usually produced formal statements from Socialist Party conferences and congresses that the party was still guided in its strategy by its undertakings to support the common program. There were occasional calls on local Socialist Party officials to conduct themselves accordingly.

The fact was that the rising strength of the Socialists at the polls combined with an apparent disorientation and confusion among Communists to produce a fundamental weakening of the ability of the PCF to profit as it had envisaged from the electoral alliance with the Socialists. In the first round of voting, a preliminary contest between Socialist and Communist candidates functioned as a measure of their relative strengths. The Communist candidate had to win in this contest with a Socialist or Radical rival to have the benefit of *désistement* in the final round against the leading candidate of the right. In the municipal elections of March 1977, there were seventeen confrontations between Communists and Socialists for control of the major city governments. The Socialists won fourteen of these contests, eliminating the Communist contenders. The Communist Party discovered that the strategy of the common program was serving to raise the Socialist Party to power in more and more electoral districts.

These developments in the period 1972–77 confirmed the analysis Mitterrand had used at the Congress of Epinay in winning the leadership of the Socialist Party: An agreement with the PCF on a common program would help the Socialist Party rise to power if the PS could achieve *rééquilibrage*, that is, establish hegemony over the PCF. Once he had won over the PS to that strategy, by appealing to deep-seated anti-Communism to win approval of an agreement with Communists, he used his long-cultivated relations with centrist elements to build the strength of the Socialist Party. This, combined with a decline in the appeal of the PCF to voters for whatever reasons, made possible the ultimate victory of Mitterrand and the Socialists in 1981.

The year 1977 proved to be a critical turning point for Mitterrand's strategy of Epinay, the strategy of committing to a common program with the Communists. The Socialist Party Congress of Nantes, which opened on June 17, 1977, once again tested the balance of forces among the different factions of the party.

Favoring Mitterrand's continued authority in the party were its spectacular gains since he had become first secretary in 1971. Recruiting had accelerated, with a gain of 100,000 members in the previous two years. Distribution of its three principal publications, *Le Poing et la Rose*, *L'Unité*, and *Combat Socialiste*, was rising. A party telephone central, "Hello, PS," was receiving hundreds of calls of inquiry every day. A National Center of training had been created. The number of Socialist Party cells or groups in work enterprises (called *sections d'entreprises* and *groupes socialistes d'enterprises*) had more than doubled. An effort had been made to attract more women by raising to 15 percent the minimal number of women named to committees of leadership. All this contributed to the improved success of the party at the polls. The *Mitterrandistes* in the halls of the Congress of Nantes could boast that since the last Socialist congress, the party had established itself as "the leading party of the left, the leading party of the country."

Nevertheless, all were aware that this growth had been achieved by the incorporation into the party of Rocard's faction, and this provoked a dangerous confrontation of two conflicting cultures within the party, threatening its unity. To CERES and Poperen followers, the Rocard faction and new arrivals from the center aggravated the tendencies toward reformism, social democracy and accommodation to capitalism. These critics were able to point with alarm at the weakness of the party's recruitment efforts among blue-collar working people. As the party grew, its social composition became more weighted toward the middle class, professionals, and managers.

At Nantes it was evident that the changes in the party since 1972 had undermined its commitment (which had always been ambivalent) to the alliance with the PCF. Calls from the CERES spokesmen for flexibility in negotiations with the Communists over an updating of the common program led to the exclusion of CERES from the party Secretariat (though Chevènement, along with Rocard and two others, was named to the team that would negotiate with the Communists). It was also the sense of the Congress that the demand from the PCF for the designation of more nationalizations should be resisted. Specifically, two CERES motions were defeated: (1) to nationalize any enterprise in which a majority of its workers called for it; and (2) to give workers a right of veto over the naming of the managers of their enterprise. In these debates Mitterrand distanced himself from CERES and accepted the consequences of the more centrist character of the party resulting from the changes that he himself had fostered. The days of the Union of the Left were numbered. If the PCF wanted to let it die, an explanation was ready at hand: The Socialist Party had veered to the right.

Negotiations over the updating of the common program dragged on over the summer of 1977. Agreement could not be reached on the minimum wage, on the number of enterprises to be nationalized, or on the rights of workers to participate in the naming of managers. On August 3, Marchais went on national television to deliver a scathing attack on Mitterrand. The Socialist press responded in kind against the PCF. Both sides were preparing their cohorts for the coming rupture. In September another round seemed staged to display a goodwill effort by the participants to find a compromise. But by then it was becoming clear to all that the indispensable will to continue the cooperation undertaken in 1972 had expired. Robert Fabre of the Left Radicals was the first to announce, on September 14, 1977, that he was pulling out.

Mitterrand was not willing to abandon the stance of unity on the left. Strongly supported by CERES and the Poperen faction, he won a mandate from the Socialist Party national convention of November 1977 to resume negotiations with the PCF. Negotiators for the Socialists were instructed to yield on the question of the minimum wage, accepting the Communists' demand to raise it to 2,400 francs (approximately $600 per month). This gesture was not enough to persuade the Communists to yield on other outstanding issues. Both parties were prepared to accept the rupture, with many leaders on both sides welcoming it.

It is impossible to know for sure the effect on the electorate of this failure to agree on an updated common program. Each party tried to lay the blame on the other. What is certain is that in the elections of deputies to the Parliament in March 1978, the Socialist Party candidates won 24 percent of the votes in the first round to the Communists' 20.6 percent. It now seemed confirmed beyond question that the Socialist Party had become the leading party of the left in the competition for votes. The other certainty was that in the final round the parties of the right retained a clear majority and therefore prolonged their control of the government.

Many rank and file Socialists and Communists were disappointed and felt an opportunity had been lost for a unified left to win the right to name a prime minister and run the government. President Giscard d'Estaing would nevertheless have had the right to continue in office until his mandate expired in 1981. Perhaps it was fortunate for Mitterrand that he would be free in 1981 to run without having to bear any responsibility for what Parliament did and did not do in the years leading up to the presidential election. Furthermore, the de facto demise in 1977–78 of the common program and Socialist-Communist unity left Mitterrand in a position to court the voters of the center without the burden of a formal alliance with the PCF.

But the nomination of a Socialist candidate to the presidency was still two years away, and a formidable rival, Michel Rocard, seized upon the breakdown of the common program to mount a campaign against the first secretary who had foisted the strategy on the party. Mitterrand with his common program was labeled passé, archaic. Rocard, with his engaging dynamism, accused those who had relied on agreements with the Communists of yielding to utopianism. What was needed was "modernism," a full recognition of the weight of "civil society" against the political illusions of those who had followed Mitterrand into unity with Communists.

Rocard, whose ambition to be elected president matched that of Mitterrand, dropped the new leftism with which he had won plaudits from anarchists and Trotskyists in the May 1968 drama in the universities. He began molding an image of himself as the champion of the modern middle class. His re-entry into the Socialist Party was seen as a strategy of preparing an electoral base on the left to which he would strive to join at election time the votes of a decisive bloc of centrist voters impressed by his appeal to the values and prejudices of the business class. Many described him as an innovator in French politics, bringing the style and sophisticated techniques of a candidate in a U.S. election. At least two important Socialist journals, *Le Nouvel Observateur* and *Matin de Paris*, were giving Rocard their support. Public opinion polls showed Rocard well ahead of Mitterrand for the presidency.

To meet this challenge, Mitterrand reorganized his general staff. He placed Paul Quilès, known for his remarkable abilities as an organizer, in charge of the immediate campaign for control of the Socialist Party. This would be a first step in the campaign for the presidency. Quilès would be aided by Henri Emmannuelli and Jean Auroux, both young and energetic. Mitterrand succeeded in attracting to his team two brilliant minds, Jacques Attali and Laurent Fabius, counselors whom he respected, heeded, and rewarded in the years to come. He made alliances with Pierre Bérégovoy and the leader of the leftist faction, Jean Poperen.

In April 1979, the Socialist Party Congress at Metz provided a test of ideas and a test of skill in political maneuvering. Paul Quilès and Laurent Fabius, playing conspicuous roles for the first time, showed outstanding ability in persuading undecided delegates to cast their votes for Mitterrand. Mitterrand emphasized the impressive advances made by the party since the Congress of Epinay. The strategy adopted there had by no means exhausted its potential, he said, and it should be pursued as the struggle to win governmental power entered the phase of presidential election. That meant hewing to the leftist line of the common program and unity of the left. As at Epinay, Mitterrand won the support of Chevènement and most of the delegates of the CERES faction with his militant anti-capitalist, pro-socialist rhetoric. Between himself and Rocard, who stressed caution and moderation in economic measures, Mitterrand gave the Congress a clear choice of rhetorical line. He employed such phrases as the necessity of "replacing" capitalism with Socialism, describing the goal as a "rupture" with capitalism.

Rocard lost to Mitterrand on all the crucial votes at Metz. The composition of the directing committee of the party, the executive bureau, and the Secretariat, all elected by the Congress, ensured that Mitterrand and his allies had decisively put down the Rocard attempt to take over direction of the party. The text adopted as the party's declaration of principles was proposed by the Mitterrand faction and negotiated with allies. And the task of drafting a "Socialist Party project," which any candidate seeking the support of the party would be expected to endorse, was assigned to Chevènement. This was certain to contain left-leaning declarations of principle unacceptable to Rocard.

Still, the party had not yet formally named its candidate for the presidency. Rocard made it clear he had not abandoned his intention to run. The polls continued to show he would have a better chance than Mitterrand in a race to defeat Giscard d'Estaing, who would certainly be a candidate for re-election. Rocard received praise in the liberal press, which saw him as capable of winning on a centrist platform and giving the country what it needed, a fresh start with safe, sensible reforms.

Rocard seemed to be positioning himself to neutralize Mitterrand's domination of the Socialist Party by giving his own candidacy such nationwide momentum that he could in effect pre-empt the field on the left, leaving the Socialist Party no alternative but to support him. Many Socialists, even some who had voted for Mitterrand's ideas at Metz, thought Rocard's campaign was the only way to defeat Giscard.

Mitterrand and Chevènement met this challenge with a draft of the Socialist project that clearly contradicted the line on which Rocard was campaigning. The draft was considered for formal adoption at a party meeting at Alfortville in January 1980. This tactic forced Rocard to choose between openly defying the party or wooing party support by a submissive vote for the project. He chose the latter course, thereby strengthening the claim of the party to be unified behind its project, but weakening his own strong appeal to center and right voters looking for a satisfactory alternative to Giscard.

Rocard had apparently decided he was not in a position to pre-empt the field and run against the clearly defined line of the Socialist Party. Instead, he sought to win endorsement of the party, accepting its project and hoping that even Mitterrand might finally step aside in favor of Rocard's candidacy in order to maximize the chances of defeating Giscard. Rocard announced his candidacy, adding that he would withdraw if Mitterrand decided to run.

The pressure on Mitterrand not to run, given the availability and the vigorous campaigning of the more popular candidate, Rocard, was brought to bear by editorial writers and commentators of the mass media. Mitterrand delayed announcing his decision until October 26, 1980. On that date, in Marseilles, he told the press he was ready to become a candidate if the Socialist Party declared it wanted him to run. He was sure the party would choose him over Rocard in a formal vote. The battles at Metz and Alfortville over the Socialist project had been mounted and fought precisely to isolate Rocard in the party and show him to be an outsider hostile to the line of the majority.

On January 24, 1981, Mitterrand was named the candidate of the Socialist Party by 83.5 percent of the ballots cast. To unify the party for the campaign, Mitterrand named Rocard (who had made good on his promise to withdraw) and Pierre Mauroy, a Socialist who had supported and voted for Rocard, to his Political Council. Mauroy was joined with Laurent Fabius in a flattering designation as the team of liaison of the Mitterrand campaign with the press. They were to be regarded as spokesmen for Mitterrand.

Mitterrand stepped down as first secretary of the party, to be succeeded by a relative newcomer, a young and vigorous supporter, Lionel Jospin. Jacques Attali continued as a close personal aide to Mitterrand in the new capacity of director of Cabinet. Paul Quilès was confirmed as campaign manager, assisted by Michel Charzat, Roger Fajardie, Michel de la Fournière, and Marcel Debarge. Jean Poperen was given responsibility for public meetings and endorsements, Pierre Bérégovoy for relations with other political parties, labor unions, and associations. Pierre Joxe was designated treasurer. Others named to positions of responsibility in preparing the campaign were Louis Mermaz, Georges Sarre, Georges Fillioud, Claude Estier, Jacques Piette, Louis Le Pensec, Jack Lang, Didier Motchane, Roger Hanin, Christiane Mora, Michel Pezet, Gérard Malfan, Nicole Questiaux, Serge Moati, Dominique Taddei. Among these names all factions of the Socialist Party were represented, balanced in a show of unity without discrimination.[2]

How could Mitterrand overcome the handicap evident in the polls taken in the early months of 1981? He was aided by a bitter division between the two principal candidates of the right, President Valéry Giscard d'Estaing of the UDF and Jacques Chirac of the Gaullist party, the RPR. Both underestimated their Socialist opponent, Mitterrand, whom they gave no chance of winning. Chirac intended to position himself to succeed Giscard d'Estaing, if not in 1981 then in 1988. He leveled much criticism at Giscard for the state of the economy and public discontent. Chirac's dynamism cost Giscard many votes in the first round of the election and seriously upset and wounded the president.

The Communist Party, still smarting from what it perceived as Mitterrand's betrayal of the common program, named its own candidate, Marchais, to run against the field, including the Socialist candidate. There was no longer a unity of the left.

During the campaign Mitterrand, accused of betraying the left, was excoriated by Marchais and other spokesmen for the Communist Party, such as Charles Fiterman. The demise of the Union of the Left was underlined by Marchais's declaration at the outset of the campaign that the *désistement* of Communist voters in favor of Mitterrand in the second round of voting was not to be presumed. This may have helped Mitterrand gain votes in the center from small-business circles and from the unemployed (10 percent of the work force in 1981), many of whom wanted nothing to do with communism. Among rank-and-file Communists were some staunch enthusiasts for the common program who refused to accept Marchais's fault-finding with Mitterrand and voted for the Socialist candidate in the first round of voting, preferring not to "waste" their vote on Marchais.

In contrast to Giscard, Chirac, and Marchais, Mitterrand campaigned in a low key manner, generating an impression of poise, depth, and self-confidence. Thus was born his identity as "the quiet force," *la force tranquille*. Occasionally he would draw blood: "Giscard of the four D's: decline, decadence, destruction and disarray," "a President at the end of his course" who "had not believed in his ideas sufficiently to put them into practice."

Giscard attempted to focus attention on the Socialist project, warning the country that it threatened rupture with unforeseeable consequences. Mitterrand parried this with his own platform of 110 propositions, more concrete and less radical, the only undertakings to which he pledged engagement. In the campaign Mitterrand thus separated himself from the sweeping Socialist project. It had served its purpose in helping Mitterrand hold on to the Socialist Party against the challenge of Rocard.

The first round of the election took place on April 26, 1981. The results were:

Giscard d'Estaing	28.3%
Mitterrand	25.8%
Chirac	17.9%
Marchais	15.3%

Giscard and Chirac, the candidates of the right, had between them only 46 percent of the votes. The final round, on May 10, pitted Giscard against Mitterrand.

Mitterrand's assiduous courtship of the Radicals, who occupied the center of the political spectrum, had been a feature of his tenure as first secretary of the Socialist Party. Aided by his own political origins, he had recruited among them and brought the Left Radicals (the MRG) into the strategy of the common program with the Communists. He was at home in those circles, and he now pitched his message to win their votes in the final round. As he expected, this did not cost him votes on the left. The Communists, recovering from shock at Marchais's poor showing in the first round, finally announced they would vote for Mitterrand as a vote against Giscard. They had the option of abstaining, but this would have definitely thrown the election to Giscard. Their votes were essential in Mitterrand's victory with 51.75 percent of the votes in the final round.

As returns came in to establish the outcome, Socialists, Communists, and throngs of working people took to the streets to celebrate all night, especially in the Place de la Bastille, the "victory of the left." Such it was, yet hardly a victory for the Union of the Left, which had not existed since 1977. More accurately, it was a victory for Mitterrand and his balanced team of Socialists formed from many factions, with grudging support from Communists and, finally, some crucial help from the center.

NOTES

1.   Mario Soares, "Frères en socialisme", *Le Nouvel Observateur* (Paris) 1593 (18-24 May, 1995): 104.

2.   Yves Roucaute, *Histoires socialistes de la Commune de Paris à nos jours* (Paris: Editions Ledrappier, 1987), 195–96.

6

Grand Disillusion

Put on the dauntless spirit of resolution!
—Shakespeare
King John

Mitterrand's victory in the election was a cause of foreboding in the Department of State in Washington, which believed it probably portended Communist ministers in the French government. Marchais's pointed emphasis on the votes of four and a half million Communists, crucial to Mitterrand in the second round, made it clear the PCF would expect some recognition. Marchais announced that his party was prepared to accept all its "responsibilities." The tone adopted by *L'Humanité*, which called the outcome a "victory for hope," showed that the PCF was eager to make peace with the victors and revive some public appearance of unity on the left. This prospect of Communists in the government of a NATO power dominated commentary in the U.S. press.

In Britain, the *Guardian* newspaper congratulated the French on their choice, but the conservative *Daily Telegraph* considered "pro-Soviet Communist ministers" in the French Cabinet to be a "frightening" prospect. It acknowledged that Mitterrand was more anti-Soviet than Giscard d'Estaing, but would he have the last word in such a government?

In France, the prestigious center-left newspaper, *Le Monde*, declared that Mitterrand deserved his victory by his frankness and realism, which bespoke a spirit of morality in contrast to the artifice and illusions employed by Giscard. The right-wing *Quotidien de Paris* deplored the defeat of Giscard and blamed it on the hundreds of thousands of supporters of Jacques Chirac who in the second round had either abstained or given their votes to Mitterrand. These "so-called Gaullists" bore the responsibility for putting into office one who had made a career of combatting de Gaulle and his legacy.

The other major right-wing newspaper, *Le Figaro*, called on its readers to prepare for the "third round," that is, the elections to a new Parliament. It was expected that the president-elect would shortly announce, as he had stated in his campaign, that the old Parliament, dominated by the two right-wing parties, would be dissolved.

Jacques Chirac immediately convened all leaders of the defeated right, including those of Giscard's party, to a council of war in preparation for the anticipated legislative elections. He thereby announced his intention to lead the struggle against Mitterrand, a role he would have to contest with Giscard, who did not appreciate Chirac's conduct toward him during the campaign and after the election.

On the foreign exchange market at the Paris *Bourse* there were signs of panic as thousands of investors moved to transfer funds out of France. The outgoing government under Prime Minister Raymond Barre felt obliged to try to stabilize the French franc by expending dollars to buy francs and to counteract the effects of the flood of offers to sell. This cost the government $5 billion, a third of its foreign currency reserves.

Mitterrand was warned that the oil-rich sheiks of the Middle East might withdraw their deposits from French banks, partly from fears for the French economy, partly in protest against Mitterrand's promise to be the first French chief of state to visit Israel. Mitterrand named his new chief of staff, Pierre Bérégovoy, to a mission of experts to make the rounds of all Middle Eastern embassies in Paris, carrying reassurances and requests not to add to the financial panic. His policies in the Middle East, he promised, would be "balanced." He sent his brother, General Jacques Mitterrand, to Saudi Arabia to confer with King Khaled and Crown Prince Fahd. As a consequence of this urgent mission to do everything possible to keep Middle East oil wealth in French banks, Mitterrand's first visit abroad as president of France was to Saudi Arabia in September 1981.

Mitterrand was the first Socialist to be elected president since the establishment of the Fifth Republic in 1958. In his inaugural address on May 21, 1981, after receiving the symbols of office from the outgoing president in the Elysée Palace, Mitterrand commented in carefully crafted phrases on the significance of this event for France and the world: "The political majority has just become identical with the social majority. In the world of today, what higher demand on our country than that of realizing the new alliance of socialism and liberty."

The emphasis on Socialism with liberty, pursuant to election by a "political majority" (contrasting, of course, with the Leninist seizure of power in Russia), evoked for many in the audience the memory of Jean Jaurès and made the event seem a kind of long-awaited vindication of his teachings. The phrases were a salute to the poorer classes, "the social majority," who certainly constituted the bulk of his "political majority" in the election. But Mitterrand was also concerned to restore national unity for the tasks ahead: "For that I will go forward tirelessly on the road of pluralism." "President of all the French, I wish to bring them together for the great causes that await us and create above all the conditions for a true national community."

Having laid a wreath on the monument to the Unknown Soldier at the Arc de

Triomphe, Mitterrand rode down the Champs Elysées in an open car, standing, wearing like a mask an expression befitting the new monarch of the republic, elected to reign for seven years.

A few hours later, in a ceremony full of symbolism, broadcast to the nation on television, Mitterrand slowly mounted the steps of the Panthéon and proceeded to lay roses (the flower of the Socialist Party) on the tombs of three of France's heroes of pluralism and progress: Jean Jaurès, Socialist martyr, founder of the SFIO; Victor Schoelcher, a leader in the movement for emancipation of slaves; and Jean Moulin, a delegate sent from London by de Gaulle to coordinate the movements of the Resistance during World War II, killed by the Nazis.

CONTROL OF THE NATIONAL ASSEMBLY

While Mitterrand was performing these ceremonies, Pierre Mauroy, the new prime minister appointed by the president, was installing himself in his offices at the seat of government in the Matignon Palace. His first major decision, taken after consultation with Jacques Delors and Pierre Bérégovoy and ratified by the president, was not to devalue the French franc. The flight of capital and the heavy sell-off of francs during the three weeks since the first round of the presidential election on April 26 made a quick devaluation logical from an economic point of view. To Michel Rocard such a step seemed not only advisable but inevitable, and the more quickly done the better. That was his advice to Mitterrand, saying the blame for such a humiliating step could be laid on the previous government.

Mitterrand and Mauroy rejected Rocard's advice on political grounds. "One does not devalue on such a day as this," said the president as the country watched the installation of a new regime. For Socialists, including Mitterrand, it was a day for euphoria and celebration, not to be spoiled by the pain and retreat of a devaluation. That could wait.

Delors was named minister of finance. Paris could hardly then see the long-range significance of this appointment. It was hoped his reputation for experience, moderation, and realism would reassure the nervous investment community. He had served on the governing board of the Bank of France. After his years in the Cabinet of Gaullist Prime Minister Jacques Chaban-Delmas, he was described as "too enlightened for the right, too much a realist for the left."[1] He had joined the Socialist Party in 1974, making it clear from time to time that he preferred social democracy to the goal of Socialism.

The naming of Pierre Bérégovoy as secretary general of the presidency (equivalent to the president's chief of staff) was also seen as a safeguard against the left ideologues to whom the president was indebted. His first assistant, on the other hand, would be Jacques Fournier, one of the brains of the CERES faction. Jean-Pierre Chevènement would thus have representation in the day-to-day deliberations at the headquarters of the president.

Mitterrand named the brilliant writer on economic and political subjects, Jacques Attali, his special counselor without portfolio, to occupy an office next to the president's. It was evident the president would be consulting with him constantly.[2]

The French Parliament had not been renewed by the presidential election and would continue to function with an anti-Socialist majority in both National Assembly and Senate until its mandate expired in 1983, or until the president dissolved it and called new elections.

Mitterrand had announced during his campaign that if elected, he would dissolve the Parliament and ask the country to give him a new Parliament with a working majority favorable to implementation of his plans for the country. Once installed as president he lost no time in setting in motion the procedure of dissolution. This involved formal consultations with the president of the Senate, Alain Poher, and the president of the National Assembly, Chaban-Delmas.

The meeting with Poher, a hard-line Gaullist, was no more than a formality. But when the president received Chaban-Delmas, he was conversing with an old friend. Their careers had been made at the center of the spectrum, and they seemed sincerely to wish each other well. In a book published in 1990, authors Pierre Favier and Michel Martin-Roland reproduce, on the authority of Chaban-Delmas, some revealing statements made to Chaban-Delmas by the president during this consultation in May 1981 regarding the dissolution of Parliament and Communist participation in the government. According to this source the president said he had need of the Communists, and that he was going to utilize them while continuing to diminish them. He expected to have them in the palm of his hand until the municipal elections to be held in March 1983.[3]

The authors also report that Maurice Faure, a Radical, told them he too had raised with Mitterrand in May 1981 the question of Communists in the government. According to Faure, Mitterrand had replied that his policy of alliance with the Communists was designed "to make them disappear." Faure said that Mitterrand from the outset tried to keep the Communists as long as possible. He wanted to compromise them by forcing them to employ a double language: solidarity within the government, criticism outside it.[4]

Henry Kissinger paid tribute to Mitterrand in 1995 for having found the right strategy for weakening the French Communist Party. Kissinger recounted in an interview with *Le Nouvel Observateur* that as U.S. secretary of state during the 1970s he had protested to Mitterrand his policy of an alliance with the Communists. Kissinger said Mitterrand had explained to him that his intention was to destroy the Communists, but that in order to marginalize them, they had to be made to participate in political life for a while.[5]

The Communists may not have known it at the time, but their own insouciant opportunism in this 1981 moment of triumph for Mitterrand, inviting his overtures and joining in the victory celebrations, led them into a fateful compromise. They underestimated the venom toward them in the calculating brain of this descendant of Pétainism, the Catholic Church, and the Socialist International.

Without delay, Mitterrand announced dissolution and the call for new elections to the Parliament, to take place on June 14 and June 21. Socialists and Communists quickly reached agreement on *désistement* in the second round of voting, thereby promising to aid the candidate, whether Socialist or Communist, who fared better between them in the first round. Since the Socialist Party, allied with the MRG (left Radicals), would be riding the wave of Mitterrand's victory, its candidates were likely to receive more votes than the Communists in the first round in most jurisdictions. By this agreement, and their disciplined fulfillment of its spirit, the Communists made it possible for the Socialists and MRG, even though together they had only 38 percent of the vote to the Communists' 16 percent in the first round, to emerge from the final round with an absolute majority of 285 deputies in the National Assembly. The number of Communists in the Assembly dropped from 86 to 44. On the right, the number of RPR deputies (Chirac's Gaullist party) dropped from 154 to 88, and of UDF deputies (Giscard d'Estaing's more centrist party) from 124 to 63.

Mitterrand and the Socialists thus would have a comfortable majority in the Assembly even without support from the Communists. Nevertheless, for reasons indicated above in the quotation from Maurice Faure, Mitterrand wanted to have the Communists formally engaged in supporting the government by giving them a certain number of ministries. The final number was negotiated with Marchais and Fiterman, who first demanded five for the PCF but finally agreed to four (out of a total of 44). The most prestigious of these appointments went to Fiterman himself. As minister of transport, he would be a minister of state, entitled to take part in smaller meetings of key ministers with the prime minister. Fiterman, formerly an electrical worker, had served as secretary to General Secretaries Rochet and Marchais. He had risen in the party to an important place on the Political Bureau. Many considered him at that time to be second only to Marchais as a spokesman and representative of the party with a good chance of becoming its general secretary.

The other three Communists named to ministries were: Minister of Professional Formation Marcel Rigout, a former a lathe worker and editor of a Communist newspaper in the Limousin region; Minister of Health Jack Ralite, who was experienced in theater productions, an elected deputy in the National Assembly, and mayor of d'Aubervilliers; and Minister of Public Functionaries Anicet Le Pors, who had degrees in engineering and economics, and had worked in the Ministry of Finance.

The Communists had asked for a more favorable distribution of some of the important ministries, especially Energy, Culture, Labor, Economy, and Planning. They had also hoped to see some of their academic luminaries, such as economist Philippe Herzog and geographer Félix Damette, as well as a female Communist, Danièle de March, named to government posts. Mitterrand and Mauroy quashed these hopes, and still the Communists went along. What did they hope to gain by accepting the humiliation of this subordinate role? Perhaps they wanted to give Mitterrand all the support he would accept from Communists as a way of encouraging him to go forward with his promised "rupture with capitalism." They must have realized they were allowing Mitterrand to put them on a leash, that they would be obligated to justify his policies and performance with the public so long as they held ministerial portfolios.

Perhaps even Communists were affected by the euphoria of the Mitterrand victory, making it difficult for Marchais and the Political Bureau to brush aside the invitation to accept some of the responsibility for the new experience the French nation was about to undergo. In the circumstances, it would have been difficult, perhaps impossible, to convince working people that Mitterrand's promise to lead the nation into *socialisme à la française* was utopian, or worse, merely an electoral ploy to win votes. It had to be tested in practice. This was the argument Marchais later used to justify his recommendation to accept "participation."

Furthermore, the Communists were anxious to lay the foundation for giving themselves a new image with the public, one of responsibility in the role of governing at the national level. But since this was going to be a Socialist-dominated government, it suddenly became necessary to jettison, or rather to suspend, the bitter attacks on Mitterrand and the Socialists with which Communists had fought the electoral campaigns since the collapse of the Union of the Left. The tone of *L'Humanité* changed markedly from one day to the next.

The PCF leadership had decided to do what was necessary to generate an image of the party as a participant and co-beneficiary in the great victory of the left. This became clear in an agreement with the Socialist Party announced shortly after the legislative elections. The document was described as an accord between the two parties on the program to be implemented by the government in which both would be participating. Its terms simply set forth propositions on which Mitterrand had run and won the presidency. Gone were the days of negotiations between the two parties over the terms of a "common program." The Communists bravely drank their bitter cup and called it bracing, just what the country needed.

Mitterrand knew that the government of the United States under President Ronald Reagan and Secretary of State Alexander Haig might react negatively to the admission of Communists into the new French government. He had a chance to convey his explanations on June 24, with the arrival of Vice President George Bush for an official visit with the new French president. From official French archives it appears that Mitterrand sought to reassure Bush and the U.S. government with the statement that his adherence to Socialism was not a commitment to Marxism but a means for the left to come to power. While within the governnment, he said, the Communists are tied to decisions of the Socialists. He believed that they would cling to their posts and that their erosion would be great.[6]

Recalling this interview with Bush eight years later, Mitterrand stated that he had told Bush he was placing Communists in posts that did not create any danger for NATO.[7]

Bush may have been reassured, but back in Washington, Haig had the ear of Reagan. While dining in Paris with Prime Minister Pierre Mauroy and new French Foreign Minister Claude Cheysson, Bush was called to the telephone to be advised that the secretary of state would be issuing a communiqué expressing the displeasure of the U.S. government with the entry of Communists in the French government. Shortly before midnight the text arrived. It bluntly warned that the tone and substance of French-U.S. relations would be affected.[8]

This rebuke did not come as a surprise to Mitterrand, and it did not alter his intentions with respect to including Communists in the government. On the following day he discussed the situation with French journalists, saying that France was still a good ally of the United States and that their common interests would prevail over the mood of the moment.[9]

The governments of Britain and Western Germany made it clear they had no criticism of the naming of Communists to the French government, which they declared to be strictly a matter for the French to decide. In Paris Foreign Minister Cheysson diplomatically called the United States communiqué "surprising and unacceptable." The former Gaullist premier, Pierre Messmer, supported him, saying it was unacceptable for the leaders of any foreign government to utter comments on the composition of a government of France. In the French press, even *Le Figaro*, bastion of anti-Socialist conservatism, expressed indignation at Haig's communiqué, saying, "Ronald Reagan will make a mistake if he confuses France with El Salvador or Santo Domingo."

Shortly after his installation as president, Mitterrand was advised by his newly appointed Minister of the Interior Gaston Defferre that the French counter-intelligence service, DST, (performing a role equivalent to that of the FBI in the United States) had for several months been receiving information from a highly placed Soviet source. Mitterrand and Defferre agreed it seemed to be important information and would probably be of interest to the United States. Here was an opportunity for the new French regime to show its solidarity with Washington, and Mitterrand seized it. In July 1981, at a summit meeting in Ottawa of the Group of Seven, the seven leading industrialized countries (with the Soviets excluded), Mitterrand and Cheysson met privately with Reagan and Haig. Copies of some of the information received by DST were delivered to the Americans with explanations regarding the source. This was appreciated and led to consultations between DST Director Marcel Chalet and Bush, a former director of the CIA, aimed at establishing an unprecedented level of cooperation between the intelligence services of the two countries.

By this course of action Mitterrand undoubtedly reassured the Reagan government, showing that he could be counted on as an ally in the Cold War against the Soviet Union. Some years later Mitterrand expressed a suspicion that the information involved may have been fed into the DST channels by U.S. agents, as a way of testing France's reliability. If so, Mitterrand, who in fact had no sympathy with Moscow's ambitions, passed the test with flying colors.

The appointment of Régis Debray as counselor to the president for Latin-American affairs seemed to show a perverse will in Mitterrand to tweak Reagan and Haig. Debray had acquired worldwide notoriety in the 1960s as the companion of Che Guevara and author of a book, *Revolution in the Revolution?* It set forth the theory of the guerrilla focus as the ideal strategy in Latin America for spreading the Cuban revolution throughout the hemisphere. Debray had been with Guevara in Bolivia, championing the cause of revolution with his considerable talents and renown as a writer. He had been seized by Bolivian police, tried, and imprisoned for three years.

It is traditional with French governments to challenge the pretension of the United States to police developments in the Western hemisphere to the exclusion of Europe. France has never consented to live by the Monroe Doctrine, whether in its nineteenth-century or twentieth-century applications. Mitterrand aimed to give this assertion of French interest in Latin America a new importance, sure of support from the French public. He invited the widows of Chilean President Salvador Allende and of the Chilean Communist poet, Pablo Neruda, to attend his inaugural ceremony in Paris. He approved a visit by his new foreign minister to Havana to convey greetings to Fidel Castro. In cavalier defiance of Reagan and Haig, he expressed support for the Sandinista regime in Nicaragua. And he announced the appointment of Debray as one of his counselors, a salute to the martyred Che Guevara.

However, Debray had lost his enthusiasm for the Cuban revolution in the dozen years since his Latin-American adventures had ended. He was trying to make a new name for himself as an independent writer on sociological and foreign policy topics of general interest. As counselor to the president, he was clearly not going to take up his long-abandoned role of speaking for Che Guevara and Fidel Castro. The furor in Washington over his appointment quickly died down.

For years Mitterrand had been critical of the United States for its concentration on the Cold War with the Soviet Union to the neglect of the pressing problems of underdevelopment and poverty in Latin America, Africa, and southern Asia. It was clear from his writings, his speeches, and his appointments that he wanted to be the generator of a new concern in the councils of the Group of Seven for relations between north and south. He aspired to act with whatever influence he could muster at these conclaves of the powerful as the "champion of oppressed peoples." This plainly manifested ambition, which he had long cultivated as a distinctive mark, made his entry into the G7 as the new president of France something less than an occasion for celebration by the other members. At the G7 meeting in Ottawa in July 1981 he was listened to politely and allowed to declaim as a tribune of the poor. It remained to be seen what difference he could make in the long run. In the African press, where Mitterrand enjoyed a reputation of enlightened engagement in their problems of development, his election was greeted with editorials expressing hope of improvement in their ability to gain a hearing for their perennial complaints of treatment by the pitiless world market.

SOCIALIST CONGRESS OF VICTORY AT VALENCE

During the euphoria of the months following the elections of 1981, there was a great deal of rhetoric from Socialists on the necessary "rupture" with capitalism. The new president gave expression to this spirit in a long conference with the press on September 24, 1981. He was determined, he said, to breach the "wall of money" that blocked progress. At the Socialist Congress at Valence in October 1981, the Mitterrand faction with Lionel Jospin, the new first secretary, as a leading spokesman, joined with CERES, the Mauroy and the Poperen factions to set a leftist tone of "breaking with capitalism." Louis Mermaz, newly elected president of the National Assembly, called for an end to the "dictatorship of the banks." Paul Quilès, Socialist deputy from Paris and manager of Mitterrand's victorious campaign, elatedly called on the government to act with revolutionary vigor in sweeping out its enemies. Speeches criticized the themes and policies of Michel Rocard, who had attempted with his own candidacy to draw the party to the right in the period leading up to the elections. This Congress at Valence was a kind of victory celebration before the television cameras of the leftist factions that had fought off the Rocard challenge and gone on to win the elections. Understandably, there were corks popping and much rhapsodizing over the new day about to be born.

Was it to be another milestone in the history of *liberté, égalité, fraternité*? France had already given to humanity the Great Revolution of the eighteenth century. From France had come the works of the inspiring utopian Socialist thinkers: Fourier, Proudhon, Cabet, Saint-Simon. And in 1871 there had been the attempt to storm heaven with the Paris Commune, model for the Bolsheviks in 1917.

In the fall of 1981, France was a public opinion state, and the spirit of the people was up. The party that had just won power called itself Socialist, and the candidate it had helped win the presidency called himself a disciple of Jean Jaurès. He had hinted time and again at his hatred of the inordinate power of the wealthy. He now had in his hands the powers of an elected government, the presidency and the National Assembly. How would he use them? The Communists were ready to give him full support, especially if he moved to defy the bourgeoisie and liberate the nation from what he called the "power of money," a power exercised through the state and the market. Was Mitterrand destined to enter history as the republican pioneer who discovered the peaceful way to free an advanced Western people from the fetters of capitalism?

Such exciting possibilities stirred hearts and fears all over the Western world. But they were only possibilities. The rest of the story is a disappointing decline from the high hopes of 1981, a grand disillusionment. What might he have done! If only he had really wanted to start a process of revolution, calling it a "transformation" or a "liberation," he could have done so. But as events would show, that was not the kind of man the French had chosen to become their president. It is the conclusion of this author, developed in the next several chapters, that the responsibility for the disillusion, for the *déception*, as it is called in French, lies with Mitterrand.

The Socialist Party, dominant in the National Assembly, was content in the circumstances to serve as Mitterrand's instrument by enacting into law what he proposed. This also seemed to be the attitude adopted by Prime Minister Mauroy, who in more normal times would have asserted the prerogative of his office to lead the government while the president looked on from above. Clearly in this first phase of the Mitterrand presidency, the president was closely supervising the activities of the government and making decisions on the details of legislative proposals. For good reason, the measures enacted in 1981 and 1982 are regarded as the substance of the "Mitterrand reforms." But the support of the prime minister was essential in moving them forward. Mauroy was always free to resign. The fact that he signed on and played his role as chief of government before the National Assembly makes them his reforms as well. Undoubtedly Mitterrand consulted with him constantly and gave his views great weight. The period 1981-84 is appropriately labeled the "Mauroy years" of Mitterrand's first term.

NATIONALIZATIONS

Of first importance to Mauroy were the nationalizations. In his view, they should and would become the distinctive mark of the Socialist regime. Jean Le Garrec was named secretary of state for nationalizations. He was a friend of Mauroy and an experienced labor leader (CFDT) who had served as a labor representative in the transnational enterprise IBM. Le Garrec worked out the details of the program of nationalizations, a program that had been under public discussion since the agreement between Socialists and Communists in 1972.

These touched nine industrial groups: steel, aluminum, glass, chemical, electrical equipment, metallurgy, computers, pharmaceuticals, and military aviation. The firms nationalized, added to those already owned by the state under nationalizations carried out in 1937 and 1945, brought the public sector to some 17 percent of the gross national product.

Private ownership of the means of production was still to be dominant in Mitterrand's France. Of great significance were the president's explanations of the aim and spirit of nationalizations. They were intended, he said, to remedy the deficiencies in French capitalism, which in some sectors showed signs of losing its will to invest and produce. Nationalizations were to serve in the defense of French production, since private investment by the French had increased by only 1 percent since 1976.[10]

In the steel industry, for example, deterioration of plant from lack of investment was notorious. During the presidency of Giscard d'Estaing, large loans had been made by the Government to two leading steel companies, USINOR and SACILOR, to aid their modernization. The funds had apparently been distributed as dividends to stockholders. This debt to the state of 14 billion francs (some $2 billion) was converted into shares of stock of the companies and delivered to the state in lieu of repayment of the loans. This gave the state ownership of 98 percent of the shares of the two companies.

Share owners of other nationalized enterprises were to be compensated on the basis of the value of their shares on the stock exchange. Here was a readily available, market-based objective standard. Nevertheless, since these shares had been declining on the exchange for years, the shareholders protested against this system of valuation. They wanted profitability and the value of physical and financial assets to be taken into account. This question proved contentious in the National Assembly and led to appeals to the Constitutional Court to declare the rights of the former owners. These appeals caused delays and in the end were successful.

Within the government the more conservative advisers Minister of Finance Jacques Delors and Minister of the Plan Michel Rocard counseled expropriation of only 51 percent of the shares of each enterprise, thereby holding down the cost to the state. They were supported by Foreign Minister Claude Cheysson, who thought this approach would be viewed more favorably in Britain and the United States, and by Minister of Justice Robert Badinter, a lawyer who argued that 51 percent was enough for control and that paying for 100 percent of the shares was simply making a gift to the shareholders. Minister of the Budget Laurent Fabius took no position, and Prime Minister Mauroy waited to know Mitterrand's decision before announcing his own. Charles Fiterman, Communist minister of transport, said he was amused by these debates among the different currents of Socialists. He and Jean-Pierre Chevènement insisted it was important to move fast despite all the technical, juridical, and financial problems. They were in favor of the single criterion, stock exchange value, and government expropriation of 100 percent of the shares.

Another element in the program of nationalizations was the availability of credit to enterprises. To ensure the government's ability to direct credit as needed to support nationalized firms and other crucial sectors of the economy, it was deemed necessary also to nationalize the major banks. Within the government there was another debate between Delors and the more leftist ministers as to the threshold that would determine the number of credit institutions to be nationalized. Delors wanted only those with deposits of more than 1 billion francs to be touched; others wanted the threshold to be lower. But the lower the threshold, the more banks that had to be included, and this meant more difficulties with the financial community. Also, said Delors, Cheysson, and Badinter, it was important to frame this program to minimize reaction abroad.

Mitterrand decided against Delors on the first question, ordering that the state should acquire 100 percent, not just 51 percent, of the shares of nationalized firms. But on the credit threshold he was content to follow Delors's recommendation. This produced a nationalization of thirty-six banks, which together accounted for 75 percent of all credit activity. All the major banks of deposit, Banque National de Paris, Crédit Lyonnais, Société Général, Crédit Commercial de France, would henceforth be owned by the state.

Pierre Moussa was president of the financial group Paribas, a kind of holding company. He fought hard, publicly and privately, for the exclusion of his group from the terms of the legislative drafts, counting on support from Jacques Attali and Delors. Moussa was suspected of secretly reducing the assets of the group, especially in Belgium and Switzerland, as a way of keeping them from being transferred to the French state. A criminal prosecution was begun, and the Socialists in their press made him the symbol of the "traitors of high finance," the modern equivalent of the *émigrés* of the French Revolution, royalty and aristocrats who had fled with their assets to Austria and England to escape the embrace of a new *égalité*. Mitterrand overruled the objections of Delors and decided to include Paribas, along with a similar financial group known as Suez, in the targeted banks.

The debate in the National Assembly on this supposedly crucial legislation opened October 13, 1981. The "opposition" parties led by Chirac and Giscard, the RPR and the UDF (Union for French Democracy), had decided to fight an all-out ideological war of words and parliamentary maneuvering in an attempt to delay and perhaps wear down the Socialist majority. They were assisted by technical experts from law, industry, and finance. Coordinator of this complicated procedural strategy of the opposition forces was a deputy of the RPR, Michel Noir, seconded by Deputies Charles Millon and Franois d'Aubert of the UDF. They were prepared to force detailed consideration of every clause of the proposed legislation, anticipating that the sessions would go on day and night without suspension, perhaps for weeks. A total of some 1,000 amendments were proposed in the course of the debates. Class warfare raged in the speeches of the deputies, though there was no echo of it in the streets, where calm reigned.

The general public did not see any fundamental importance in this legislation. The French were already familiar with nationalized enterprises (the Renault auto plant, airlines, the railroads, coal mines, gas sources, electricity, some banks and insurance companies), and these did not seem to function differently from those owned privately.

The opposition had the enormous satisfaction of delaying a final vote on the legislation in the National Assembly until the Socialist Congress at Valence had come to an end, thus frustrating some Socialist expectations of an additional reason for celebration. On October 26, 1981, the Law on Nationalizations was adopted by a vote of 332 votes (PS and PCF) to 154 (RPR and UDF). Three days later the Senate, where the RPR and UDF were in the majority, rejected the legislation. This was followed by conference deliberations between representatives of the two chambers. The Senate again disapproved, so the legislation returned to the National Assembly, which had authority under the Constitution to enact it at that stage without Senate approval. The opposition was ready with another 100 amendments and recourse to procedural delays. On December 3, 1981, the bill was passed a second time.

But this did not end the debate. Opposition deputies and senators filed an appeal with the Constitutional Council, alleging violations of the Constitution. This served to suspend implementation. In January 1982, the Constitutional Council issued an opinion declaring the legislation to be "in conformity with the Constitution" except as to the manner of compensation of share owners. The Council of State, asked by the government to give its advice, replied that it would be necessary to revise the legislation and start anew in the National Assembly. It was not clear whether the government was bound under the Constitution to abide by the judgment of these two Councils on the validity of legislation. Mitterrand decided to respect their decisions and present a new draft, altered to incorporate the additional criteria recommended for fixing (and thereby increasing) the value of compensation of shareholders. In ordering that this be done, the president overruled the objections of the two CERES ministers, Chevènement and Nicole Questiaux.

To forestall another long parliamentary debate, Mitterrand instructed Mauroy to employ a seldom-used procedure authorized by Article 49, line 3, of the Constitution, known as "the 49-3." This permitted the government to declare a proposal to be law without debate, unless condemned on a motion of censure. The government had more than enough votes to defeat the motion of censure. This sent the new legislation to the Senate, where it was rejected as before. It went back to the National Assembly, where the government did not have to employ "49-3" to have the bill passed a second time. The opposition had finally been outmaneuvered. It did make another appeal to the Constitutional Council, which in light of its earlier opinion could now only give its approval to the revised legislation. It finally became law on February 13, 1982.

How little this legislation was to mean for the average French citizen began to become apparent. The newly nationalized firms, including the banks, were to continue to function under the old constraint of profitability. They were simply to have new chief executive officers, men of business experience willing to accept appointment by a Socialist government. It proved to be an exercise in musical chairs as well-known practitioners of high finance and business management slipped into their new places with instructions to revive these failing enterprises and make them competitive in the marketplace. No revolution had taken place. There was no new criterion of social welfare to qualify managers' paramount concern for solvency and return on capital. It seemed that Mitterrand wanted to show that his Socialist regime understood very well how state-owned enterprises were to be administered in a capitalist country. The hegemony of the investor-class was not to be challenged.

DECENTRALIZATION

The second *grande affaire* to which Mauroy attached historic significance in his years as prime minister was decentralization, the redistribution of governmental power and responsibility from Paris to regions, departments, communes, and municipalities.[11]

The Jacobins of the French Revolution had given France a tradition of concentrating power in the capital. Revolutionary Paris had seized the initiative, created an Assembly and then a Convention asserting authority throughout the country, making the unity of the Republic against its enemies—royalist, clerical, and foreign—a supreme goal of government. This revolutionary centralization was one feature in the destruction of the old feudal order wherein the aristocracy, through regional *parlements*, had for centuries resisted the growing power of the monarch. Centralization vanquished aristocratic, feudal regionalism in one of the triumphs of the French Revolution.

Napoleon had strengthened national unity, developing the tradition of centralized administration of the whole nation. One of his laws created the institution of the prefect, representative of the central government permanently in place in the administrative *départements* into which the Revolution had divided the map of France. The prefect was the supreme local authority throughout the nineteenth century, and this continued under the Constitution of the Fifth Republic. In the two centuries since the Revolution, as the administration of national policies in education, taxation, social security, and dozens of other areas became more complicated, power was distributed and redistributed among the ministries of the central government in Paris, most of which for greater efficiency established their representatives in the other major towns and cities of the nation.

What were the agencies to be enhanced in authority by the proposed decentralization? The answer to this question is indicated by France's constitutional structure, which includes communes, *départements* and regions. Communes (towns and sections of cities) elected their councils and mayors, and each of the ninety-five *départements* had an elected general council but no executive. Regional general councils had emerged here and there, with no clearly defined authority, to bring together representatives of several *départements* to discuss common problems, especially those related to the attraction of investment in industries that would create jobs. Legislation in the 1970s had given these regional councils official standing but little authority.

It should be kept in mind that Mitterrand, in calling for a revision of the French tradition of central power, was not undertaking to downgrade the role of the state in meeting the problems of the nation. He was not echoing in France the call from Republicans in the United States to "get the government off our backs!" Ronald Reagan became president of the United States in 1980, one year after Margaret Thatcher became prime minister in Britain. In France the parties of the right and much of the press campaigned against Mitterrand and the Socialists with arguments based on this impressive resurgence of "liberalism" in the United States and Britain. In Europe, "liberalism" refers to an unhampered freedom for investors to seek their profits in the market with a minimum of state interference. Reagan and Thatcher were champions of this classic liberalism, but Mitterrand was not a "liberal" as the word is used in France. His readiness to rely on state power to advance national goals was demonstrated by his recourse to nationalization of privately owned banks and industries.

Many Socialists had served as mayors of their communes, and many as members of the general councils of *départements* or of regions. They knew first-hand the impotence of these entities to deal adequately with local problems because of lack of financial resources and dependence on approval from prefects or ministries in Paris. Thus Mitterrand evoked an enthusiastic response from his party when he announced as the fifty-fourth proposition in his campaign platform the suppression of the authority of prefects over "local collectivities," that is, over local governments. "The decentralization of the state will be a priority," he declared. The regional councils were to be given a new prestige and authority by electing their membership directly through universal suffrage.[12]

Except for the fact that the Socialists would be making the proposals, an attempt at decentralization was not necessarily an offense to the principles of the parties of the right. De Gaulle had unsuccessfully proposed giving more importance to the regions, in 1969. Three years later, during the Pompidou presidency, regional assemblies had been created. (They were composed of members chosen indirectly, that is, from among those who had been elected by direct popular vote either to the National Assembly or to the General Council of a *département*.) And in 1980, in the final year of Giscard's presidency, another step toward decentralization had been taken by giving local collectivities a greater latitude in fixing tax rates for local revenue. Giscard had also given the city of Paris an exceptional authority over its affairs, relatively free of supervision by the national government. There was an underlying consensus that some new steps could be taken in the movement toward decentralization already begun in the years since the creation of the Fifth Republic.

That did not mean, however, that any proposal would be spared partisan political opposition when it reached the floor of the Assembly. Clearly, the opposition would seize upon any Socialist proposal to decentralize as endangering national unity. Mitterrand and Mauroy took precautions to moderate the legislation so as to weaken the arguments against it. The "unity of the Republic" was not to be undermined, said Mitterrand. Even after decentralization, there was to be only one state, not many states in a federal system.

In some areas, Socialists' ambitions to make policy changes prompted them to keep control in the national government. This applied to the management of forests and to expenditures for cultural projects. Mitterrand had plans for action on a national scale that could not be left to local authorities. "Democracy" was not affected by keeping these decisions centralized, or was it? Such exceptions raised the question whether there is any connection between decentralization and democracy. Nevertheless, ignoring inconsistencies, the campaign for decentralization was based on the need for more "democracy."

It is interesting to note that French Communists, who generally claim the right to wear a mantle inherited from the Jacobins of the French Revolution, had abandoned the Jacobins' attachment to centralization of state power. The Communists supported Mitterrand's call for decentralization. In their analysis, the subordination of local entities to the national government constituted a "lack of democracy."[13] It was necessary to modernize French society in the pursuit of more democracy by reducing the authority of the central government. This was connected with the Communists' decision to place *autogestion* at the center of their strategy for moving the nation onto a vaguely defined French road to Socialism.

The Communists had apparently lost hope by 1981 of ever taking over the reins of the state through elections of the president and the National Assembly. And of course they had long since renounced any strategy of a revolutionary seizure of power in the manner of the Paris Commune or the Bolsheviks. *Autogestion* came to mean an increased assertion of authority at the level of the workplace and local institutions. The Communists could hope to guide working people in particular enterprises into campaigns for workers' "rights to intervene" in managerial decisions. This could lead ultimately to worker authority over every facet of an enterprise's operations. Accompanying this aspect of *autogestion* was a hope to win control through elections of local assemblies or councils: municipal, communal, perhaps even departmental and regional. This was now the Communists' vision of a French road to Socialism. Therefore "democracy" in their definition should include a large measure of freedom for local entities to establish laws with a Socialist content and orientation, immune from control and restraints by national authorities in Paris.

The legislation proposed by the Mauroy government through new Minister of the Interior Gaston Defferre did not go nearly far enough to create any real possibility of nurturing some future Socialist commune installed by Communists on the morrow of a local electoral victory. That "road to socialism" remained a chimera in France, even after the decentralization carried out by Mitterrand.

The most important element in the legislation of 1981–83 was the transfer of some of the old executive authority of the (Napoleonic) prefects to the presidents of the twenty-six regional councils. Since these presidents were elected by the councils of the region, that is, by council members who were themselves elected directly by the people of the region, the regions could become entities with a sense of separate identity and potential independence. But to make sure this continued to be more potential than actual, the prefect, with a new title of *Commissaire de la République*, continued to have important functions as chief agent of administration for the national ministries.[14]

Debate in the National Assembly proved much less heated over this legislation than over nationalizations. Defferre, himself the mayor of Marseilles, and Mauroy, mayor of Lille, negotiated compromises with opponents in the course of debate. They were able to convince leaders of the opposition parties that nothing earth-shaking was under discussion, especially nothing that would favor the left over the right. Philippe Séguin, a spokesman for the RPR, congratulated Defferre on his readiness to compromise. Michel Noir said that the reform was "indispensable," and that he had simply wanted to be sure it was not being used for political advantage.

After passage in the National Assembly, the Senate had its say, and since there the Socialists and Communists were a minority, the bill was disapproved by a vote on party lines. Then it went back to the Assembly, which had the authority (without any need in this case to resort to the "49-3" tactic) to enact final passage. It became law on March 2, 1982.

Though local entities (communes, *départements*, regions) now had more freedom for acting on their own initiative without prior approval by the central government, they were still subject to *a posteriori* control through the retained power of the national institutions to declare local legislation and regulations invalid. Further, in their planning for their locality they would be required to coordinate their plans with the national plan prepared by a ministry in Paris.

The newly renamed *Commissaires de la République* would represent the national government in all regions and *départements* with the responsibility to ensure there was no conflict between local and national plans. They would also have power to represent the national government in negotiations of contracts defining rights and responsibilities involving different levels of government. The general intention was to have a power of final decision within the region, eliminating the necessity of referring every problem to Paris. Nevertheless, the *Commissaires* and their staffs would inevitably have to seek guidance from the relevant ministry and keep it informed. Since the state was to remain unitary, with no region or *département* gaining a share in sovereignty as in a federalist system of states, no definitive authority could be conferred on a region or *département* exclusive of central control from Paris. Clearly, the oft-stated intention "to bring authority with power to decide closer to the citizen asking for a decision" would still depend on how far each ministry went in delegating power to its local agencies.

It was not at all clear how local entities were going to find the resources, human and financial, to use their new liberties. It remained to be seen whether the National Assembly would follow through and agree to transfer some of the revenue at its disposal.

In regard to the city of Paris, the battle over decentralization pitted the Socialist president against Chirac, mayor of Paris, leader of the RPR, former prime minister, and already a candidate to oust Mitterrand from the presidency at the first opportunity. The problem was that the mayor of Paris had inherited a unique status of power and independence rooted in a centuries-old struggle between the chateau and city hall, going back to the days of kings and the *prévôt*, who represented the merchant and manufacturing classes against the crown and his ministers.

To minimize resistance to the first steps toward decentralization, the government exempted Paris from its terms and allowed the established order, called "the common law," to continue in effect. This meant that the twenty sections of Paris, the *arrondissements*, were lumped together and treated as one entity for purposes of electing the mayor of Paris. The arrangement gave Chirac a firm hold on the whole city, even in those *arrondissements* where the Socialists felt they were in a majority. Understandably, the Socialists were not happy with a system that largely nullified their dominant position in a few *arrondissements*. How could they change it to their advantage?

On June 30, 1982, the Mauroy government, with Mitterrand's approval, announced that it was necessary to treat each Paris *arrondissement* as a commune, with its own municipal council that would elect the mayor for that commune. These municipal councils and mayors of communes would have increased powers, in accordance with the new laws on decentralization. There would also be a Council of Paris, with vague powers of coordination, made up of representatives from the municipal councils of the communes. It would elect the Mayor of Paris. Clearly, the status and powers of this latter office were being reduced, to the advantage of the councils and mayors of the twenty communes created out of the old *arrondissements*.

Chirac immediately sent word to the president that if this proposal were not withdrawn, it would lead to war between them. He was not going to accept it. On the following day Chirac convened the press to denounce Mitterrand for violating formal engagements not to undermine the unity of the capital. The city of Paris, he said, "is threatened with dissolution and dislocation." Almost all Paris newspapers rallied around the mayor, seeing in the government's proposal a political maneuver to win advantage for the Socialists. A solid majority of Parisians had voted against Mitterrand and the Socialists in the 1981 elections, so the climate was difficult for implementing changes denounced so vigorously by Chirac. Once again it was the *prévôt* against the chateau. The government tried to counter the charge that it was aiming its legislation against the mayor of Paris by making it applicable to Lyon and Marseille as well.

In this form it was passed into law and ultimately took effect without a "war." This controversy probably contributed to the poor showing of the Socialists in Paris in the municipal elections of March 1983. The opposition, led by Chirac, triumphed in every one of the twenty communes, and people still called them *arrondissements*.

The focus on increasing the powers of communes under the new legislation raised the question of making them more democratic. Smaller parties were seldom represented in municipal councils, since it was necessary under the voting law as it existed in 1981 for a candidate to win a majority of votes cast for election. France is a country of many different parties, yet some of them were in effect being excluded from local governments. The question the Socialists asked themselves was: Should the chances of the minor parties for representation be improved by distributing the seats on the councils in proportion to the votes won by each party? This is called proportional voting. Mitterrand had many times described it as a more democratic system of electing representatives to governing assemblies and councils.

Here was an opportunity to act on a high-sounding principle without any great consequence to himself or the country. No one cared a great deal about the distribution of a few seats in the municipal councils. The Socialist government therefore took a small step in that direction by introducing a "dose of proportional." Henceforth communes with more than 3,500 inhabitants would elect their councils by the proportional method. Whether the Socialists would continue along this road of electoral reform, however, was by no means certain. Introducing proportional representation into national legislative elections would affect the composition of the National Assembly, sure to leave the Socialists without their absolute majority and dependent on alliances with other small parties.

KEYNESIAN STIMULUS

The Socialist Congress at Metz in April 1979 had shown the Party to be divided between a more radical majority (Mitterrandists, CERES) and a more cautious minority (Rocard, Mauroy, Delors). As Mitterrand's campaign developed, the candidate for the presidency had distanced himself from the Socialist Party program drafted by Chevènement of CERES and adopted a reassuring tone of moderation. It was not clear that Mitterrand was really a Mitterrandist in the Metz sense of the word. What would his election bring in the way of a rupture with capitalism? Uncertainty on that question in May and June 1981 was widespread and led to the flight of capital that prompted Mitterrand to send Pierre Bérégovoy into a round of reassuring interviews with investors and bankers.

The naming of Mauroy as prime minister, Delors as minister of finance and Rocard as minister of planning, together with Bérégovoy as chief of staff and Jacques Attali as special counsel to the president, were signals that no "rupture with capitalism" was being prepared. Laurent Fabius, a Mitterrandist in the Metz definition, was named minister of the budget. His slogans during this initial period of the Mitterrand mandate gave a very accurate summary of the legislation that was under preparation: "A goal, employment; a method, economic stimulus [*relance*]; a means, solidarity." Each of these needs to be explained.

Unemployment in May 1981 was estimated at 1,795,000, an increase of 21 percent over May 1980. This manifestation of continuing economic crisis as the mandate of Giscard came to a close posed a severe challenge to the new government. All of Mitterrand's principal economic advisers agreed on a package of measures that were clearly inspired by Keynesian theories. The economy would be given an injection of new purchasing power by increasing the resources of the most poorly paid. The minimum wage (SMIC) was raised 38 percent between

June 1981 and March 1983. To help employers meet this increased wage bill, the state reduced some of the required employer contributions to social security funds. Family allowances from state funds for housing and the expenses of raising children were raised by 25 percent, along with an increase of 20 percent in allowances for the elderly. These measures increased purchasing power of some of the neediest sectors of society by some 30 billion francs (approximately $6 billion). It was hoped this would lead to the creation of jobs.

The economic stimulus also took the form of 200,000 new jobs on public payrolls, distributed among different ministries. The newly nationalized firms were encouraged to hire by improving their capitalization from public funds. Some aid also went to private industry, aimed at creating new jobs. The government stressed the vital importance of growth in the economy, not only to absorb the currently unemployed but to prepare for an expected influx of new job seekers in later years. Funds were appropriated for research and job training. The total cost of these various measures of stimulus during 1981–82 was 60 billion francs, approximately 2 percent of the gross national product. By French standards this was not a dramatic, all-out effort. As a percentage of gross national product the total was something less than the expenditures of the Chirac government in 1975–76 to stimulate the economy, approximately 50 billion francs, mostly as investment in private enterprises and in infrastructure. (Chirac spent as a liberal, Mitterrand as a Keynesian.)

Measured by results, the Keynesian stimulus was inadequate to accomplish its purpose. No decline in the net number of unemployed appeared. In fact, the number increased during the first year by 12 percent to 2,000,000 in May 1982. By then it was clear to all that the Mitterrand strategy was not going to eliminate or even reduce unemployment. The Socialists could only express deepest regrets and add the boast that they at least had reduced the rate of increase from what it had been under Giscard d'Estaing. This seemed cold comfort and added to the feeling of deception that mounted in the country.

Another measure projected was to reduce the length of the working week to thirty-five hours by 1985. A beginning was made in 1981 with a reduction of one hour to a thirty-nine-hour working week. In "solidarity" with workers, employers were urged to continue to pay wages of a forty-hour week. It was expected that further reductions would include a call for solidarity from workers in the form of a reduction in wages corresponding to the reduction in time worked. The second stage was never reached.

A fifth week of paid vacations became a right written into law. This caused employers to shake their heads in disgust but naturally was well received by worker beneficiaries, excepting only those who already enjoyed five weeks of paid vacation. They were disappointed not to acquire the right to yet another week. The Popular Front government in 1936 had been the first to provide in law for two weeks of paid vacations, a wonderful gift enabling thousands of French workers to see their country for the first time. This had been increased to three weeks during the Fourth Republic and to four by the Gaullist government of Georges Pompidou. The Socialists, strongly supported by the Communists, could do no less to mark their accession to power.

The reform of the Labor Code gave another expression to the social-democratic character of the new regime. Mitterrand selected Jean Auroux, a provincial school teacher and Socialist mayor of the commune of Roanne, to take on the portfolio of minister of labor. His principal task would be to negotiate with the labor unions and representatives of employers of both large and small enterprises to find an acceptable reform. Mitterrand in his campaign had promised to strengthen the rights of workers in their workplaces. This would involve widening the competence and the authority of workers committees (*comités d'entreprise*).

Mitterrand had included in the 110 measures on which he ran a promise to give these committees the right in each enterprise to veto a decision by management to hire or fire workers. During his first months as minister in the summer of 1981, Auroux came to the conclusion this was too great a concession to ask of management. He was fearful that the workers committees could not be trusted to give sufficient weight to the imperatives of the market and would leave managers without authority to make the harsh decisions enabling a company to compete and prosper. In the end, said Auroux, many more companies would go bankrupt, a risk workers were inclined to underestimate until too late. Mitterrand went along with this argument and accepted the much more modest Auroux alternative: a "right of alert." The unions and the workers committees were to acquire the right to have the company's accounts examined by auditors of their choice. The decision to hire and fire remained with management, subject as before to the terms of labor contracts negotiated with the labor union.

Mitterrand also backed down on another issue. He had promised to give worker committees of health and safety the authority to stop a machine or even a whole plant on grounds of protecting the security of workers. The alternative solution proposed by Auroux and accepted by the president was to give workers, when declared by the committee to be endangered by the condition of equipment, a "right to retire" with a pension, not equal, of course, to full pay while working. Again Auroux persuaded the president that he had gone too far in proposing an infringement on the freedom of managers to run their enterprises.

In these negotiations with business leaders over workers rights, Mitterrand and the Socialists were beginning to cultivate an image of realism, of prudent and understanding accommodation to the constraints of competing in a capitalist market. They yielded to the argument that the market was now Europe and the world, and it was essential not to handicap French industry. If there was to be any hope of meeting the fundamental problem of unemployment, French companies must be able to compete successfully in a wide market. It would be gratifying to give the unions all they wanted, but that was not the way to govern a capitalist country like France. Mitterrand quickly made this kind of compromise with his Socialist hopes.

In their final form the Auroux laws proposed:

1. A right for workers to express their views on the organization of their work. Annual negotiation on this became obligatory.
2. A definition of the right to organize workers committees and the role of labor unions in their functioning.

3. Clarification of rules on collective bargaining and settlement of conflicts.
4. An extension of the competence of the committees on health and safety to include the power to confer a "right to retire" on an endangered worker.

The limits on these pitiful new workers' rights, after the years of competition between Communists and Socialists for the right to lead in the establishment of a new order of worker *autogestion*, made abundantly evident what the leaders of neither party would yet confess: This "French road to Socialism" vaunted by the Union of the Left had been oversold in political rhetoric.[15] President Mitterrand, with support from the Communist Party, was spelling out in his program nothing more than some social-democratic reforms to make life somewhat more bearable under a capitalist system which in its fundamentals was not to be challenged.

Nevertheless, the opposition parties were prepared to resist these reforms with another long parliamentary debate in which some 3,500 amendments were proposed to the 101 articles of the legislation. One of the favorite arguments of these saviors of society from the threat of revolution was that Communists were behind the reforms. They therefore must have the approval of Moscow. Though in fact Mitterrand and the Socialists had an absolute majority in the Assembly and were not consulting with the Communists before proposing legislation, opposition deputies and press had labeled the regime "socio-communist" and were exploiting the resonance of this phrase in public debate.

By joining the government, the PCF had made itself appear to be a sponsor of these social-democratic proposals. It even took an active part in the debates, defending them as if indeed they were an expression of Communist analysis of the needs of the French nation in its crisis. During the period 1981-84 the PCF refrained from openly criticizing Mitterrand and the Socialist Party and referred to itself as a "party of the government." This was in fact an exaggeration that bordered on deceit, since the Communists were given virtually no role in formulating key policies and proposals.

It was only after the Communists had withdrawn from the government in 1984 that their reservations about the famous Auroux laws could be expressed. Fiterman, who as a minister of state had to remain silent while this debate was taking place in the Assembly in 1981, has since condemned the program as merely social-democratic: "Proceeding from a formal and juridical *démarche*, they [the Auroux laws] were in no way a taking of power by workers in an enterprise."[16]

Another ideological debate raged around the Quilliot law, which aimed to give increased protection to tenants against eviction by landlords. A principal consequence of the outcry raised in the conservative press against this measure was a generalized dread of renting houses and apartments to anyone except foreigners, who, it was supposed, could be counted on to leave in due time. The Quilliot law was debated and enacted in the summer of 1982. It would be years before the availability of rentals to French newlyweds began to recover from the panic caused among landlords and owners of dwellings. This was a new case of the characteristic "great fear" always suffered by the French bourgeoisie in times of change.

Such modest reforms, greatly overblown in opposition rhetoric, served to frighten investors, with the result that new starts in building rental housing suffered a severe drop. This made more urgent the Government's own housing construction plans. Mitterrand had promised 450,000 units per year. For budgetary reasons, this goal had to be reduced to 343,000 for the year 1982. Since the private sector was refusing to carry its share of the burden in a situation it deemed uncertain and perhaps "socio-communist," the need was even greater for the government to step in and provide the financing and the initiative for a large-scale building program. Such a program would have provided jobs for the unemployed and housing for the poorer sectors of the population. But Mitterrand and the Socialists were not up to such a challenge. By 1982 they were in the throes of knuckling under, of casting aside the brave talk of breaking with capitalism, of adjusting their policies to the severe limits placed on them by the market economy in which they chose to compete and seek salvation.

BOWING TO EMPLOYERS

The crisis forcing the Socialists to define themselves revolved around budgetary deficits, inflation, and the declining value of the French franc in international currency markets. Mitterrand had tried to reassure business circles by naming Jacques Delors to the post of finance minister. Such an appointment was itself a signal that the new Government was not going to continue very long in its Keynesian policies of stimulus through increasing government expenditures. Given the recession in the international economy, it was a virtual certainty that France would not be able to increase its exports significantly without a drastic devaluation of the franc. As mentioned earlier, such action (advocated by Rocard on the morrow of the installation of the new government) was rejected by Mitterrand; one does not devalue at such a happy hour, he had said. Devaluation would make all imports cost more in francs and sharply push up the cost of living for the French.

Mitterrand had promised much in his campaign, and he began to deliver with projects that had to be financed from public funds. Nationalizations by seizing and compensating owners of 100 percent of shares of target companies increased government debt and interest costs. These companies, many of them suffering from lack of resources, had to be aided with government credits if they were to prosper and hire. Every ministry presented plans for increasing its activities; government hiring was a key feature of the Keynesian *relance*, stimulus through increasing the buying power in the public. The first budget prepared by Budget Minister Laurent Fabius envisaged an increase in government spending of 27 percent.

To help increase revenue, a new *impôt sur les grandes fortunes* (IGF), a property tax on real and personal property, was imposed on the largest fortunes, defined so as to affect approximately 200,000 of the richest families. The rates were moderate, progressing from 0.5 percent to a maximum of 1.5 percent. To avert a removal of works of art from the country, they were exempt from the tax. So were properties employed in industry, agriculture, and commerce, up to a limit of 2 million francs. Income taxes were also increased for those earning more than 15,000 francs annually (approximately $3,000). Tax receipts from corporations were increased by eliminating some business expense deductions.

These new revenues did not cover the increase in expenditures. The deficit contemplated in the Fabius budget for 1982, prepared in the summer of 1981, was some 95 billion francs, compared to 51.6 billion francs for the previous budget year. In Germany, by contrast, deficit reductions were being achieved with a freeze on government expenditures and a reduction in social services. Conditions were thus being created, or rather exacerbated, for a higher rate of inflation in France than in Germany. This would inevitably raise the question of a devaluation of the French franc. France, as a member of the European monetary system (SME) could not expect to employ a Keynesian-type stimulus, inevitably inflationary, without paying the penalty of devaluations.

The first such devaluation (8.5 percent with respect to the German mark) took place on October 4, 1981, through an application of the rules of the SME by the minister of finance, the director of the Treasury, and the governor of the Bank of France. It was a first step in Delors's campaign to persuade the president to bow to reality and bring the French economy into a posture that would win back the confidence of private investors.

Fabius, carrying out the wishes of the president, had prepared the budget for 1982 without the participation of the minister of finance. This was to be the budget celebrating the Socialist victory, the budget of euphoria. Mitterrand and Fabius probably knew Delors would disapprove, so he was circumvented and therefore "spared" from sharing in the responsibility. It was important, in Mitterrand's view, to try to keep Delors from resigning, because the Socialist strategy expressed in the budget counted on an active participation by the private sector. There was reason for anxiety in the government over whether that cooperation from the private sector would be forthcoming.

The Fabius budget, added to the debate over nationalizations, fed the spirit of resistance in business circles. The new president of the National Council of French Employers (CNPF), Yvon Gattaz, found that his executive committee was in favor of a strike by investors with a halt in hiring.

Polls taken among employers in November 1981 confirmed the strongly negative attitude toward investing and hiring in the new circumstances created by the election. All Socialists lamented what many called a deliberate "sabotage" of the government's program for economic recovery. Chevènement was in favor of a strong reaction by the government, going to the country with a militant condemnation of the freeze on investment by private enterprise and molding an adequate program of public projects to provide more employment and needed production.

The president did not agree with Chevènement, a sign that he was looking for a formula of accommodation in which Delors would be given a leading role. He directed his ministers to attempt to restore the confidence of investors. The prime minister spoke to this purpose in Brest on October 26, 1981, and on December 8 Mitterrand undertook to assure the private sector that he, as president, would govern with full appreciation of the importance of business profits to the welfare of the nation.

On November 29, 1981, Delors began to go public with his protest against the spirit of euphoria expressed in the Mitterrand-Fabius budget. It was necessary, he said, to *faire une pause* (make a pause) in the presentation of reforms, while implementing those already approved. The word "pause" was seized upon by all commentators as an echo of Léon Blum from 1936, announcing a critical suspension, a confession of defeat, in the reform program of the Popular Front government. The reference was valid, but it was not yet clear that Delors had convinced the president to accept a "pause."

By the beginning of 1982, statistics on rising prices, on rising unemployment, and on foreign trade and budgetary deficits forced the technicians surrounding Mitterrand and Mauroy to sound alarms to their chiefs. This created the atmosphere for the decisions on strategy sought by Delors. He and his assistants spent many hours with the president and the prime minister discussing what was to be done. In preparing a new budget, Delors was this time a major participant. Probably under Mitterrand's direction, Budget Minister Fabius moderated his enthusiasm for *relance* with Keynesian reforms. In February it was decided to limit the budget deficit to 3 percent of gross domestic product. This was announced publicly after the meeting of the Council of Ministers on March 10, 1982.

The president commenced a series of private meetings with spokesmen for private entrepreneurs, especially with Yvon Gattaz, president of the CNPF (Employers Council). On April 16, 1982, in an all-day meeting held in the Matignon, the prime minister, with the participation of Delors, Fabius, Jean Auroux (author of the Labor Code reforms), Nicole Questiaux of CERES, and Pierre Dreyfus, reached an understanding with Gattaz and his chief of staff. The resulting change of course for the government had been worked out between Gattaz and Mitterrand, advised and assisted by Delors, a week earlier in the Elysée Palace. Gattaz has said that he was urged to keep the agreements secret to avert criticism of the government from the Communists.[17] In this fashion were the Communists treated by Mitterrand and Mauroy as "a party of the government."

The agreements provided several concessions demanded by business leaders: No further reductions in the work week, thus forcing Mitterrand to give up on his promise of a reduction to 35 hours; a reduction of some 12 billion francs in taxation on business for the years 1982–83; and no increase in charges on employers for social security for at least one year.

Gattaz called the day "historic." For him, it marked the turning point in the attitude of the government toward private enterprise. Mitterrand explained to his Council of Ministers on June 16, 1982, that he had decided to cooperate with business employers because any other course would violate many liberties. Since the choice had been made to continue to live in a free economy, it was necessary to draw the consequences. He did not want to run the risk of being swept away.[18]

The steady increase in the cost of living was hurting wage workers, many of them not fully under the control of their unions. Strikes broke out despite opposition from union leaders at the Renault plant in Flins, at Citroên in Aulney-Sous-Bois, and at the Talbot plant in Poissy. These were the first strikes since the installation of the new government.

Union leaders appreciated the measures enacted on behalf of the poorer sectors of society during the first year of the Mitterrand-Mauroy government:

1. Increase in minimum wage and family allowances.
2. Reduction of work week to 39 hours.
3. Fifth week of paid vacation.
4. The Auroux laws increasing worker rights in the work place.
5. Right to retire with pension at age 60.
6. Training programs for unemployed youth.
7. Property taxes on the wealthy.

The Communist Party was engaged in its charade of being a party of the government. Through Henri Krasucki, chief of the CGT who was also a leading member of the Communist Party, the Mitterrand-Mauroy government had the benefit of political support from some key labor leaders. Socialist Edmond Maire and André Bergeron of *Force Ouvrière* (a strongly anti-Communist labor union federation) were also inclined to help the government with a period of social peace. Minister of the Interior Defferre and the prime minister were in frequent contact with these leaders, who cooperated to the best of their ability to inculcate an attitude of patience toward the government among working people. This was not always effective, as the strikes of April-June 1982 in the auto construction plants demonstrated.

TO STRENGTHEN THE FRANC

The steady rise in the cost of living consequent on the measures taken in 1981 to increase consumption soon wiped out the correction in exchange rates ordered on Delors's initiative in October 1981. By April 1982, a second devaluation was in the air. This time Delors was determined to make it a turning point in the government's economic policy. This was to be the moment to accomplish not only the "pause" he had recommended without success in November 1981, but a permanent turn away from the Keynesian *relance* of 1981 to an acceptance of the necessity for severe government economies and restraints on wages and prices, all of which came to be summed up with the word "rigor" (*rigueur*). Delors saw his task to be that of bringing Mitterrand to a recognition of the economic realities that made the turn onto a new road essential.

Mitterrand, like de Gaulle, did not claim to understand the science of economics, but he did have years of experience as a politician, especially as a minister in governments of the Fourth Republic. He was aware that a change of course like that demanded by Delors might be such a humiliation for the government, such a confession of failure, that it could bring on irresistible demands for his resignation and a call for new elections.

Delors knew there were Socialists in Mitterrand's entourage, especially Chevènement and the CERES faction, who were advocating a voluntaristic radicalization of policy, including, if necessary, a departure of France from the European monetary system and the application of rigid controls on foreign exchange. The spirit in this faction was a defiance of the pressures from the business community and the world market. France would go its own way toward a rupture with capitalism and a decision truly to embark on a French road to socialism.

A key figure for Delors in the campaign to sway Mitterrand toward capitalist "realism" was Prime Minister Mauroy. He too was primarily a politician rather than an economist, and Mitterrand would know that Mauroy weighed questions from a political standpoint. At the Matignon Palace (office of the prime minister) Delors had allies in the economists Jean Peyrelevade and Henri Guillaume. In April 1982 they began the siege of Mauroy to approve a new devaluation, to be accompanied this time by the array of changes designated *rigueur*. They maintained liaison with Delors and kept a sympathetic economist in the Elysée Palace, François Stasse, informed of the developing campaign.[19]

In April and May 1982, Mauroy was won over to the views of his economists and made his recommendation to the president, in a note dated May 28.[20] It advocated adoption of all the elements of *rigueur* as conceived by Delors: devaluation, freezing of wages and prices, budgetary restrictions, tightening of credit. Mauroy sent copies of this note to Lionel Jospin, first secretary of the Socialist Party, Pierre Joxe, another key liaison of Mitterrand with the Socialist Party, and Delors.[21]

This proposal came at an especially inconvenient moment for the president. He would be receiving at the Versailles Palace on June 4 the heads of governments of the Group of Seven, the leading industrial nations of the capitalist world. His plea there would be for an acceptance by these principal political leaders of market economy countries (and especially by Ronald Reagan, Margaret Thatcher, and Helmut Schmidt) of France's attempt at recovery with a Keynesian-type stimulus. From the United States Mitterrand hoped to have help in the form of a lowering of interest rates, which would lower the cost of the dollar on foreign exchanges. From West Germany France was asking for a re-evaluation of the German mark upward, which would greatly reduce the pressure for a devaluation of the French franc. Cooperation in these forms was justified, Mitterrand would argue, in view of the benefits to German, British, and American exporters from France's program of stimulus, some of which went to increase its imports from abroad.

Mauroy was skeptical that Mitterrand would have any success at the economic summit, but his was not the office of decision on such an important matter. In discussing the note of May 28 with Mauroy, Mitterrand urged patience. "Let me have my summit," he said, "and then we'll see." At Solutré, where Mitterrand hiked to a summit with journalists on May 30 in an annual rite over the Pentecost holiday, he assured them there would be no major change of direction in economic policy. However, policies might be modified "according to circumstances."

The summit at Versailles was a gala affair, but it produced no help for the Socialist government of France. There was perhaps some satisfaction among the others in the reports of Mitterrand's economic troubles, since he had chosen to row against the current of the worldwide recession, trying to turn it around prematurely before the bankers of Bonn, New York, and London could read any signs in the market that such a purely political initiative was justified. France still had pretensions at being independent of domination by the world market and was testing its potential to choose its own course in these new political circumstances. The rebuke Mitterrand received at Versailles was a lesson in the limits placed on a social-democratic government that wishes to enjoy the good will of the other leaders of the capitalist world.

On the last day of the summit, Mitterrand confided to Mauroy that he was ready to give the green light on the policy changes advocated by the prime minister since his note of May 28 to the President. Mitterrand would undertake the task of preparing the public for the changes soon to be specified and announced in implementation of *rigueur.* This he began to do with a press conference on June 9. In a long monologue before 300 journalists and in his answers to their questions, the president did not mention *rigueur,* devaluation, or freeze. His theme was that the government was about to enter its second phase, which he named that of "effort." He drew an analogy with the cyclists in the annual *Tour de France,* who pass from a phase in their race on the flat lands to a phase in the mountains. It sounded normal and reassuring, and he insisted no change of objective was taking place.

Still, in the measures Mitterrand said would be forthcoming there were some significant new elements. He advocated changes to:

1. "Restructure our industry"
2. "Improve our competitiveness"
3. "Stimulate savings"
4. "Develop risk capital"
5. "No new taxes"
6. "Give priority to investment and innovation"
7. "Get control of the state budget and of social security"

Gone from his discourse was the aim of government help to the poor to stimulate demand and generate jobs. Also missing was a reference to the goal of giving "priority to jobs," a principal theme in 1981. In fact, the problem of unemployment was downplayed. The failure to check its rise was a humiliating defeat for the government at the end of its first year in office. Mitterrand chose to shift the focus to the problem of inflation, which, he said, had to be brought under control. Putting the new elements beside the omissions in his analysis, it was fairly clear that Keynesian stimulus, the Fabius *relance* of 1981, was being abandoned for a return to supply-side economics, with a search for ways to help business cut its costs and improve competitiveness.

Thus began the great turning back from the brave attempt to revive the French economy and reduce unemployment with a home-made stimulus to consumer demand. The new theme of competitiveness implied that the French Socialists were preparing to knuckle under to the dictatorship of the world market and move France back onto the road of liberal capitalism. The Socialists had come to power shortly after the election of Ronald Reagan and Margaret Thatcher, political champions of supply-side economics. With de Gaulle's independence in their memories, the French Socialists thought they too could enjoy the satisfaction of acting out a French difference, quixotically and provocatively called "the French road to Socialism."

But it was easier to remove the French military forces from the command of NATO, as de Gaulle had done, than it was to free the French economy from domination by the United States, Britain, and West Germany through the world market. The Labor Party in Great Britain under Harold Wilson had tried such a gambit, which ended with Britain accepting the tutelage of the International Monetary Fund as the price of restoring the value of the pound in capitalist markets. Delors and Mauroy were fearful a similar humiliation might be visited on France if it did not change course drastically and impose austerity on itself.

Editorialists commenting on Mitterrand's press conference were not quite sure that a turning had begun. Socialist Party organs insisted on the constancy in the president's goals. But Michel Rocard, showing some signs of satisfaction, declared to *Le Nouvel Observateur* on June 6: " The hour of socialist *rigueur* has arrived, the time for a balance between economic lucidity and social imagination." But Mitterrand and Lionel Jospin agreed it would be inadvisable to make any further attempt to alert the party to what was coming. For Socialists, Jospin explained later, it was difficult to admit the turning, which came too soon and seemed to contradict what had been said up until then. Anyway, he insisted, the new plan of *rigueur* did not abolish the social measures taken previously.

Most striking was the attempt by the Communists to assure their supporters that there was a perfect continuity with the programs launched in 1981. Any "turning" of the kind maliciously proclaimed by Rocard would have forced the Communists to consider giving up their ministries and their respectable role as a "party of the government." A spokesman for the party, Pierre Juquin, commented on Mitterrand's declarations, saying that the president had expressed his will to continue the policy of the past year with the same objectives and the same orientation. That, said Juquin, was what the party had demanded.[22]

Marchais stated on television his agreement with this assessment of Mitterrand's program: "He is staying the course." *L'Humanité* continued to behave like an official journal. Marcel Rigout, one of the four Communist ministers, was struck by the fact that austerity or *rigueur* came on without causing any problem in the Communist Party. So far as he knew, the leadership of the Party did not at that time even discuss the idea of quitting the government.

Delors, as minister of finance, was above all a spokesman for a "realistic" acceptance of the constraints placed on France by its dependence on its exports, its imports, and its financial transactions with the other countries of Western Europe and with the United States. Without his consent, even behind his back, Mauroy and Fabius in 1981 had launched France on an attempt to spend its way to economic progress. The enactment of these inflationary economic measures during the leftist euphoria created by the elections of 1981 had frightened investors and money market dealers in France and its principal trading partners. The resulting flight from the franc caused its sharp decline, exacerbating inflation by raising the cost of all imports.

On June 12, 1982, Delors was consulting in Brussels with the other finance ministers of Western Europe (the community then known as "the Ten"). Under the rules of the European monetary system (SME), the weakness of the franc and the strength of the German mark on the exchange markets made a general readjustment of rates imperative. Delors participated in the setting of the new rates, which produced a new net devaluation of the franc *vis-à-vis* the mark of 9.75 percent.

Delors returned to Paris with the message that the community expected France to get its inflation under control and take measures to restore investor confidence. Delors thus spoke with the voice of the international finance community, which was totally unsympathetic to the first year of initiatives taken by Mitterrand and Mauroy. It seems likely that Mitterrand had foreseen this criticism from the other leading capitalist countries and named Delors to the Finance Ministry in order to make sure France did not continue its "Socialist" euphoria for too long. Delors did his job of bringing into public consciousness the limits placed on France by its membership in a Western European community in which the sacrifice of sovereignty was demanded as an economic imperative of capitalism. Mitterrand agreed with Delors in reading the destiny of France precisely in the emerging economic unification of Western Europe. The "French road to Socialism" proved to be a short-lived mirage, forgotten by the Socialists themselves as the hard realities of seeking common ground with Germany, Great Britain, Italy, Belgium, the Netherlands, and Luxembourg became the principal focus of French policy for the remainder of Mitterrand's term in office. "Austerity" was the first installment required for membership in the Western European pool, which promised to pay high dividends in the form of profits to be taken from the world market.

Delors promised in Brussels that France would do its duty to restore investor confidence. This was exactly what he had been urging for months. Through Mauroy he had convinced Mitterrand that an "adjustment" was necessary. It need not take the distasteful names of *rigueur* or austerity, since these would make acceptance by the public, especially workers, even more difficult. In meetings of the Council of Ministers from June 13 to June 16, the measures proposed included:

1. Freeze of prices for four months, excepting prices for energy and for those farm products that were already subject to price controls from Brussels.
2. Freeze of wages for four months, except for legislated rises in the minimum wage.
3. Restraint on government spending to ensure that the deficit did not exceed 3 percent of the gross domestic product.
4. Increase in the value added tax (TVA).[23]

The strongest opposition to these measures in the Council discussions came from Chevènement. He was fundamentally at odds with the sacrifice of French independence to proceed along the path laid out in 1981, which above all aimed at creating jobs. He argued that France should withdraw from the European monetary system and go its own way. Delors pointed out this would further weaken the franc and exacerbate inflation. This debate was an indication of the developing isolation of Chevènement in the Socialist Party on the question of sacrificing French sovereignty to the institutions of Western European unification.

Mitterrand offered some consolation to Chevènement by indicating to his ministers that if the Mauroy-Delors revisions did not produce results, he would consider a "third phase," involving France's withdrawal from the SME. This came to be known as "the other policy," always held in reserve. It would have been closer to the spirit of the Mitterrand of the Metz Congress when he was battling, with help from Chevènement, against the conservatism of Michel Rocard. At some point in these months of 1982 and early 1983, Mitterrand made the fundamental choices that fixed the character of his regime and his place in French history. Perhaps he already knew what his choice was going to be when he gave such an important role to Jacques Delors in the first government headed by Pierre Mauroy.

Delors hoped that the labor unions would accept the new measures, since they included controls on prices. Krasucki of the General Confederation of Labor (CGT) called them mistaken but, following the line of his party, the PCF, accepted them temperately. There would be no campaign of union-inspired strikes, assuming, that is, the government could enforce the controls on prices.

Although businesses were critical of the increase in the TVA at the time of controls on prices, they were generally pleased with the turning toward restraints on government spending and short-term controls on wages. They applauded Delors and Mauroy for making the fight to get inflation under control a first priority.

In the National Assembly the opposition parties, pleased at the turning, nevertheless condemned the government for its "incompetence." The government's proposals, with the votes of Socialists and Communists, became law on July 20, 1982.

NOTES

1.   Alain Duhamel, *Les prétendants* (Paris: Gallimard, 1983), 243.

2.   Jacques Attali's first book was *Analyse économique de la vie politique* (Paris: PUF, 1973). From 1973 until 1981 he had published a book a year, to critical acclaim. On taking up his duties with President Mitterrand he began keeping notes of all his consultations with the president. These form the basis of a valuable account of the Mitterrand years from 1981 to 1986. Jacques Attali, *Verbatim: Chronique des années 1981–1986*, Vol. 1 (Paris: Fayard, 1993).

3.   Pierre Favier and Michel Martin-Roland, *La décennie Mitterrand*, Vol. 1 (Paris: Editions du Seuil, 1990), 66.

4.   Ibid., 66–67.

5.   Henry Kissinger, "Il avait raison contre moi," interview by Sara Daniel, *Le Nouvel Observateur* (Paris) No. 1593 (18 to 24 May, 1995): 98.

6.   Favier and Martin-Roland, *La décennie Mitterrand*, 91; Attali, *Verbatim*, 46.

7.   Favier and Martin-Roland, *La décennie Mitterrand*, 91.

8.   Favier and Martin-Roland, *La décennie Mitterrand*, 92; Attali, *Verbatim*, 46.

9.   Favier and Martin-Roland, *La décennie Mitterrand*, 92–93; Attali, *Verbatim*, 47.

10.   Favier and Martin-Roland, *La décennie Mitterrand*, 131–132.

11.   See Vivien A. Schmidt, "Decentralization: A Revolutionary Reform," in Patrick McCarthy (ed.), *The French Socialists in Power, 1981–1986* (New York: Greenwood Press, 1987), 83–105.

12.   François Mitterrand, *Ici et maintenant* (Paris: Fayard, 1980), 173–175.

13.   Anicet Le Pors, *L'Etat efficace* (Paris: Robert Laffont, 1985), 170.

14.   Favier and Martin-Roland, *La décennie Mitterrand*, 146.

15.   "No one—excepting, perhaps, the CNPF [Employers' Association], would have mistaken these measures as steps toward *autogestion* and socialism. In short, the Auroux laws might turn out to be something of a Gallic Wagner Act." George Ross, "Labor and the Left in Power," in Patrick McCarthy (ed.), *The French Socialists in Power, 1981–1986* (New York: Greenwood Press, 1987), 116–117.

16.   Favier and Martin-Roland, *La décennie Mitterrand*, 168.

17.   Ibid., 413; Attali, *Verbatim*, 161, 200.

18.   Favier and Martin-Roland, *La décennie Mitterrand*, 429.

19.   Jacques Attali indicates that Stassi, an economist in the entourage of the president, was supporting the views of Delors in the debates over economic policy. Attali, *Verbatim*, 204.

20.   Attali, *Verbatim*, 234.

21.   Favier and Martin-Roland, *La décennie Mitterrand*, 415.

22.   Ibid., 424.

23.   Attali, *Verbatim*, 251–252, 254–255; Favier and Martin-Roland, *La décennie Mitterrand*, 426-428.

7

In the Name of Rigor

The construction of life lies far more in the power of facts than in convictions.

—Walter Benjamin

The decision taken in June 1982 to fight inflation by limiting the deficit forced the government to abandon the Keynesian strategy of stimulating the economy with an increase in demand financed by the state. This set the Mitterrand-Mauroy regime on a new course associated with the name of Jacques Delors, who had won over the prime minister to his view of the overriding need to strengthen the franc. The full consequences of that basic reorientation were working themselves out during the remainder of the period left to Mauroy as prime minister. Mitterrand emerged from this reorientation, which took some two years to be fully grasped by him and by the country, with a new acceptance of the constraints placed on France by its dependence on the international investment community. Before this lesson had been assimilated into his thinking, he clung for many months to his dream of an independent France, strong enough and clever enough to plan its way into prosperity with strong government intervention and guidance despite disapproval of such Socialist-oriented ambitions by Reagan, Thatcher, and the moguls of international finance.

By the autumn of 1982, Mitterrand had entered into this painful period of education. To reporters on August 2 he expressed some preoccupation with the situation created by the new budget and the restraints it imposed. The drop in the popularity of Mauroy and the government, who were in the front line, was natural, he said, in view of the sacrifices that were now being demanded of almost everyone. His own ratings in the polls had also been dropping. If the municipal elections were to be held with the country in this mood, the left would be severely beaten, he admitted. But those elections would not be taking place until March 1983, so he and his colleagues still had several months to show the electorate the benefits of the measures being adopted. If only inflation could be brought down a few points, everyone's confidence in the future would improve. This was now, he said, the primary task of the government. This new orientation was reflected in the "budget of rigor" of which he approved.

But the problem of unemployment, which had been proclaimed the government's primary concern when it took office, was by no means forgotten. Jean Le Garrec, who had succeeded in developing the program of nationalizations and getting it enacted, was named to take charge of what would prove to be an even more difficult task, promoting the creation of jobs. Mitterrand told him it was essential that an improvement be registered in the statistics of unemployment in time to affect the outcome of the March 1983 elections.

Le Garrec studied carefully the ways unemployment was measured and decided it would be reasonable to eliminate from the tally certain categories of people, such as those unemployed who had put in their names for job training. There was a certain logic in arguing that such trainees and prospective trainees were occupied for the time being and therefore not unemployed. This high-handed bureaucratic revision provoked derision and protest, but it improved the statistics issued by Le Garrec's agency, which was just what Mitterrand had commanded.

When the post of minister of industry became vacant by the resignation of Pierre Dreyfus (at seventy-five years of age), Mitterrand nominated Chevènement as his replacement, in addition to the portfolio he already held as minister of research. Chevènement was known to favor an acceleration in the government's attempts to stimulate jobs in industry despite the deficits attributed to such policies pursued under the first budget. Delors and Mauroy could not have been pleased at this appointment of a leading representative of a leftist current that identified itself as "revolutionary Socialist." The attitude of this left Socialist, Chevènement, toward the series of governments to be named by Mitterrand over the seven years of his first term as president will provide us from time to time with an interesting point of view on the evolution of policy.

Mauroy was given some satisfaction by a change of personnel surrounding the president at the Elysée Palace. Pierre Bérégovoy, who had been serving as general-secretary, a chief-of-staff post that placed him in daily contact with Mitterrand, was now given a portfolio as minister of social affairs. This removed from the president's immediate entourage one who had expressed his objections to the new "rigor" of Delors-Mauroy, and declared his preference for France's departure from the European monetary system if necessary to continue the 1981 strategy of stimulus and job creation. Bérégovoy's transfer to a ministry was hardly a demotion. He was replaced in the Elysée Palace by Jean Luis Bianco. These appointments suggested that Mitterrand was still not giving up his hopes for a return to the strategy of economic stimulus that had marked the first few months of his regime.

On the suggestion of Jacques Attali, Mitterrand in the autumn of 1982 ordered that certain of his principal advisers meet with him in restricted sessions once each week for discussions of economic strategy. Attending these meetings, besides the president and the prime minister with their staff economists, were Delors, Fabius,

Chevènement, Defferre, Jobert, Rocard, and Fiterman. The discussions frequently turned into debates between defenders of market-dominated "rigor" and advocates of stimulated growth and industrialization with heavy reliance on planning. Mitterrand used these debates to clarify his own understanding of the economic factors in the problems he confronted.

According to Jean Peyrelevade, who attended these meetings as an adviser to the prime minister, Mitterrand expressed from time to time his strong desire to protect France from the cold-hearted domination of the financial markets. He did not want his government, he said, to adopt the policies of Thatcher.

The moment was critical for France and for Mitterrand's place in history. From his writings, his speeches, his private conversations, we know what his dreams were, his vision of France's future and his own role as leader. These can be summarized roughly in four goals:

1. Full employment
2. Stable prices
3. Integration of immigrants
4. Generosity toward the Third World

These were the chief characteristics of what Mitterrand hoped to achieve with the support of the Socialist Party, the Communist Party, and a majority of the French electorate. In their ensemble these four goals clearly implied that France's system of production and distribution must be revived from the crisis conditions that had given Mitterrand his chance to be elected. It was essential that all the residents of France, immigrants as well as native-born French, be enabled to work for a livelihood and to produce for the nation's growing needs and for export onto a world market.

Failure throughout the next decade to achieve anything close to full employment greatly hampered the government's ability to carry through on the third and fourth goals. It is not premature to raise fundamental questions about the Mitterrand years: Why did this leader of the Socialist Party fail to lead the French out of the grip of a stagnant economy that left millions unemployed? Was it a failure of character? Could a more resolute Socialist have striven, with some prospect of success, to make France an inspiring vanguard in the industrialized countries of Western Europe? How?

This would have entailed accepting the consequences of an invigorating declaration of independence from the domination of international capitalism represented by Thatcher and Reagan. There were advisers in the internal debates of 1982 who would have welcomed such a radical spirit of defiance in the president. They envisioned implementation of a French-style "rupture with capitalism" once commended by Mitterrand. This would have been very different from the Bolshevik Revolution in Russia. All his party supporters on the left, including the Communists, were committed to respect for pluralism. There was to be no resort to dictatorship. Mitterrand had an opportunity to try, in the bold spirit of the French Revolution, to open a new road leading to a new social and economic order for peoples of the advanced countries plagued by unemployment, racial tensions, and insecurity. He chose not to seize the opportunity.

Mitterrand's four goals expressed a strongly felt imperative to change the system that made their achievement impossible. Mitterrand had frequently inveighed against the power of money. He had given voice to a morality of equality that deplores the right of the owners of capital to exclude millions from the opportunity to earn a livelihood. The question was, would he use his authority as president to actualize that morality? Would he base his policies on his Socialist ethics? Let us reject the hypothesis that he was merely a hypocrite and opportunist in his ethical professions of judgment on capitalism, never intending to act on them once he had succeeded in rising to the presidency. His life does not show him to be such a villain in his heart.

A more plausible explanation of the conservative role he came to play is that he felt himself a prisoner of the economic system that held France in its grip when he came to power. His definition of what could be done was determined by what had been done. In this he was a victim of his own prejudices, and these undermined his freedom of action. The moneyed powers won a victory over Mitterrand by standing on the argument of "necessity," defined by the past and called a "providence" working through the invisible hand. If only Mitterrand had been more strongly imbued with the spirit of the Enlightenment, if only he had attached more importance to progress, if he had chosen to break with the past and orient his administration toward the future, on a project capable of inspiring and energizing his nation, what might he have done! He had an electoral mandate to do something absolutely new, inspiring, energetic, and if Washington was displeased, so much the better for awakening the effort of a great nation with a challenge the world would watch with sympathy and engagement.

He could have used the state as a means of providing work for the millions left unemployed by enterprises subjected to the demands of investors who profit from the competition among these enterprises to produce for sale in national and world markets. Instead, he chose to resign himself and his government to the inevitability of unemployment, since this was one consequence of cost-cutting measures essential to keeping French industry competitive. Reason condemns this despotism of the investors. The opportunity to work for a livelihood is now felt to be a human need denied to millions. Mitterrand had said as much, and several Declarations of Rights at the United Nations show that mankind is ripe for action aimed at implementing a new step forward.

A historic opportunity was lost, but not inevitably. This experience did not prove that history has come to an end in Western Europe. It can also be read to show the enormous importance of the human factor, of the character of leaders, in determining the outcome.

THE OTHER POLICY

The months leading up to the municipal elections of March 1983 came to be called the months of indecision (*flottement*). Thierry Pfister, counselor in the cabinet of Prime Minister Mauroy from 1981 to 1984, has given an account of Mitterrand's dissatisfaction with the course adopted in June 1982 on the recommendation of Delors and Mauroy.[1] The president was encouraging the elaboration of what came to be called "the other policy." Mauroy suspected that the president was being influenced in that direction by "night visitors," who were advising him to order the departure of France from the European monetary system (SME). This step, they argued, would permit France to modernize its industry by lowering the cost of borrowing money. Under the constraints of the SME, France had to keep its interest rates high (15 percent to 18 percent) in order to support the exchange rate of the franc. Such a move, though not very radical in itself (Britain did not adhere to the rules of the SME), would have been seen in the financial markets as a declaration of independence and would surely have provoked a run on the franc. Delors was opposed to such a measure, and he was supported by Mauroy.

"The other policy" was designed to stimulate French enterprises by improving their profit opportunities. This was the promise seen in lowering the cost of borrowing by throwing off the constraints of the SME. Moreover, a reduction in the costs of production was to be achieved by alleviating the burden of social security charges paid by employers. Some of this would be shifted to the government's budget. Wage costs would be held down by abandoning the "indexation" of wages. In other words, wages would not necessarily rise at the same rate as prices. Finally, barriers to imports would be raised to provide protection for French industry from foreign competitors in the national market.

None of this was very radical. It expressed a continuing respect for the rights of business leaders to make their investment decisions with a view to maximizing their profits. There was no suggestion that the government itself should assume the responsibility of investing in the production system with some criteria other than maximum profit. Even the nationalized industries were to continue to measure their performance by their *rentabilité*, the bottom line of profits and losses. In fact, some of the "night visitors" who were advocating a shift to "the other policy" were business leaders.

Among these was Jean Riboud, who had been managing a family enterprise known as Schlumberger.[2] He was a longtime friend of Mitterrand. From his personal experience of trying to compete on the international market he argued, with support from his economic counselor, Jean Denizet, that French enterprises were being asphyxiated by the high cost of borrowing money. Under Pompidou and Giscard they had managed to survive only because the high rate of inflation had enabled them to repay debts in devalued currency. It was time to put an end to that vicious circle. To bring down inflation was fine, but while that was being attempted French enterprises should have a quick shot in the arm made possible by leaving the SME. This and other cost relief measures would enable them to modernize with new equipment and plants; a protected national market for their products would encourage them to invest. Once they were converted and functioning at a higher level of productivity thanks to their new capital investment, France could re-enter the SME, remove barriers on imports, and engage its competitors in a world market.

Jean-Jacques Servan-Schreiber, author of books vaunting the computer-based "revolution" in Silicon Valley, California, also favored "the other policy" as the best way to put French industry in a condition to compete in the emerging world-wide capitalist market. He was another of the "night visitors," supported in his presentations by Minister of the Interior Defferre.

Among Mitterrand's advisers at the Presidential Palace, Charles Salzmann and Alain Boubil were the strongest advocates of these proposed changes.[3] Among his ministers, Jean-Pierre Chevènement (industry and research), Pierre Bérégovoy (social affairs), and Laurent Fabius (budget) added their voices to that of Defferre in deploring the constraints of the SME.

This was perhaps the last time Mitterrand was seriously tempted to take a leaf from the Gaullist tradition and defy the rest of Europe and the United States. Pierre Bérégovoy saw the political appeal in such a course. He was in favor of leaving the SME, accompanying this with strict austerity. With support from the Communists, he said the blame for the hardships could be placed on the Germans and the Americans.[4]

The implementation of austerity measures went forward during the final months of 1982. When the four-month period of controls on prices and wages came to an end on November 1, the government used its good rapport with the labor unions to foster wage agreements that did away with the practice of raising wages automatically each quarter on the basis of the predicted rate of inflation for that quarter. Thus began the process of *désindexation* of wages, which aimed at cutting production costs by holding down the rise of wages to a rate below that of inflation.

In a speech on September 27, 1982, at Figeac, Mitterrand declared himself in full agreement with the goal of helping French industry improve its competitiveness by lowering the burden of payments to the government and to banks.[5] It was an important moment in the definition of his policies for meeting the growing crises of unemployment, deficits, inflation, and declining value of the franc. He urged the nation to recognize a common interest in helping these entrepreneurs lower their costs of production, which would help them compete in export markets, reduce trade deficits, strengthen the franc and thereby lower the costs of imports. He argued that everyone would benefit from a lowering of the rate of inflation. These French companies, he said, were fighting a battle for the welfare of all. In the course of this speech, so full of solidarity with the concerns of private entrepreneurs, the President made a new and significant declaration: "*Socialisme à la française*, I do not make it my Bible." His apostasy from Socialism was steadily to emerge as a new feature of his public image. This is the man who would put his stamp on France of the 1980s.

In his new post as minister of social affairs, Bérégovoy had the unpleasant task of implementing the spirit of "rigor" in the social security system. This meant changing the direction of liberalization launched by the newly elected government in 1981. Formulas for calculating payments were tightened to achieve savings, hospitals were instructed to cut costs, and beginning in 1983 all patients would have to make a co-payment from their own funds of twenty francs per day. To restore funds to the hard-pressed unemployment insurance program, a special

"solidarity" assessment of 1 percent of wages was levied and eligibility requirements were rewritten to exclude about 100,000 new claimants. André Bergeron,
leader of *Force Ouvrière*, a labor union with no ties to the Socialist Party or the
Communist Party, protested and proclaimed that in his view, wage workers had
nothing to anticipate from the government in the way of an improvement in their
standard of living and social security. This statement was published in the newspapers and contributed to the gathering discontent in the ranks of labor. Leaders of
the other major unions, CFDT and CGT, strove to help the government retain
support among their members as the March elections approached.

Prime Minister Mauroy tried to persuade the country that the left had not abandoned its ideas. "We remain loyal to our objective of social justice and solidarity,"
he said in the Pas-de-Calais on October 12, 1982. "We will show both rigor and
imagination as necessary." And to the Council of Ministers on October 27, he
insisted that the government had not changed its perspective.[6]

Nevertheless, in the president's traditional New Year speech to the nation,
Mitterrand emphasized the new theme, "the objective which commands all others": solidarity with business enterprises. "It is necessary to produce more and to
produce better," he said. Workers must recognize their responsibilities. The burden of charges borne by the enterprises must be lightened. They must become
more competitive by investing, inventing, and learning how to sell in the world
market. They should receive government help in the training of workers, he said.

Mitterrand seemed to have reoriented his thinking about the challenge to the
country. What now "commanded all others" was industrial modernization, translated into the goal of improving France's performance in the international competition for markets. And the forces on which he saw the country dependent for its
future prosperity and welfare were the private entrepreneurs, investors and business leaders. The year 1982 had worked this fundamental change of focus and
with it a sweeping change of priorities in the president. Since he had been elected
as a leader of Socialists with support from the Communists, serious questions of
continued support would certainly arise as the implications of the reorientation
became more and more manifest. Could the Communist Party continue to call
itself a "party of the government"?

It was not the Communist Party which first drew conclusions from Mitterrand's
reorientation. Throughout 1983 it continued its public expressions of satisfaction
with the government and expressed satisfaction with itself as a responsible party
of the government. Fiterman, a Communist who was minister of transport, has
since said that he wished to resign in early 1983, but that the leadership of the
party, specifically Marchais, urged him to remain. Fiterman said that in his ministry he was allowed no freedom of action, because "rigor" blocked everything.[7]

But Marchais told him the Communist electorate placed very high hopes in the
Union of the Left and was not ready for a rupture with Mitterrand.

However, Minister of Industry and Research Chevènement, leader of the CERES
faction of the Socialist Party, expressed his discontent with the new orientation by
submitting his letter of resignation as minister in February 1983. He stated two
grounds. First, the president had criticized him and other ministers for interfering

in the management of the nationalized industries. Mitterrand had accused these ministers of confusing Socialism with bureaucracy. The managers, said the President, should be left to run their enterprises as they knew best. To Chevènement, this defeated the social benefits sought in nationalizing. Second, Chevènement objected to the economic change of course to "rigor," expressing his support for a policy of stimulated growth with a strong concern for social justice and national independence. His letter was a reiteration of the views he had maintained in the economic debates of 1981 and 1982 in which he was the most outspoken opponent of the changes urged by Delors and Mauroy.

Mitterrand could not have been too surprised to receive this letter. The policy views that Chevènement championed had been put on the shelf. However, the government was not making any such confession to the public. Mitterrand asked Chevènement to remain until after the municipal elections, which were to take place on March 6 and 13. Their conclusion would be the moment for a general appraisal and reorganization. Perhaps some different post could then be offered to persuade Chevènement to remain in the government. It would be a blow to the Socialists to have his resignation announced a few weeks before the elections. Chevènement acceded to the president's request and waited for the elections to pass.

Chevènement could read the logic in the events and decisions of 1982. He wanted to register his protest publicly, but out of loyalty to his party he consented to wait for a less critical moment. Edmond Maire, chief of the Socialist-oriented union, CFDT, created a similar problem for Mitterrand, but one not so easily averted. He emerged from a meeting with the president on January 31, 1983, with the statement for the press that a second plan of "rigor" now had to be envisaged. This was exactly the possibility the Socialists did not want discussed at the moment.

Mitterrand suspected that Maire, frequently a champion in the labor movement for Rocard, was trying to hurt the Mitterrand-Mauroy team as they approached the elections. Maire, however, maintained innocently that he was only trying to prepare his members for the new demands soon to be made on them. In early February, Rocard publicly gave his approval to what Maire had done. In the review, *L'Expansion*, he said, "When one senses difficult times coming, it is necessary to give people a warning."

An attempt by Mauroy to counteract the mood of anxiety fed by Maire's statement further undermined the government's credibility. In a television appearance on February 16 he denied that there was any plan to tighten austerity in the new year. The big problems are behind us, he said, and all the signal-lights are turning green.

The trouble with this statement was that many signal-lights were plainly flashing red: unemployment, trade deficit, inflation. It was hard to see in this situation any evidence that the left was on the way to succeeding. Mauroy had spoken as a cheerleader and was now mocked for his analysis with the term much employed by the right against the government as the election approached: incompetence.

A THIRD MAUROY GOVERNMENT

The first round of the municipal elections on March 6, 1983, was marked by a high rate of abstention of voters in the leftist sector. This generated euphoria in *Figaro* and other papers of the right, together with disappointment and apprehension in government circles. It appeared that the government had not been able to mobilize a majority of the electorate to come out for candidates supporting its program. Three ministers who were also mayors, Defferre (Marseilles), Bérégovoy (Nevers), and Chevènement (Belfort), had failed to win enough votes in their respective cities to be re-elected mayors in the first round of voting. They found themselves in *ballotage*, meaning their re-election would depend on the outcome of the second round on March 13. This was also the situation of Prime Minister Mauroy, under challenge as mayor of Lille.

How many of the larger cities (with populations over 30,000) would the left have lost after the second round of voting? This was the criterion by which the outcome would be assessed. Between the two voting dates the opposition in its euphoria foresaw victory for its candidates in forty to forty-five of these cities. But in fact the outcome of the second round proved much more favorable to the government, which suffered a loss of thirty of the larger cities. Compared to what might have happened, it was a kind of victory for the left. Mauroy won re-election in Lille, as did Defferre, Bérégovoy, and Chevènement in their cities. Edith Cresson, a Socialist who won in Chatellerault, entered the ranks of mayors of large cities.

But there were important defeats for the left, especially in Paris, where Jacques Chirac won in all twenty *arrondissements*. And in one *arrondissement* Jean-Marie Le Pen, playing on the theme of "France for the French" and calling for the exclusion and expulsion of Arabs and blacks, won 10 percent of the vote. Henceforth his party, the National Front, playing on racism and insecurity, would be a factor in French political life. This raised new obstacles to Mitterrand's hopes for policies of generosity toward immigrants.

With the municipal elections behind him, Mitterrand had to decide what policy and personnel changes were to be made, if any, to prepare for the next three years, a period that would lead to the decisive moment of the legislative elections in 1986. Much has been written about his ordeal of decision in March 1983. According to some observers, he had come to the conclusion that France should adopt "the other policy" recommended by the "night visitors." This would mean cutting French policy free from the restraints imposed by participation in the European monetary system. France would temporarily withdraw from the system in order to escape the obligation to devalue the franc arising from the failure to control inflation. (At 10 percent per year, inflation in France was still causing speculators to move funds into German marks or U.S. dollars, where they could enjoy high interest rates and a relatively stable currency.) Departure from the SME would be accompanied by increased government expenditures to help French industry to modernize and a raising of barriers to imports. This was the program recommended by Mitterrand's confidant, Jean Riboud.

If such policy changes were to be introduced, Mitterrand would have to name a new prime minister, because Mauroy had long since been won over to the views of Minister of Finance Delors, or, to state the point more cautiously, that was the stand Mauroy had championed in the economic debates of 1982. These views went against the grain of Mauroy's lifetime devotion to Socialist principles and even to his 1981 reliance on a Keynesian strategy of stimulating recovery by increasing the purchasing power of the poorer classes.

Perhaps Mitterrand, with good reason, saw Mauroy as only partly committed to Delors, as an unenthusiastic supporter of the conservative, orthodox economic policies of the minister of finance. This would explain why Mitterrand might find it plausible to make a surprising proposition to Mauroy: that he continue as prime minister in order to implement "the other policy." He had already shown a remarkable capacity to adapt to political necessity. Having changed in one direction, toward Delors, could he not be persuaded to change again, this time toward the businessman Riboud? Such a proposal was bound to be resented by Mauroy. Stay on, to implement the policy he had been arguing against for months? Assuming that Mitterrand did ask such a favor of Mauroy, as the investigative reporters Pierre Favier and Michel Martin-Roland argue in their book, *La décennie Mitterrand*, Mauroy refused the offer and was prepared to step down. These authors describe Mauroy's state of mind with the quotation, "I was determined not to be had" (*decidé à ne pas me laisser faire*).[8]

Jacques Attali in his book *Verbatim* (1993) expresses the view that during the week between the two rounds of the elections, Mitterrand had decided in favor of "the other policy."[9] He also reports that Mauroy absolutely refused to take responsibility for implementing such a policy, as did Delors. This firm opposition from Delors and Mauroy (and from Attali himself) apparently convinced Mitterrand that "the other policy" was not a viable option since it would cause a rupture he did not want. He allowed the possibility to remain alive for a few more days in order to gain better terms from the German government, which did not want France to withdraw from the European monetary system. Fabius, perhaps sensing that the president had decided to stick with the Delors-Mauroy policy, let himself be persuaded that France did not have the foreign exchange reserves needed to risk a withdrawal from the SME. He withdrew his support for "the other policy," ensuring its demise.[10]

The certain fact is that Mitterrand, some eight days after the municipal elections, announced that Mauroy would continue as prime minister. In a reorganized government (known as the third Mauroy government), the number of ministers was reduced from thirty-four to fifteen. Delors would continue at finance and add to it the portfolios of economy and the budget. He was given the cabinet rank of second to the prime minister. It seemed evident that in the vital area of economic policy he had won over to his views not only the prime minister but the president as well. The resignation of Chevènement, on the president's desk since February, was now accepted. Chevènement announced publicly that he was opposed to the course the government had chosen in the change from stimulus to "rigor."

The Communists, who were accorded two places in the new distribution of ministerial posts (Charles Fiterman and Marcel Rigout), announced they would continue as a "party of the government." But this was becoming a question of debate, it seems, within the party leadership. Rigout has said that the retention of Mauroy as prime minister weighed against any Communist departure. Yet many Commmunist leaders knew that by remaining in the government, the PCF was underwriting an increase in unemployment.[11]

The presence of the Communists in the government was exceedingly useful to Mitterrand and Mauroy because it ensured that the CGT, the powerful labor union headed by Henri Krasucki, member of the Politburo of the Communist Party, would continue to support the government despite growing discontent of the rank and file with the policy of "rigor." Bérégovoy, who was consulting closely with Mitterrand on the makeup of a new government, formed the opinion that the president renewed the mandate of Mauroy as a way of prolonging this useful Communist presence. They would remain, Bérégovoy said, thanks in part to the president's decision not to replace Mauroy.[12] This is a most illuminating demonstration of the relations among Mitterrand, Socialists, and Communists. The president was making use of the uncritical support of both parties gradually to introduce the conservative economic policies of Delors.

In a luncheon conversation with the four principal leaders of the Mitterrand faction in the Socialist Party, Louis Mermaz, Louis Joxe, Charles Hernu, and Claude Estier, the president indicated that the alternatives he was considering to Mauroy were Delors, Rocard, and Fabius. These men were not favorites with the Socialist Party. Though Fabius in 1981 had drawn up the budget to implement the policy of stimulating recovery through aid to the poorer classes and had expressed some support for the idea of France's leaving the SME, he was ready in March 1983 to implement Delors's policies if that was what Mitterrand wanted.

The consideration of Delors or Rocard for the post of prime minister indicates that as early as March 1983 the president had settled into a strategy of moving toward the center, with policies aimed at reassuring financial markets and preparing France to seek its fortunes in the capitalist competition of a common European market. The goal of *socialisme à la française* was being quietly buried. Viewed in retrospect, the years 1982 and 1983 show Mitterrand reshaping his view of his place in history. Whatever the flaws in French capitalism, its guardians, he concluded, were too firmly entrenched to be confronted and defied. Instead, he would seek to modernize it by giving it a European, a continental arena of opportunity. That way lies salvation? Such became his hope. If Mitterrand was ever to join his former hero, Jean Jaurès, in the Panthéon, that could hardly be as a Socialist but rather as one of the political architects of a capitalist Europe.

The president addressed the nation on the evening of March 23, 1983. He asked for a redoubling of effort from all in a mobilization against inflation, trade deficits, and unemployment. He explained his decision to stay in the European monetary system by saying he did not want to see France isolated from the European community.

Two days later at a special meeting of the Council of Ministers, Delors presented the new plan to pass from rigor to austerity. It was designed to reduce consumer demand by 2 percent of gross national product. (This was twice the increase in demand legislated in 1981 and 1982.) Taxes were raised; an "obligatory loan" of an additional amount (10% of taxes payable) was to be paid to the government by the wealthier households, to be repaid in three years; new taxes were levied on alcohol and tobacco; the twenty franc per day co-payment at state hospitals, held in suspension pending the March elections, was put into effect; some of the major public work projects in progress were suspended; and the budget deficit was to be reduced by 20 million francs.

Raymond Barre, who had been prime minister under President Giscard d'Estaing, enjoyed national prestige as one of the country's leading orthodox economists. During 1981 and 1982 he had been a severe critic of the Mitterrand-Mauroy government. His speedy declaration of praise and support for the austerity measures announced following the March 1983 elections helps the historian measure the importance and the character of the turning that was being accomplished. Led by Delors, the government had abandoned the Socialist longings of 1981 and the Keynesian stimulus of the first budget. It had now returned, judging from Barre's praise, to the conventional liberal-capitalist policies of the parties of the right. Barre congratulated Mitterrand on having resisted the temptation to take France into an adventure of independence by leaving the SME. Praise from this quarter was not entirely welcome, since it fed the stirrings of suspicion in the labor unions and the parties of the left that Mitterrand was destined, despite his campaign promises and his protests, to ratify pro-business, trickle-down policies like those of Reagan and Thatcher in the United States and Britain.

The first secretary of the Socialist Party, Lionel Jospin, had the task of explaining to his fellow Socialists, and particularly to his leading committees, the logic and the utility of the course being adopted. He was in frequent contact with the president, who counted on him to sustain unity and morale in the party.

Jospin urged the members of his directing committee to employ the line that the changes were only temporary, a "parenthesis." In retrospect, he admitted that he had invented that theory in order to calm both himself and his troops. It was a way of giving an accounting for the change of course without criticizing the government. Socialists would feel bad under the plan but they would be inoculating themselves with realism.[13]

Prime Minister Mauroy in *L'Express* of April 1, 1983, took a similar line. This was a period of adjustment, he said, of which the harvest would come in 1985 and 1986. He insisted the government would be maintaining "our policy of the left."[14]

Thus with the words, "realism," "afterwards," "parenthesis," and "the harvest will come," Socialist leaders tried to convince themselves and their voters that nothing fundamental in the way of a change of course was under way. Years later Jacques Toubon of the right-wing RPR slyly offered them a poisonous tribute:

The change of economic policy was carried out without great difficulty. It is remarkable. For a year Jospin repeated that the Government had not changed its policy. Mitterrand can be very grateful to him for having caused this swerve to take place without pain.[15]

MODERNIZATION OF INDUSTRY

One of the new ambitions with which government spokesmen sought to reassure the country was modernization of French industry. During the summer of 1983, the management of the privately owned automobile manufacturing group, Peugeot-Talbot, announced that it was going to modernize by reducing its work force. Nearly 7,400 jobs were going to be eliminated.

The minister for employment was a Communist, Jack Ralite. He began negotiations with management and labor unions to try to diminish the magnitude of this disaster. The company agreed to postpone the start of the layoffs while negotiations were taking place. It agreed to reduce the number of layoffs in the first phase from 3,000 to 2,000. Ralite signed off on this arrangement, supported by the leadership of the CGT. But Edmond Maire of the CFDT characterized the agreement as "governmental trickery," and this encouraged rank-and-file members of all the affected unions to go on strike and occupy plants in protest against the planned layoffs.

In December 1983, this controversy had reached its crisis. Jacques Calvet, president of Peugeot-Talbot, demanded that the agreement he had signed with Minister Ralite be respected and that the occupation of the plants be brought to an end by the armed police using force as necessary. Ralite was opposed to the use of force and made his views known in a written appeal to the president. Mauroy foresaw that modernization, for example in the shipyards and in the steel industry, would generate similar crises. It was important to show the country that the government meant business, even if this aggravated the climb in unemployment. Delors agreed, as did Bérégovoy, Georgina Dufoix and Joseph Franceschi, secretary of state for security. Mitterrand overruled Ralite, and at 2 a.m. December 31, 1983, the police entered the occupied plants and evicted the strikers.

Mitterrand spoke to the nation that evening, saying that this was the way to make of France a great modern country. His action against the strikers was essential to the effort of national recovery on which the government had embarked.[16]

The initiative taken by Peugeot-Talbot in the summer of 1983 to modernize by substituting new machinery and reducing its work force crystallized in the government a will to undertake for the whole French economy the wrenching ordeal of modernization. Onto the back shelf went the old Mitterrand-Mauroy slogan, "priority to employment." Mitterrand returned from a period of reflection with a clear new orientation, conveyed to his prime minister in October 1983: It is necessary to clean up our industry, help it to modernize, and cut back on subsidies for outdated enterprises. These were goals that had finally moved to the forefront of his thought. Mauroy realized that his new mandate as prime minister placed upon him the responsibility for some painful and unpopular measures.

Minister of Industry Fabius found himself called upon to implement what had become Mitterrand's top priority. It was a golden opportunity for a talented and ambitious young minister, graduate of the prestigious National School of Administration (ENA), to win a place among the leading figures of the regime. His impressive performance over the next nine months made him a favorite with Mitterrand

and led to his designation as prime minister to replace Mauroy in July 1984.

Before the National Assembly in October 1983 Fabius laid out the government's proposals for preparing French industry to compete in national and world markets. He had earlier won the approval for these plans of the Council of Ministers, with only the Communist Ralite dissenting on the ground that they would entail massive layoffs. Fabius announced what he described as a straightening out of the nationalized enterprises with the goal of making them more competitive and profitable. Steel production would be greatly reduced, and the government would provide financial help to enable firms, public and private, to move rapidly into automation and the use of robots. The successes of Japan and Silicon Valley were held up as models for emulation by French industry. Fabius named as the three orienting priorities research, training of personnel, and capital investment.

This strategy, which plainly presaged large-scale layoffs in nationalized coal mines, shipyards, and steel production, all of which cost the government large sums in subsidies, posed an issue of fundamental importance to the alliance between Socialists and Communists. Ralite's opposition to Fabius and Mauroy on the industrial modernization announced the coming end to Communist participation in the government. The Communists, through the economic writings of Paul Boccara and Philippe Herzog, were developing a theoretical basis for changing the criterion of performance by industrial enterprises from profitability to social benefit. The PCF supported the workers' instinctive opposition to all layoffs. This meant that the Communists had to be free to condemn implementation of what had become the government's priority program for the country. Over the months of Fabius's rise to prominence, with full support from Mitterrand, criticism of the government from Communist spokesmen began to be given public expression, veiled at first but ever more outspoken.

By the end of 1983, Marchais on several occasions had said, or at least insinuated, that the government was not adhering to the promises it had made in the campaign of 1981 and in the signed agreements between the Socialist Party and the Communist Party in June 1981 when the Communists became a party of the government. For example, Marchais was asked during an interview over Radio-Monte-Carlo in November 1983: "Since workers are discontented, as you have said, is another policy possible, and if so what would it be?"

Marchais replied: "Yes, there is another policy. It is that on which we reached agreement in 1981."

The leadership of the Socialist Party took exception to this criticism of Mitterrand from a party bound by a commitment to support the government and represented in the Council of Ministers. Relations between the two parties were clearly deteriorating. Could this be checked? In December 1983, at the halfway mark in the five-year term of the legislature elected in 1981, the principal leaders of the two parties, headed by Marchais and Jospin, met in an attempt to show the public that the Union of the Left still existed. The meeting began with long statements by Jospin and Marchais, both expressing loyalty to their alliance, but each loaded with criticisms of the other.

Jospin complained that the Communists' public declarations of support for the government lacked clarity and conviction. He argued that the measures of "rigor" adopted in March 1983 were absolutely necessary. The storm of speculation against the franc had to be confronted with a vigorous effort to correct the imbalances. The government could not in the short term, he said, promote strong growth, reduce unemployment, reduce inflation, and correct the trade deficit all at the same time.[17]

Jospin relied on a clause in the June 1981 agreement signed with the Communists that provided that the changes to be undertaken by the new government of the left would take place "in stages, keeping in mind the need to maintain economic and financial equilibrium and the fact that the French economy was open to foreign trade." Jospin insisted that the government was acting in the spirit and the letter of those accords. Therefore it was false for the Communists to convey to the public the notion that a policy faithful to the agreement of 1981 would be different from the one being followed.

Jospin laid a major part of the blame for the decline in electoral support for the government, demonstrated in the March elections, on the negative influence of the Communists:

If an important part of the left expresses its support in a whisper, emphasizing its criticism, and concentrates more on arguing for its own program than for that of the Government, I do not see how we can mobilize in our favor a majority opinion. Because if you convey doubt toward our common program, toward the orientations proposed by the President of the Republic, that weakens all of us, that damages our credibility.

Marchais in his statement spoke of the Socialists and the government in an overall positive tone. He emphasized that the Communist Party wanted the Union of the Left to continue. On balance, he said, its performance had been encouraging. He did not threaten a withdrawal of Communist participation in the government. The task, he said, was to give a new *élan* to the Union of the Left. In spelling this out he called on the Government to do what, in Jospin's view, it clearly could not and would not do. Marchais cast these demands as nothing more than the fulfillment of promises made to each other and to the country in the accords of June 1981. Thus in a veiled form Marchais was making the case, softened with handshakes and ambiguities, that Mitterrand and the Socialists had changed course and in doing so had broken promises that were the basis for a Union of the Left.

Marchais, continuing this stiffly formal exchange (really a debate between rivals who hated each other), assumed the role of constructive interpreter of the electoral setbacks suffered by the left, both Socialists and Communists, in the preceding months. He alluded to the recent strikes and demonstrations by workers as evidence that something had gone wrong with government policy. He proceeded to lay out a bill of particulars:

We said in our accord that we will carry out an effective struggle against unemployment. It has been stabilized, something which needs to be underlined. But it still afflicts two million men, women and youth who placed confidence in the left that this drama would really be reduced. Total employment has diminished. The decrease in employment in industry continues at an alarming rate.

He then quoted more clauses from the accords, each followed by allegations that they had not been fulfilled. These were:

1. An engagement to create conditions for new economic growth. Yet industrial production, said Marchais, was the same as at the beginning of 1981, with very little growth envisaged for 1983 and 1984.
2. A promise to reduce social inequalities. Yet the purchasing power of working people had stagnated or declined while income from capital had steadily risen.
3. Financial and economic equilibrium was to be established and maintained. The size of the foreign debt showed this had not been done. Capital flight and speculation were not being adequately controlled.
4. An engagement to "further the development of liberties." To the Communists this included more opportunity to air their views on government-controlled radio and television. This had not taken place. On the contrary, anti-Communism continued to be "the daily bread of news reporting by radio and television."

It could have come as no surprise to the president and the Socialists that the Communists were opposed to the method of modernization advocated by Fabius and ratified by Mauroy and Mitterrand. As this became the centerpiece of Socialist strategy, the threat of massive layoffs provoked deep discontent in the workforce of declining base industries like coal, steel, and shipbuilding. By the end of 1983 it was clear the Communists were not going to side with the government in trying to avert strife on the issue of reducing workforces.

Marchais concluded his speech to Jospin by calling for joint action between Socialists and Communists against the closing of enterprises and for the creation of jobs. Clearly the two parties were now going in different directions on a fundamental issue. This gave a hollow ring to their "Joint Declaration" issued at the end of the meeting:

The two parties consider that the left majority in the service of the people and of France has accomplished important work which on balance is already superior to the great conquests of the Popular Front and of the Liberation. The right is trying to rally the country to its anti-egalitarian, authoritarian, racist policies. The best answer of the left is its union to sustain the action of the Government, to continue its reforms, to continue the policy of change undertaken in June 1981.

There would be another six months of stiff smiles for the cameras, accompanied by veiled criticisms and growing signs that both parties were preparing to let the Union of the Left be buried.

Within the Socialist Party, Chevènement, having resigned from the government on principle in March 1983, was in a position to criticize it throughout the rest of the year. In the pages of *En jeu*, the review of the CERES faction of the party, and in public debates Chevènement labored to save the Socialists from the error, as he defined it, of adopting as government policy the liberal economic orthodoxy of Delors. He framed his argument with emphasis on the political: The legislative elections of 1986 were being decided by Government policies in 1983. By following Delors, the Socialists were abandoning their electorate and would pay the consequences by losing their majority in the legislature. Delors had shown himself to be a Raymond Barre in the Socialist camp. He was willing to sacrifice growth and employment in the attempt to bring down inflation and strengthen the franc. Such a policy inflicted too much pain on working people and would immobilize them, with fatal results for the vision cherished by the left in its victory of 1981. Chevènement rejected the argument of Jospin that all Socialists had the duty to "get behind the government." Rather, he said, it is the duty of Socialists to "get ahead of the government" and lead it onto a different road, because the road chosen by Delors road led to disaster for the Socialist Party.

Chevènement had been minister of industry and research, so he spoke from some experience and authority. It was absolutely essential, he argued, to recover and develop the French market for French industry. Making the revitalization of French industry depend on its ability to win export markets, as Delors advocated, opened a long period of sacrifices, unacceptable to the French people, with no assurance of success for France. It was necessary to confront immediately the crisis of unemployment as it existed. Otherwise, the policies of liberal capitalism would leave the French at the mercy of the stronger economies of Germany and the United States. France should safeguard the French market for French companies by installing protective measures as necessary, he argued. The government should use its control over nationalized industries and banks to generate the creation of jobs by conditioning low-interest loans and favorable terms of repayment on expansion of the workforce and maintenance of prices without inflation.

These were ideas that Delors had been resisting for over a year in the internal debates of the government. He now publicly dismissed them with a different logic, one that Mitterrand came to adopt as his own: The "interior market" is really the European common market. It is necessary, he said, to change mentalities, to innovate, invest, and set down roots in other countries. On February 12, 1984, Mitterrand appeared on television with a defense of the new policy that might have been written by Delors himself. Modernization and reduction of workforces today, he said, are the way to create jobs in the future. The crisis arises, he said, from our failure in the past to adapt to the requirements of competing in the international market. That is what France was undertaking to correct.

THE PCF BEGINS TO REBEL

Workers in the steel industry knew they were marked for force reductions. In Longwy (Department Nord) and in Metz (Moselle), with support from the CGT of Henri Krasucki, they marched and protested. On the walls of steel-industry towns appeared slogans that would soon be adopted by the Communist Party itself: "Mitterrand, keep your promises!" "Mitterrand, you have betrayed us!"

In 1981 coal miners were told the government planned to increase production to 30 million tons per year, yet in 1983 it stood at only 18 million tons. Costs of production were high by world standards; therefore, given the way the industry was functioning, the government would have to cover large deficits every year into the indefinite future. As there was plenty of coal available for import, Fabius, with support from Mauroy and Mitterrand, decided to scale down French coal production drastically. As announced in the autumn of 1983 the workforce in coal would be reduced by 6000 per year for five years. This in effect announced a reduction of the workforce by a half or more.

Insecurity and anger seized the coal-mining communities. This was exacerbated when Georges Valbon, a Communist who in 1981 had been named by Mitterrand and Mauroy to head the principal group of coal-mining enterprises (*Charbonnages de France*), announced in November 1983 his resignation, a clear protest against the new government policy. He was on record as favoring an expansion of production with an expansion of the workforce. It was a significant demonstration of the difference of approach to the overall problem of employment, with Valbon, the Communist Party, Chevènement, and CERES on one side and Delors, Fabius, Mauroy, and finally Mitterrand on the other. Thousands of coal miners, wearing their coveralls, caps, and lanterns, marched in the streets of Paris on March 2, 1984, to demonstrate their anger.

In March 1984 a plan for restructuring the shipbuilding industry was announced, designed in the new spirit of "modernization." Over a period of three years the workforce would be reduced from 18,000 to 13,000, with important credits granted to management to promote automation. Ironically, Secretary of State for the Sea Guy Lengagne announced simultaneously that five important new orders for ship construction in French yards had been received. With these orders in hand it would be necessary to lay off "only" 5,000 shipyard workers.

Mitterrand returned from a week's trip to the United States in March 1984, during which he declared his enthusiasm for the introduction of the newest technical advances to make industry competitive. He seemed to be forgetting the costs and the social consequences of replacing workers with labor-saving machinery. The state of discontent in the steel-producing zones, particularly the regions of Lorraine and Northern France, gave the president a rude shock at his homecoming, aggravated by serious differences between Industry Minister Fabius and Prime Minister Mauroy over the measures to be taken in modernizing steel production.

Fabius favored construction of a "universal train" plant in Gandrange in the Lorraine. This would increase production capacity and entail the closing of steel plants in other regions. It would also be expensive. Mauroy, who continued to be the mayor of Lille in Northern France, preferred a balance between his region and the Lorraine by modernizing four plants with the less expensive conversion to electricity. Both plans aimed at reducing the workforce drastically in order to lower labor costs and create conditions of profitability without state subsidies.

As minister of finance, Delors sided with Mauroy in this debate, since the Fabius plan was going to be more difficult to finance. Mitterrand, confessing that he was attracted to the technical sophistication of the "universal train" concept, nevertheless supported his prime minister and his finance minister. Anyway, he said, the real weakness in both plans was that they did not deal satisfactorily with the need for substitute economic opportunities for people living in the regions to be afflicted by these modernizations. The debate in the Council of Ministers on March 29, 1984, was marked by some anguished reflections from the president. Nothing was being offered to the affected populations, "who can only choose to revolt." He would take responsibility for the decisions made, but he could see troubles accumulating.[18]

The modernization decided upon, though less expensive than the "universal train," would cost some 5 billion francs plus the still undetermined amount to cover the costs of maintaining and retraining thousands of workers dismissed from their former jobs. Delors announced that additional measures of austerity would have to be introduced into the 1984 budget. To the consternation of all ministers, he said that in the new circumstances, reductions totaling 11 billion francs (in a budget totaling 940 billion francs) would have to be imposed, sparing only defense, social security, scientific research, the postal service, a reconversion program in the mining regions, and certain grand architectural projects dear to the president.

A few hours after this modification in the 1984 budget had been announced, Henri Krasucki of the CGT declared it "unacceptable. There is more than discontent. There is anger." He indicated that the anger should be expressed in massive union actions.

Almost immediately violence broke out in steel towns. In Hagondange, several hundred workers entered the city hall, seized the portrait of the president and burned it in the streets. Workers responded to the tear gas grenades of the police by hurling showers of bolts and steel balls. At Longwy, steel workers sacked the local headquarters of the Socialist Party and the tax collectors' office. At Gandrange, steel track serving the plant was torn up. Barriers were set up across roads in the region. A one-day general strike of political protest throughout the Lorraine was voted. The regional press called the government actions "treason," showing a hidden goal of euthanasia for the steel-making population.

In Paris, *Le Monde* showed itself sympathetic to the plight of the Government. The Socialists were doing what previous governments should have done but had always feared to do.[19]

The Communist Party was now well into the strange phase of keeping its ministers in the government while making it plain to all that it did not like the government's austerity policies or the plan of restructuring at the cost of jobs. This posture of the Communists irritated the Socialists, who ridiculed it as "one foot in and one foot out." Marchais persisted: The decisions relating to the Lorraine, he stated on television on April 2, 1984, were a "tragic error." The government should return to the policies agreed to between Socialists and Communists in June 1981. He called on Socialists to join him in that demand. In the meantime the Communists, he said, despite their critique, did not intend to leave the government.

On April 13 a march in Paris of 30,000, many from the Lorraine, demonstrated against the decisions affecting the steel industry. Many banners condemned and insulted the president. Conspicuous in the crowd of marchers was Marchais. "My presence here does not have the character of hostility toward the government," he declared to the microphones.

Over the next few days, as the prime minister fumed over the ambiguities in the positions adopted by the PCF, other Communist leaders, Marcel Rigout and Paul Laurent, reiterated that the PCF had no intention of leaving the government. *L'Humanité* declared in its headline, "We are with the government and with the workers." In his irritation, Mauroy decided to force the Communists to vote for or against the government's policies in a parliamentary vote of confidence. Marchais warned the prime minister that the party reserved its right to criticize: "We are not unconditionals [*des inconditionnels*]. The Communist Party is not a cleaning lady." Nevertheless, the party supported the Socialists in the parliamentary vote.

There were some Socialists, among them even Minister of Interior Defferre, who now urged the president and prime minister to hold their tempers and show continuing tolerance toward the Communists in order to keep them in the government. If they were forced to leave they would be in the streets and the situation would be much more difficult to handle. Lionel Jospin also favored indulgence. He found it understandable that the PCF was dragging its feet, considering the policy changes that had been made "under the constraint of events." It was in the best interests of the government to keep the Communists in, despite their discordant words.[20]

These final few months of the Mauroy government shed a clarifying light on the real character of the Union of the Left. Mitterrand had seen that Communist support was indispensable to the election of a Socialist as president. He won control of the Socialist Party with his strategy of Socialist-Communist alliance in a Union of the Left. Once he was elected to the presidency, he rewarded the Communists with four ministerial portfolios of secondary importance. As Socialists like Jospin and Defferre were frankly admitting in 1984, this was seen in the upper ranks of the government as a way of keeping Communists on a leash. It kept them out of the streets, and (at least until 1984), it served to hamper their freedom to criticize government policy.

Mitterrand politely ignored the Communists in the government and gave more and more authority on economic questions to Delors and Fabius. This was a signal that Communist hopes for the Union of the Left, which was to start the country down the road to a French Socialism, were misplaced. The Keynesian measures of 1981 were abandoned, not to move on toward Socialism but to move back into liberal capitalist policies. Mitterrand accepted this reorientation without apology, promoting Delors and Fabius following the March 1983 municipal elections. The Communists had no grounds for holding on to their illusions after that reorganization. The resignation of Chevènement, who knew Mitterrand intimately, was another signal that this regime could not be supported in the name of Socialism.

Delors was developing his vision of France as a participant in a strengthened European Economic Community, organized as a common capitalist market. This was totally inconsistent with the vision of *socialisme à la française* developed in the theoretical writings of the Socialist Party and the Communist Party. By 1983 this incongruity between a European common market and reform into a French

Socialism was too plain to be denied. By choosing Delors and the common market, Mitterrand repudiated his hankering after Socialism. That he did not proclaim this openly is to be attributed to a perception that the French electorate was not ready to join him in abandoning the goal for which he had been elected.

The restructuring in the Lorraine, unavoidably painful, involved cutting the workforce in the steel industry by 25,000. The government chose as prefect to oversee the implementation of the Fabius program an experienced labor leader from the CFDT metalworkers union, Jacques Chérèque. He believed in the Fabius reforms. These included social measures to soften the hardships on workers who were to be dismissed. Half of these workers were given early retirement. One quarter were transferred to different posts. The remainder were placed in retraining programs for two years at 70 percent pay. With the state paying one-third of the salary cost, some 1,500 new jobs were created in the plants at Sollac. From this combination of stern-willed closing down of old production lines and humane measures to open new opportunities to those laid off, Fabius and Chérèque launched into modernization. It went relatively smoothly, winning credit with Mitterrand, who had named Fabius "super-minister of modernization" in April 1984 and would soon promote him again to the post of prime minister. Chérèque was asked to stay in his post by Fabius. His performance over the next few years made a favorable impression even on Chirac, who would later reward him with the same post under a right-wing government.

The evolution in economic policy will again be taken up in a later chapter. The focus now shifts to the problem of reforming the system of education.

NOTES

1. Thierry Pfister, *A Matignon au temps de l'Union de la Gauche* (Paris: Hachette, 1985).

2. Jacques Attali, *Verbatim: Chronique des années 1981–1986*, Vol. 1 (Paris: Fayard, 1993), 301.

3. Ibid., 322.

4. Pierre Favier and Michel Martin-Roland, *La décennie Mitterrand*, Vol. 1 (Paris: Editions du Seuil, 1990), 442.

5. Attali, *Verbatim*, 322.

6. Favier and Martin-Roland, *La décennie Mitterrand*, 449.

7. Ibid., 490.

8. Ibid., 468.

9. Attali, *Verbatim*, 408.

10. Ibid., 411.

11. Favier and Martin-Roland, *La décennie Mitterrand*, 490.

12. Ibid., 475.

13. Ibid., 489.

14. Ibid., 488.

15. Ibid., 489.

16. Favier and Martin-Roland, *La décennie Mitterrand*, Vol. 2, 47.

17. *L'Humanité* (Paris), December 23, 1983.

18.   Quoted from minutes of meeting of Council of Ministers, March 29, 1984, in the archives of the general secretariat of government. Favier and Martin-Roland, *La décennie Mitterrand*, Vol. 2, 58.

19.   Favier and Martin-Roland, *La décennie Mitterrand*, Vol. 2, 62.

20.   Conversation of Jospin with Favier and Martin-Roland on April 27, 1984. Favier and Martin-Roland, *La décennie Mitterrand*, Vol. 2, 66.

8

The Catholic Church and School Reform

The problem of reforming the educational system in France had been included in Mitterrand's 110 propositions put forth for the 1981 presidential campaign. Number 90 vowed that a "great public service of national education, unified and secular" would be constituted, but only "through negotiation and without spoliation or monopoly." To understand fully what this issue meant to the French would necessitate a study of the role of the Catholic Church in the development of French history and culture. Proposition 90 presented to the French electorate Mitterrand's approach to an unresolved issue, the relationship between the state and private schools. Since 95 percent of these private schools (long called "free schools" to distinguish them from schools of the state-run system) were being directed by the Catholic Church as Catholic schools, any program to create a service of national education "unified and secular" seemed to imply an intention to diminish the freedom of the Catholic Church to educate as it wished in the schools under its direction.

During the eighteenth century the struggle of French thinkers such as Voltaire, Diderot, d'Alembert, and d'Holbach to liberate the human spirit from the authority of the Catholic Church served as intellectual preparation for the "de-Christianization" of France undertaken during the French Revolution. That tumultuous period in French history (1793–94) was a late development in the years of revolutionary rule by Jacobins before their overthrow in July 1794. It was a fascinating period on many counts. Jean-François Lyotard in a 1975 essay saw in the anti-religious agitation of 1793 an expression of strong pagan instincts, manifested again in the rebellion of French youth in May–June 1968.[1] It is not necessary to accept that thesis, interesting as it is, to feel the continuing importance in the French psyche of the revolutionary effort undertaken 200 years ago at "de-Christianization." That historical memory was an element in the problem of educational reform in 1981.

NEGOTIATIONS TOWARD REFORM

The Concordat with the Vatican negotiated by Napoleon I had been brought to an end in 1905 with the Combes law, which formally proclaimed the separation of church and state. Since the early nineteenth century, the contest between the Catholic Church and those who want to reduce its influence in education has been a permanent issue in French politics. In 1959, during the de Gaulle presidency, the Church won an important victory. Under a law prepared by Michel Debré and approved by the National Assembly of the new Fifth Republic, private schools became eligible to receive financial aid from the state under a contract negotiated between the school and government authorities. These contracts were to allow the state a certain degree of supervision over the quality of instruction.

In 1977 the right of the Church to receive additional financial support from local governments, the communes, was written into a law proposed by Guy Guermier, RPR deputy from Finistère (a Catholic stronghold) and president of the Parliamentary Association for Freedom of Teaching (la liberté d'enseignement). This law also confirmed and increased the rights of the Church in the appointment of directors and staff of religious schools.

Both the Debré law and the Guermier law had been strongly opposed by Socialists, Communists, and advocates of secularization of education. The common program agreed to by the leaders of the Socialist Party, the Communist Party, and Radicals of the Left in 1972 stated: "Private schools receiving public funding will, as a general rule, be nationalized."[2]

In judging Mitterrand's handling of this issue of integration of private schools into a unified national system of education, it is relevant to note that only one-sixth of the school population attended private schools. But this sixth was drawn mainly from the wealthier classes. Further, most of the private schools (approximately 95 percent) were Church-supported. Any modification of the Debré and Guermier laws would surely meet resistance from the Church and from the more conservative sectors of society, claiming the liberty to use their superior means to educate their children as they chose.

Mitterrand's promise in his 110 propositions to create a "great unified and secular system of public education" was taken verbatim from the program of the Socialist Party published on July 23, 1977.[3] A factor in the formulation and publication of this undertaking was the need to accommodate the powerful teachers union, the Fédération syndicale de l'éducation nationale (FEN), a major pillar of the Socialist Party. Its inclusion by Mitterrand in his propositions undoubtedly helped him mobilize Socialists, especially teachers in the public school system, for his presidential campaign. But because of the origin of the phrase and its associations in the public's mind with the FEN and therefore with hostility toward religious schools, it was likely to alienate many centrist voters, unless Mitterrand could somehow qualify its threatening implication.

With the first round of the election behind him, Mitterrand sought to strengthen his chances of beating Giscard in the second round by writing a letter to all the associations of parents of private school students "clarifying" his stand on education reform. He may also have met secretly with "an eminent representative" of the Church hierarchy.[4] In the letter he declared his intention "to convince and not to constrain." Any modification in the law would be the result of "negotiation" and not a unilateral decision on the part of his government. He promised that no private school would be compelled against its wish to join in the integration. This letter was a part of his successful campaign to distance himself from the Socialist Project and thereby win crucial support from voters who wanted a moderate centrist who could be trusted to face down Communists and the FEN.

Mitterrand was himself a product of Catholic schools. He had many times expressed great respect and affection for the teachers in his primary and secondary schools. In the final days of his campaign to become president he seemed to promise to approach the education reform question with a primary concern for the sensibilities of the most zealous Catholics and for the anxieties of the wealthy classes over their freedom to educate their children without social control. This was the dominant tone of his final communication to the parents of private school students on the eve of the election. Needless to say, this letter was not cleared with the FEN, which would never have consented to promise to respect in the Church a final right of veto over any reform proposed by the government.

Jean Poperen has said that the Socialists, who with the Communists had a commanding majority in the National Assembly, were ready to repeal the Debré and Guermier laws, despite the inevitable opposition from Church authorities and representatives of wealthier sectors.[5] Instead, Mitterrand chose to engage in interminable negotiations that only served to prepare the ground for a massive challenge of the government in a street demonstration in June 1984 by those charging it with violations of liberty.

During the summer of 1981, the camp of the *laïcs*, secularizers anxious to use the Mitterrand-Socialist victory to create a public education system "unified and secular," organized to carry through their program. The principal figures in this camp were Michel Bouchareissas, Jacques Pommatau, and Jean-Claude Barbarant. They were the general secretaries, respectively, of the National Committee for Secular Action (CNAL), the National Syndicate of Teachers (SNI), and the FEN. The first dash of cold water on their euphoria came from the palace of the president and from his newly appointed Minister of Education Alain Savary: *Rien ne se ferait dans la précipitation.*("Nothing is to be done in haste"). Immediately a sense of frustration began to arise, accompanied by questions as to what the president's true intentions were. It was evident to these militants that a resolution promoting secularization would have to be implemented over the opposition of the Church and much of the right. Was not this goal every bit as important to Socialists as nationalizations? Why should there be a longer search for an impossible consensus on one issue than on the other?

Mitterrand's sister, Geneviève Delachenal, director of Christian publications of Bayard Press, was known for her piety and served as a consultant to the president on this matter. She has said the president did not want to treat the problem as urgent. Above all he wanted time to reflect before deciding on an educational project: "My brother did not wish to force anyone, but he did wish to make some progress."

On the issue of colonialism in the 1950s, Alain Savary had distinguished himself with his patience, discretion, and willingness to listen to all sides. He understood that as Mitterrand's first minister of education, it was his task to listen and negotiate, with the primary aim, which he soon found to be an imperative in his assignment, of fulfilling the letter of Mitterrand's pre-electoral commitment: "Convince and not constrain." He named as his principal aide in charge of the reform dossier Jean Gasol, a practicing Catholic, something of a rarity among Socialist leaders.

Savary issued a statement on July 16, 1981, strongly emphasizing that the policy of the government was not to be dictated by the unions of teachers in the public schools. Though their point of view was worthy of respect because it expressed a conviction, the minister said he would be guided by the propositions announced by the president and adopted by the government. He intended to open discussions, to be followed by negotiations, with a view to creating a great national service of public education, secular and unified, without exploitation and without monopoly, and maintaining respect for the liberty of teaching.[7]

Savary was simply quoting his terms of reference laid down by the president. What they would actually produce in the way of proposals for legislation remained to be seen.

The difficulty that confronted Savary could be inferred from the results of public opinion polls on the question: "Would you like to see private schools integrated into the public school system?" In 1978, in surveys conducted by experts, only 33 percent of respondents had answered in the affirmative. This percentage had held steady in later surveys on the same question. Further, surveys in the 1970s had shown that a clear majority of the French were in favor of some financial subsidies to private schools from public funds.[8] Among those who had voted for Mitterrand in 1974 ("the left" in that election), 55 percent were in favor of partial or complete subsidization of private schools, including the religious schools. This will surely seem surprising to most American readers. Even those French who voted for Communist Party candidates were split, 47 percent to 47 percent, on this question. The established French practice of public subsidies to private schools does not seem, in the opinion of a clear majority of persons polled, to be a violation of the principle of separation of church and state. The slogan of the secularizers, "For public schools, public funds; for private schools, private funds," clearly did not have majority support.

In the early months of 1982, Savary ordered another survey to establish a basis of judging the state of public opinion on a series of questions related to school reform. The sample interviewed was drawn from three populations: the general population of France; parents of students in the public schools; and parents of students in private schools. One conclusion drawn from the study was that approximately 80 percent of parents of students in public and private schools gave moral support to the defenders of private schools. The existence of these schools was seen as a guarantee of larger choice to parents. And among the general population it seemed clear from this survey that the struggle of the secularizers was not viewed favorably. Even among those who voted Socialist, only 15 percent to 20 percent identified with this struggle. Savary could read clear signs of trouble ahead in the indication by 85 percent of the parents of private school students that they would participate in "active resistance" to any reform that seemed prejudicial to private schools.

When Savary communicated these results to the leaders of the secularizers, they dismissed the survey as poorly designed and unworthy of credit.[9]

In obedience to Mitterrand's wishes, Savary let the autumn months of 1981 pass without beginning negotiations, but he did invite the Church to formulate its positions and name its representatives. The Church agreed and named Canon Paul Guiberteau, general secretary of Catholic Education (CNEC). He would be accompanied by Pierre Daniel, president of the National Union of Parents of Students in Free Schools (i.e., private).

Beginning in January 1982, Savary and Gasol (with the frequent participation of Bernard Toulemonde, another high official of the Ministry of Education) began formally to receive delegations who wished to express views on the question of reform. These consultations lasted five months. They revealed three contentious issues:

1. The desire of the ministry to integrate private schools receiving state aid into the requirements imposed on all public schools (*la carte scolaire*). This proposed imposition of state-defined norms was declared by the representatives of private schools to be an infringement of the freedom to teach (*la liberté d'enseignement*).
2. The inclusion of teachers at private schools in a national law dealing with the qualifications required to receive a teaching certificate (*la titularisation*).
3. The obligation placed on local governments (communes) by the Guermier law (1977) to pay subsidies to private schools under "contracts of association." This practice, said the advocates for public schools, was cutting into funding needed by the public school system.

The Catholic Church in France administers its network of parochial schools from a kind of Church-supported ministry for Free Schools in Paris. The priests who were in charge of this work in education of the young (vital, they believed, to the future of Catholicism in France) saw in the first two issues listed above the threat of a dangerous transfer of power from their ministry to the state. Father Guiberteau had been named to head the Church's representatives in the negotiations with Savary because of his experience as a director of education in the diocese of Loire-Atlantique. Such directors, appointed by the bishop, were guided in their work by the Catholic ministry in Paris. It soon became clear to Savary that Father Guiberteau was closely controlled by superiors in his role as representative of the Church for talks with the government. Guiberteau made it clear that the Church's opposition to a "unified" system of education to be administered by the national Ministry of Education was not negotiable.

The question remained, would the government through a parliamentary vote legislate against the opposition of the Church? This seemed to most observers in 1982 the likely outcome of the impasse. To influence public opinion on the issue, the organization of parents of students in private schools in Île-de-France (the region of Paris), with support from the archbishop of Paris, Monsignor Jean-Marie Lustiger, organized for April 24, 1982, a public gathering near the Porte de Pantin. The campaign of the opposition political parties RPR and UDF to discredit the Mitterrand-Mauroy government was in full swing in the Parliament and in the press. Somewhat to the surprise of the organizers of the meeting, 100,000 people arrived, many with banners condemning the government and all full of enthusiasm for the political speeches they heard by Alain Madelin, Jacques Toubon, Jean Lecanuet, Jean-Claude Gaudin, and Bernard Pons denouncing Mitterrand and the Socialists. Some of the organizers, including the archbishop, later expressed concern at the political character of the meeting. Since on a strictly partisan plane the opposition parties could not prevent legislation, the Church preferred to keep the debate focused on the loftier issue of "freedom for teaching," which seemed to put constitutional restraints on those who wished to "unify" the system.[10]

The impressive Porte de Pantin meeting, with its political attacks on the Socialists and the government called for a response. This came two weeks later at Bourget on the occasion of the 100th anniversary of public school legislation bearing the name of Jules Ferry. Prime Minister Mauroy and Education Minister Savary were to be the principal speakers. Some 200,000 supporters of the Socialist program of education reform gathered in a combative mood. Their banners called for "Immediate abrogation of the anti-secular laws!" and "The only solution: nationalization!"

The speeches they heard gave them little satisfaction. Savary simply read the text of a speech written for him by his aide, Jean Gasol, assisted by François Furet, who was making a name for himself internationally as a revisionist historian of the French Revolution.[11] The excesses of the de-Christianizing atheists in 1793–94 provided a negative example for Furet, from which he drew his conclusions for the Socialists of the 1980s. The content of their promised "secularization" (laïcité) should be "tolerance and pluralism." Above all, Savary read from his text, we must appease passions and rise above divisions. The crowd hissed and whistled in a French expression of disapproval.[12]

Savary was followed by Prime Minister Mauroy, who provoked the same reaction with a similar message calling for patience and open minds toward the values and views of both sides in the debate. He made himself the spokesman for Mitterrand's option for moderation: "It is necessary to convince, not constrain." Mauroy went further and made explicit the only conclusion to be drawn from Mitterrand's electoral letter to the parents of private school students and from his instructions to his ministers on the issue: There could not be a single and uniform, "secular and unified" system of schooling in France. Those words from Mitterrand's campaign promise had, in fact, been sacrificed to his determination to "negotiate to a consensus."

In the meetings of the teachers union, the FEN, many expressed regrets that their long-standing goal, expressed in the formula *grand service public unifié et laïc de l'éducation nationale* (great unified and secular public service of national education) had been abandoned. By the summer of 1982 there were no longer any illusions on this score. But there was still hope that something in the way of reform would soon be proposed and enacted. Teachers could be appealed to with the values attached to pluralism and tolerance. The leadership of the Socialist Party was still united behind Mitterrand and Mauroy. The Communist Party, a dutiful party of the government, also withheld its criticism.

Any change at all, if it was to be achieved with the consent of the Church, would have to be formulated with its full participation, prior to formal proposal to the Parliament. This was the course discreetly adopted by the president. He arranged for his sister, Geneviève Delachenal, who had the confidence of the religious party in these negotiations, to receive in her apartment Guiberteau, with Jean Gasol and Bernard Toulemonde, Savary's principal aides, for a series of secret meetings in the autumn of 1982.[13] Gasol and Toulemonde were the architects of the proposal, ratified and presented by Savary, which was announced to the public on December 20, 1982. They have stated they thought the proposal, which became known as the "Savary Project," had the approval of Guiberteau.[14]

The proposal contained a new concept, *l'établissement d'intérêt publique* (EIP), "a public interest establishment." This would be a grouping in a particular geographical region of public and private schools. Private schools were clearly not to be nationalized. Within each EIP the school calendar would be uniform for all schools. Parents would continue to have the right to place their children in private, including religious, schools. No reduction of the rights of private schools to public financing (as mandated by the Debré and Guermier laws) was proposed. The *titularisation* of teachers, that is, the granting of certificates giving a teacher membership in the national corps and therefore eligibility for transfer to other schools and a salary paid from public funds, Savary proposed to open to teachers in private schools who wanted it. No requirement of such status would be imposed on teachers in private schools.

The concessions to the secular camp in this proposal were minimal. The concept of the EIP was sufficiently vague as to be capable of development in practice. It did promise an advance in formal coordination between the public and private sectors. This could be seen as a crack in the door. And the number of teachers with national certificates would be increased by those from the private schools who wished to acquire such status. This would lead gradually to a circulation of teachers between public and private.

If the Church agreed to this proposal, it would mean that Savary's eighteen months of negotiations had produced what the president had asked him for, a plan of "reform" that would avoid conflict with religious authorities. The secret meetings with Guiberteau had been aimed at preparing the ground for this resolution. Savary, Mauroy, and Mitterrand thought they had it in their grasp. They were prepared to override the complaints sure to be heard from the camp of the secularizers.

To their dismay, Guiberteau announced by communiqué to the press within twenty-four hours that the Savary proposals were unacceptable, saying, "They undermine [*portent atteint aux*] the conditions for exercising freedom of teaching." The "public interest establishment," he declared, would lead to the intrusion [*la mainmise*] of public power into the academic life of Catholic schools.

What had happened? Perhaps Gasol and Toulemonde had misread Guiberteau's attitude in the discussions *chez* Geneviève Delachenal. Perhaps the Church hierarchy had declined to accept Guiberteau's recommendations and ordered him to reject the Savary project. Whatever the explanation, it was clear the Church had decided to take a hard line with Mitterrand and Savary. Viewed in retrospect, the Church had every reason to read Mitterrand's statements on the issue literally, especially his assurances that he aimed to convince, not constrain. The Church was not convinced, and it saw no need to give up any of its gains under past administrations to a president who was promising not to seek legislation except with the full support of the Church.

It seems likely Mitterrand attached little importance to the demands of the FEN and the secularizers to create a unified and secularized public school system. He had included proposal ninety in his 110 propositions because something of the kind was expected of a candidate relying on support from the Socialist Party and the teachers unions. From his own experience as a youth, he had a deep sympathy with Church schools. From the time of his letter to parents of the private school community between the two rounds of the presidential election, it was clear he would go forward with reforms only if the Church gave its assent. The Church had decided to exploit its strength with this new president to the fullest degree possible.

But Mitterrand could not abruptly concede defeat on the morrow of Guiberteau's repudiation of the negotiations with Gasol and Toulemonde. His obligations to the Socialist Party and to Savary required that the minister of education be allowed to continue his attempt to draft legislation that would be satisfactory to all parties.

Savary was not ready to give up. "Today we start anew," he told his staff. Did he then foresee that he had entered into a humiliating ordeal that would end in his resignation with bitter feelings against the president? The following eighteen months contained some high drama.

In many communes where the Socialists were in power in the municipal government, it had been possible, without waiting for national legislation, to put an end to the payment of subsidies to private schools. The subsidies were to be paid, according to the Guermier law of 1977, on the basis of contracts between the commune and the school. Some 400 commune governments failed to approve or renew contracts and then used this ambiguous situation as a pretext for stopping subsidies.

In some regions proceedings were begun by religious schools to demand their subsidies, before the new regional "courts of account" established by the laws on decentralization. In some cases orders were issued in favor of the schools, directing the municipal governments to make payments; in others the proceedings were dismissed without relief. André Lagnet, Socialist mayor of Issoudun, defied the prefect of Indre to produce the text of any law forcing him to pay the subsidy. It was easy to find evidence of bad faith in the recalcitrant municipal governments, and the issue proved damaging to the Socialists in the municipal elections of March 1983. It also helped establish the case against Socialists that they opposed the right of parents to educate their children in schools of their choice. This was used as the foundation for the powerful slogan, *atteinte aux liberté d'enseignement*, ("[the

Socialists] are undermining the freedom of education").

The issue stirred passions in both camps. The secularizers had concluded by 1983 that conciliation was proving a one-way street and still producing no agreement. The teachers unions and the CNAL (Comité National d'action laïque) held public meetings to put pressure on the president and the government. Savary continued his search for a formula that would be acceptable to all parties.

On October 18, 1983, Savary announced his new proposal. He retained his concept of the "public interest establishment" as the framework for coordinating public and private schools in the same locality. He had incorporated this into new proposals for a more sweeping and radical decentralization of the national education system. The diversity of pedagogical needs of pupils, he said, and of the choices of parents necessitates schools with greater autonomy and greater responsibility. He proposed that private schools consent to become participants in this new, decentralized system.

This time it was the secularizers who refused to go forward on such a basis. Savary had pulled a surprise on the teachers unions with the proposal for decentralization. They were organized on a national basis, a source of their strength and influence. They were uncertain how they might fare under a regime of local autonomy and responsibility. They based their rejection of the new proposal on the ground that it did not unify national education but left two systems of schools in existence.

Monsignor Jean Vilney, president of the Conference of Bishops in France, met Mitterrand secretly in the apartment of Geneviève Delanchel in November 1983 as this impasse continued to appear intractable. Vilney has stated that the president assured him at the meeting that, whatever happened in the Parliament, the Church could be sure that the freedom of Catholic schools would not be suppressed.[15] It is plain from the interview that Mitterrand did not want to foster legislation that did not have the approval of the Church. If such was his stand, the president was at odds with the Socialist-Communist majority in the Parliament. A drama was in the making.

DEMONSTRATION OF JUNE 24, 1984

Archbishop Lustiger of Paris has said that the president told him in December 1983 or January 1984 that the Savary law would be withdrawn before Parliament could approve it.[16] These revelations, which were never contradicted by the president, indicate that he was prepared at that early date to oppose his minister of education and his prime minister and frustrate the Socialist Party on the issue of secularization.

From month to month during the first half of 1984, the Church and the organizations of parents of private school pupils showed their ability to mobilize impressive demonstrations of support for "freedom of education," their battle slogan against the Savary reform law. In January, Bordeaux produced a crowd of 80,000; in February there were marches of 300,000 at Lille and 400,000 at Rennes. On March 4, 800,000 assembled at Versailles. At this last gathering, thousands of small stickers were placed on windshields of cars, showing children behind bars. This made Mitterrand furious, and Father Guiberteau, organizer of these manifestations, insisted he was not responsible for it. "One cannot control everything," he said. The Church authorities also expressed some dissatisfaction with political leaders of the right, who seized these opportunities to show their support for the demonstrators. At Versailles Jacques Chirac, Michel Debré, Jacques Barrot, Jacques Toubon, and Charles Pasqua marched wearing their conspicuous deputy sashes.

On April 4, 1984, one month after the demonstration at Versailles, the president answered questions at a press conference, saying that the "propositions of M. Savary are good ones." But he began to hint at a possibility of accepting their defeat, saying the Savary project had encountered a "difficult reality," public opinion that ran very deep. "This political reality, which is that of the French nation, I must respect," said the president.

Nevertheless, the president chose to let the process move forward. The Council of Ministers formally approved the Savary text on April 18 for submission to the Parliament. It contained a new concession to the Catholic Church and other sponsors of private schools: formal recognition of the state's obligation "through contract" to subsidize such schools from public funds. This was worded in such a way as to reduce the power of municipal governments to frustrate the subsidies. Further, the text declared the state's respect for the particular character of private schools. On the other hand, the reform program of state licensing of all teachers was retained, leaving it voluntary for teachers in private schools.

Guiberteau immediately advised Savary that the text was totally unsatisfactory and that the Church would oppose its enactment. This meant there were sure to be more marches and demonstrations.

In the Parliament, Socialist deputies met in caucus and decided to demand that the text be amended. They were displeased with the retreats made to win support from the Church. It was unacceptable to force the communes to subsidize private schools. Such money would surely be taken from public school financing. The old hostility to the Debré and Guermier laws dominated debate: Public financing should be reserved for public schools, on which the future of France depended. The spirit of the "de-Christianization" movement of 1793 began to express itself in the modern form of total secularization of education, a unified education system from which all religious teaching would be excluded.

The government had to face the fact that henceforth it could not count on support for the Savary text, as it then stood, from the Socialists in Parliament. This made the issue even more troublesome in the eyes of the president. The first secretary of the Socialist Party, Lionel Jospin, a Mitterrand protégé in the party, began in the spring of 1984 to urge in party leadership meetings that the project of education reform simply be dropped. It was not worth the difficulties it had provoked, he argued, and it was clearly serving the interests of the opposition parties. Undoubtedly the president was thinking along the same lines, although he was not saying so publicly.

Mitterrand in his meetings with Socialists found himself on the defensive. He received in his mail packets of Socialist Party cards from resigning party members with letters of protest against the Savary text for its retreat from secularization. The teachers unions and the CNAL organized public meetings to bring pressure on the government. That these were not well attended was a sign of division and confusion in the Socialist ranks. It was also possible to infer from the small size of these crowds that secularization was not an issue of great importance to the vast majority of those French citizens whose children attended public schools. The issue mobilized one camp, but not the other.

The president, in discussing the issue with Socialist leaders and his Council of Ministers, began raising another argument against incorporating all schools in one unified system: The independent existence of private schools assured all families that their children would have a second chance in case of failure or expulsion from one of the two systems. Mitterrand had obviously reached a firm conviction that the idea of a "unified" school system, even though a staple in Socialist platforms and his own campaign promises, was a bad one.

Savary still had the public support of Mitterrand for the text presented to Parliament. A commission of deputies led by Socialists proceeded to formalize the amendments to be proposed against the wishes of Savary and the president. These amendments provided:

1. The principle of state certification of teachers in private schools (still on a gradual and voluntary basis) was moved from the preamble to the text of the law.
2. Subsidization of a private school by the commune was made conditional on the certification of at least half of the teaching staff of that school.
3. A private primary school could not be opened in a commune that had no public primary school.

Prime Minister Mauroy faced a dilemma. If he refused to accept these amendments they would nevertheless be under discussion in the Parliament. If they were not made a part of the text, the Socialists could not be counted on to save the government from a vote of censure, sure to be proposed by the opposition deputies. The latter would certainly vote against the Government whether or not the text was amended. The prime minister had to foresee this moment of decision. Support from the Socialist deputies was vital to utilization of Section 49-3 of the Constitution, the only way to avoid an endless parliamentary debate. Mauroy decided to overrule Minister of Education Savary by giving his approval to the proposed amendments.

The president could have overruled the prime minister and supported Savary. He chose not to do so. Perhaps he felt it was impossible to deny the secularizers their will in the Parliament. He sent word from his hotel in Angers after visiting a new industrial installation of Honeywell-Bull that the prime minister should do what he thought best.[17]

On May 22, 1984, in the National Assembly, the Socialist amendments were added to the Savary text. The government, under Section 49-3 of the Constitution, proclaimed the proposal enacted. On the following day the opposition parties RPR and UDF proposed a motion of censure, which the Socialist majority defeated, adding to their own sufficient votes those of the Communists. There would have to be further votes in the Senate and a final passage again by the National Assembly.

The Church had reason to believe it could win in a contest carried out in the streets. The impressive demonstrations by hundreds of thousands of people in a half-dozen cities on behalf of "freedom" for private schools, compared to the inability of the teachers unions and supporters of secularization to mobilize forces in the streets, undoubtedly set the stage for a major confrontation between Church and state, or rather between the Church and the Socialist-Communist majority in the National Assembly. The opposition political parties were of course delighted at this challenge developing outside Parliament and were eager to exploit it to their political advantage. Another source of strength to the Church was the position of the president, who on several occasions had conveyed in person to high authorities of the Church his own neutrality on the issue, a virtual promise that he would allow the humiliation of Savary, the Socialist Party, and the secularizers if the Church could carry it off. It was plain that the revolt of Socialist deputies (with formal ratification from the prime minister) against Savary made them rebels against Mitterrand. They would not have his support in a confrontation with the Church.

The national mass demonstration to protest against the school reform legislation was announced by the private school movement, to take place in Paris on June 24, 1984. The titular head of this movement, Pierre Daniel, warned the president that the Socialist deputies' amendments (known as the Joxe-Laignel amendments) had provoked a wrath among private school pupils' parents and supporters that could hardly be controlled. The president counseled patience. When Daniel said he thought the law would be condemned by the Constitutional Council, Mitterrand did not disagree. That was a reason, he observed, for not taking the question into the streets. His "reason" expressed a hope, but in vain.

The archbishop of Paris, Monsignor (later Cardinal) Lustiger, entered the fray publicly to put the Church's stamp of approval on the call for a national demonstration. He gave an interview to *Le Monde*, published on June 5, in which he accused the prime minister of having gone back on his word given to Guiberteau on May 15. This was a very effective way to throw the moral authority of the Church into the preparations for a demonstration against the prime minister, who had given his approval to the Joxe-Laignel amendments. The ground was thus prepared to make the demonstration a protest against Mauroy himself and a demand from the street for his removal as prime minister.

All, including the private school organizers of the demonstration, feared it might be exploited by the National Front of Jean-Marie Le Pen and perhaps by fascist forces looking for an opportunity to launch something similar to the fascist league street march of February 6, 1934. Pierre Daniel cooperated with he Minister of the Interior Defferre and Paris Prefect of Police Guy Fougier in working out march routes from Paris's six railway stations to the Place de la Bastille. He thus obtained the government's formal authorization to hold the demonstration. In return Daniel issued strict instructions to all parents attending: "Order and dignity are absolute requirements of this manifestation." He called for "the most absolute discipline" throughout the day.

On June 24, a rainy Sunday morning, the crowds began to arrive from all over France. The National Railway system had put 150 extra trains in service; these were supplemented by 6,000 interurban buses. In the Place d'Italie, near the station where trains arrived from the west, the Church concentrated its symbolic presence in the persons of Archbishop Lustiger, Bishop of Lille Vilney, President of the Catholic Commission for School and University Students Honoré, and Guiberteau. Vilney delivered the message: "You have come in crowds to Paris to defend the freedom of teaching." He hoped the day would prove to be a decisive step toward resolving the school question.

Some 1,300,000 people took part in the Paris march, according to its organizers. This figure was not contested by the police. Mitterrand said the numbers were greater than he expected. He himself spent the day far away in the southwest (Latche) in the peace and quiet of a farm in the Landes region. He was not worried, he said. In Paris, for the photographers, all the leaders of the opposition parties marched with parents from their regions: Chirac, Girard, Veil, Lecanuet, Léotard, Gaudin, Barre, Chaban. The crowds were festive, shouting, *Pays libre, école libre* ("In a free country, free schools," that is, religious schools) and *l'école libre vivra* ("free schools will live"). There were also political slogans denouncing Mauroy, Savary, the Socialists and Mitterrand himself, whom the crowds supposed to be in the camp of the "enemy of religious schools" since he called himself a Socialist and had not publicly repudiated the law still before the Parliament.

A DEFINING CONFRONTATION

The president did not admit publicly that the demonstration changed the prospects for the enactment of school reform. Mauroy gave the date of August 15, 1984, as a reasonable target for completing its course through Parliament. The government called on the leadership of the Senate, which was controlled by the opposition, to go forward with consideration of the law as amended and approved by the National Assembly.

But the opposition parties were striving to make more of the June 24 demonstration. Chirac called for an immediate dissolution of the Parliament and new elections. He probably knew there was absolutely no chance of such a dissolution by the president, who still had a secure majority in the National Assembly. Still, the call prolonged the impression of crisis exploited by the press. President of the Senate Alain Poher, one of Mitterrand's fiercest critics, called on the president to order the withdrawal of the reform law from the Parliament.[18] Perhaps he knew that some of the president's advisers, notably Jospin, had been counseling such a course even before the June events.

Mitterrand had every reason to seek some way out of the predicament that made him subject to verbal abuse as a violator of "freedom of education." Such charges seemed to him extremely unfair, as indeed they were. He was not really a secularizer, and he had even given up the goal of unification as he yielded to the recalcitrance of the Church. The problem for the president had become not how to get the legislation enacted, but how best to get himself and the government out of the box that the Savary law, as amended by the Socialist deputies on their own initiative, created for them. The opposition was having a field day. Mitterrand found himself being spat upon in public by parents fearful that they were to lose their choice of schools for their children.

Though the president was undoubtedly searching for a convenient way to bring the matter to a close by abandoning the attempt to legislate, Poher met a curt defiance when he took his proposal to the Elysée Palace for discussion. This set the stage in the Senate for a proposal by Charles Pasqua (RPR) that the president submit the question of school reform to a national referendum under Article 11 of the Constitution. "With a great majority of the French," proclaimed Senator Pasqua, "we refuse this pretension of the state to consider children to be its property."[19] The opposition parties had every reason to believe that the Socialist reform would be voted down in such a referendum and that this would be interpreted as a cutting defeat for the president. It might lead to Mitterrand's resignation in the manner of de Gaulle, who resigned in 1969 after one of his proposals was defeated in a national referendum. On the other hand, if the president refused to submit the question to a referendum, he could be accused of acting in contempt of public opinion. In the eyes of the opposition, the Pasqua motion was an excellent way to make the most of a promising situation.

The Pasqua motion revived a debate over the scope of the president's right to invoke Article 11 as the ground for a national referendum. The words of the article allow such a procedure with reference to any "project of law dealing with public powers." When de Gaulle in 1962 had proposed using this article as the basis of a referendum on direct election of the president, many deputies, including Mitterrand, had called this extension of the article a violation of the Constitution. This had been the view of the Senate in 1962. It could logically be said of the Pasqua motion that it too asked the president to go beyond the limit set down in Article 11. Nevertheless, in a purely political vote the Senate, to no one's surprise, approved the Pasqua motion. The following day, the Socialist-Communist majority in the National Assembly rejected the Senate's initiative and called on it to take up the Savary law already sent to the Senate after its passage by the National Assembly.

During the first week of July the president traveled to the Auvergne region. Opinion surveys reported in the press that he had become the most unpopular president since the founding of the Fifth Republic. Six out of ten people polled declared their lack of confidence in him. In Puy-en-Velay, Mayor Roger Fourneyon (UDF) spared the president no criticism for the offenses being attempted against "free schools." Mitterrand answered sharply in defense of the Savary law. He denounced the parties of the opposition for their attempts to reap a political advantage from this troubling question of conscience regarding the education of children. He gave no sign of any change of position. This seemed to mean the government would go forward in the National Assembly with the final passage of the Savary law.

During the week of July 7, 1984, Mitterrand revealed in the strictest secrecy to two of his advisers how he intended to deal with the crisis. One of these was Michel Charasse, an expert on the French Constitution, serving on the president's

staff at the Elysée Palace. The other was Lionel Jospin, first secretary of the Socialist Party. They were summoned from their vacations to join the President on
twenty-four hours' notice at Latche. It is their testimony that the president was
clear in his own mind as to what he wanted to do.[20] The surprising and innovative
turn he boldly gave to the situation was therefore his own. It deserves study as an
expression of his character.

The president could not simply withdraw the Savary law. That would have
infuriated the secularizers and most of the Socialist deputies in the Parliament, the
prime minister, and the minister of education. Yet, he told his confidants, it was
absolutely necessary to bring this affair to a close. At the heart of his proposed
solution to this conundrum was a national referendum on the school question, as
urged by Pasqua and the Senate majority. But, since Article 11 of the Constitution
did not allow a referendum on such a question, he would call for a preliminary
referendum to amend the Constitution to make it include "public liberties" in the
scope of Article 11. This idea had several strengths:

1. It would concentrate public attention on the proposed "referendum on the referendum."
2. It would leave the decision on school reform to a vote by the general electorate, a recourse which the secularizers could not publicly condemn.
3. The Savary law would be suspended in its course and withdrawn from the Parliament to
   be reworked into the form of questions for a referendum.
4. It was likely the nation would vote against the secularizing school reform, and it could
   then be dropped.
5. With the Savary law withdrawn from the Parliament, it would not matter what happened
   to the "referendum on the referendum." The likelihood was that the public, if it had the
   opportunity, would vote in favor of such a change in Article 11. But it was also likely the
   Mitterrand project of a referendum on the referendum would die in the Senate, which
   had the power to kill it. The opposition parties would see that such a preliminary referendum, assuming that it received a favorable vote from the public, would strengthen the
   position of the president. He would have won a political victory. This, more than anything else, the opposition wanted to prevent.

By laying the basis for withdrawal of the Savary law, Mitterrand showed that
he was independent of the Socialist Party. In this, he gave his own interpretation to
the office of the president under the Fifth Republic and, like de Gaulle, placed it
above the parliamentary party struggle. Mitterrand left the Socialist Party "to make
itself a reason," as the French say (*se faire une raison*), while he pursued his own
course. He had already made fools of the Communists, to the great satisfaction of
Socialists. Now the Socialists were discovering their own subordination to the
president they had put into power.

Mitterrand instructed Jospin and Charasse to reveal his plan to no one during
the president's trip to Jordan and Egypt. On his return to Paris on July 11, he was
met at the airport by Mauroy. The President took the occasion of their ride to the
Elysée Palace to inform the prime minister of his plan and that he would announce
it to the nation by television the following evening. According to Thierry Pfister,
counselor to Mauroy, the prime minister was stunned.[21] The moment was clearly

approaching for the withdrawal of the Savary law from the Parliament. If that precipitated the resignation of the minister of education, what would be the effect on the prime minister?

The president gave no advance notice to Savary of his plan. He undoubtedly foresaw that Savary's resignation was inevitable. As Mitterrand prepared to move before the cameras to deliver his address from the Palace, he remarked to Mauroy, "You are to remain prime minister." Apparently he still hoped to avoid a major crisis in the government. The decision was to be Mauroy's.

In his address, the president stated: "I have the supreme duty to preserve in all circumstances national unity, respect for the Constitution and the continuity of the state. Nothing will be possible if you allow yourselves to be drawn into excessive divisions."

He considered it reasonable, he said, that the Senate majority on the Pasqua motion had proposed submitting the question of school reform to a referendum. However, "in the present state of the law" it was not possible to consult the nation on such a question under Article 11. It had long been his opinion, he continued, that the scope of referendum should be enlarged, and he had heard the same opinion expressed by many others, including members of the opposition. The moment had come to do just that. He was therefore calling on the Parliament to approve a referendum amending the Constitution to expand the scope of Article 11 to include all "great questions touching public liberties." If that amendment were approved, it would be possible to move forward on a referendum on the school question itself.

In these remarks the president did not mention the Savary law then before the Parliament. At the Ministry of Education, the minister heard the president speak on television. Savary realized that this brought to a close the project at which he had been working for three years. He told his aides, "I need to think," and retired to his study. There was really no honorable course for him except to resign.

Some inferences are to be drawn from the president's willingness not only to sacrifice a Socialist minister, but to defy a Socialist majority in the National Assembly.

The president who emerged from this defining confrontation had declared his independence of the Socialist Party. He continued to use the party as it served his purpose, but he had begun to carve into the public consciousness the image of a man who above all else took seriously his commitment to the nation at large. He had left behind his years as first secretary of the Socialist Party. He had now three years of experience as president and would run for re-election, and he endeavored to show the country an administration that rose above partisan politics, however it may displease his Socialist and Communist supporters. He was no longer the political deputy of the Fourth Republic striving to win the office of prime minister and head a government responsible to the Parliament. He had become in the trials of his new position a president concerned above all for national unity, not for the Socialist project and not for his own 110 campaign propositions. He was laying the foundation for his own continuance in office after the 1986 legislative elections, which might well return the right-wing parties to control of the National

Assembly. He was also making plausible the campaign platform on which he would run for re-election in 1988: "France united." This slogan conveyed the solicitation for votes from any and all sectors, left, center, and right.

By July 1984 France no longer had a Socialist president, but a president who had passed through the Socialist Party.

FABIUS SUCCEEDS MAUROY

The Savary law had not yet been formally withdrawn from the Parliament on July 14, when the president gave his annual interview to Yves Mourousi on the national holiday. Asked what was to happen to it, the president replied, "The Savary law will disappear when the referendum process reaches the Parliament." It was his first explicit reference to withdrawal. The president knew this would bring Savary's resignation. Would it also prompt the prime minister to resign? Though in retrospect the president has said he assumed it would, the prime minister has made it known (for example, through his aide, Thierry Pfister) that the president urged him not to resign. This he did several times during the period between July 12 and July 17.[22]

But Mauroy had discussed the question with Savary and agreed with him that the two of them would announce their resignations jointly. This would have been a public demonstration of Socialist pique. The president probably suspected what was brewing and managed to avert it. When Mauroy gave the President his final answer on the 17th, Mitterrand was ready with the name of the man to be nominated to replace him as prime minister. The President would meet Mauroy that afternoon to announce the latter's resignation and the nomination of Laurent Fabius. The Mauroy-Savary linkage was astutely pre-empted. The resignation of the indignant minister of education passed almost unnoted on the day the newspapers were filled with discussions of the dissolution of the Mauroy government and the naming of Fabius.

The nomination took all the experts by surprise. It nevertheless fitted perfectly into the emerging strategy of the president to move toward the center, away from the Socialists and the memory of the common program. Fabius was a relatively inexperienced Mitterrand recruit and protégé. At thirty-seven years and eleven months, he was the youngest prime minister in the history of republican France. As minister of the budget in 1981–82 and then as minister of industry in the third Mauroy government (1983–84) he had shown himself fully adaptable to the great turning in economic policy known as "rigor" and "modernization." Had Mitterrand named the principal author of these policies, Delors, to become prime minister, it would have been too clear a break with the electoral promises of 1981 to be palatable to the Socialist Party. Perhaps some Socialist deputies would have refused to vote for his confirmation.

In Fabius, Mitterrand had a prime minister whose youth left him free of the heavy heritage of the Socialist Party and of the Fourth Republic. This made him a more dependable ally in the period that Mitterrand foresaw clearly, since he was helping to give it direction. Socialists and Communists could no longer be counted on to bring a majority of voters to the polls. The euphoria of 1981 had led to disillusionment so deep that many years would be required to recover the hopes formerly placed in a Union of the Left.

It was necessary for Mitterrand, who was looking ahead to the presidential election of 1988, to build his appeal on a broader basis by attempting to add major sectors of center-right voters to his electorate. Michel Rocard had a strong appeal to this sector, but he was an ambitious rival with his own eye on 1988. Therefore he could not be named prime minister in 1984. His nomination to the office would come only in 1988, after Mitterrand had won reelection. By then his designation seemed logical and preordained, a perfect expression of the triumphant centrism of Mitterrand. The alliance formed in the 1990s between Rocard and Fabius sheds light on Mitterrand's choice of Fabius in 1984. He had recognized in Fabius a centrist with a Socialist Party card, an ideal ally in the new order of presidential politics, in which a reputation as a Socialist ideologue was a handicap.

Fabius was born in Paris in 1946 into a family of comfortable wealth accumulated from purchase and sale of antiques. He was raised in a home of culture and bourgeois privilege that might well have prepared him for political options to the right of the Socialists. He had a distinguished record as a student at the Superior Normal School, the University of Paris (in Political Science), and took an advanced degree in modern literature. He prepared for a career in government by attending the prestigious ENA, the National School of Administration. His first post following graduation was that of an auditor in the Council of State. During these years he had a reputation for dandyism, based partly on his impeccable style of dress. He was in his element in discussions of art and literature.

What prompted him, in 1974, to join the Socialist Party? Perhaps it was disillusion with the prospects of a career in the service of the state as it was being governed by Pompidou and Giscard. He found no inspiring role models in the parties of the right. Undoubtedly the most important influence in his decision was the emergence of Mitterrand as the leader of the reconstituted Socialist Party. Here was a cultured centrist from a privileged background similar to his own who had found in the Socialist Party promise of exciting possibilities.

Fabius was soon making a career as a functionary and then a leader of the Socialist Party. After two years as an adviser on economic questions, he became Mitterrand's "director of Cabinet." With this sponsorship he moved into the political activities of a working-class district, Seine-Maritime, and there won a seat as deputy in the National Assembly in 1978. In 1979 he became a member of the executive bureau of the Socialist Party and soon thereafter became the press spokesman for the party. This meant he had won the confidence of First Secretary Mitterrand. Alain Duhamel has written that Fabius "entered into Mitterrandism as others into the Company of Jesus."[23] He championed Mitterrand against all opponents, including those inside the Socialist Party. He was brilliant in his barbs at Giscard and in parliamentary debates with Giscard's prime minister, Raymond Barre, an economics professor who had hitherto not met his match. Fabius's refined manners covered a willingness and an ability to slaughter an adversary with brutal facts, irony, and compelling rhetoric.

By 1981 he had become one of a small group of advisers closest to the president. Fabius had the full support of Jacques Attali. Despite his youth, Fabius was rewarded after the election of Mitterrand with the budget assignment and promoted in the reshuffle of 1983 to minister of industry. He distinguished himself during this three-year period as one devoted to Mitterrand, rather than to firmly fixed principles of his own, and capable of negotiating with impressive *sang-froid* the changes of course dictated from the Elysée Palace.

Pierre Mauroy had warned the president when informed of his intention to name Fabius as the new prime minister that this would drive the Communists from the government. Perhaps the President did not care much if this happened. Perhaps he believed the Communists could be kept leashed and muzzled for yet a few more years with the offer of ministries in the new Government. Mitterrand urged Charles Fiterman, Communist minister of transport, to use his status and influence in the PCF to persuade the Politburo to stay aboard. Fiterman was thought to be one of the Communist leaders who did not want to bring to an end the participation that enabled the party to claim to be a "party of the government."

Marchais had also invested years of effort at the head of the PCF striving to justify to his comrades the alliance with the Socialist Party. However, he had recently been giving more and more public support to working class discontent with the loss of jobs attributed to "modernization." Marchais had been mocked regularly in the Socialist press and especially by Lionel Jospin for his efforts to function as party leader with one foot in the government and the other foot in the ranks of protesters against the government. This "great straddle," Jospin warned, could lead to painful muscular injury.

Taking note of the Communists' many expressions of discontent, restrained though they were and usually balanced with praise for the overall record of the government, it would seem that Marchais and the Politburo began to foresee after the spring of 1983 and the turn to "modernization" an inevitable rupture with Mitterrand. The designation of Fabius as minister of industry and then as "super-minister" to implement the program that Communists saw as a deliberate sacrifice of large sectors of the working class to the bourgeois goal of competitiveness made continuance in the government ever more questionable.

The nomination of Fabius as prime minister could only be interpreted as a signal that the change of priorities from jobs to competitiveness was being consolidated. It gave the Communists a decision, and they utilized it as a moment of clarification. Fiterman told the president that the Communists would accept posts in the new government only if assurances were given that jobs would be restored as the dominant priority of policy.[24] When this assurance was not forthcoming, the Communists announced their refusal to participate in the new government as a principled protest against the turn in policy accomplished under the names of "rigor" and "modernization."

How much opposition there was in the Politburo and the Central Committee to this decision for departure is an interesting question. At the moment of crisis in which Mitterrand named Fabius prime minister, Marchais was on vacation in Romania. He returned hastily. According to Favier and Martin-Roland, sentiment in the Politburo had already crystallized in favor of a departure from the government. They name Roland Leroy, Gaston Plissonier, and André Lajoinie as the principal advocates of this position. Fiterman was of the same view, partly for personal reasons: He did not want to continue serving as a minister. The other three Communists who had held ministerial posts, Marcel Rigout, Anicet Le Pors, and Jack Ralite, thought participation in the Government should continue. Marchais and Fiterman conducted negotiations with Fabius, handing him a written statement asking for a formal commitment of a change of economic policy. Mitterrand instructed Fabius to give no such commitment. When this was reported to the Politburo and the Central Committee, it was apparently enough to put an end to divisions of opinion. The vote was reported to be unanimous against participation. The Central Committee issued the text of the adopted resolution:

We do not believe we have the moral right to allow millions of women, men and youth in the grip of anxiety and disappointment to believe that we would be able to respond to their hopes with this government. We refuse to deceive them and to deceive ourselves.[25]

Thus came to an end the attempt of the Communist Party, at the sacrifice of its independence of criticism, to influence government policy from within. The experience was not really a test of whether a rupture with capitalism as a preparatory step for the transition to socialism is possible in France through an electoral alliance, through a Union of the Left. As the previous chapters have shown, the process of changing goals and policies during the period 1982–84 was dominated by the will of Mitterrand, whose roots were in the center of the political spectrum. By 1984 many Socialists saw him to be an independent figure quite ready to abandon goals they still held dear.

The history of France in the 1980s is the history of Mitterrand's accommodation to external and internal forces to keep France a loyal participant in European and world capitalism. It cannot be regarded as a test of the possibilities in a Union of the Left, since as early as 1977 it was clear that Mitterrand was using the Union simply as a way of undermining voter support for the Communists. In his campaigns he made no attempt to win a mandate to implement the common program. As Mitterrand rose in the three years leading up to his election in 1981, he was steadily moving away from the common program. He was not elected as a candidate of the Union of the Left. That had been dissolved in 1977–78, and the Communist Party ran its own candidate in the presidential election of 1981 (Georges Marchais, who received 15 percent of the vote in the first round).

It may have been a mistake on the part of the PCF to join in the euphoria of May 1981 and to lead its members to place their hopes in Mitterrand by consenting to join in the governments headed by the president and his prime minister, Pierre Mauroy. It was a deceit for the Communist leaders to continue to describe the PCF as "a party of the government" when it quickly became evident that Mitterrand gave it no voice in the real councils of decision at the Elysée Palace. As time went on, and more and more policy changes of the government defied Communist choices, their self-labeling as "a party of the government" became a source of mockery and ridicule.

The lesson to be learned from the experience of 1981–84 is only that the Socialist commitment of a professional and ambitious politician, formed by years as a minister in centrist, pluralist, bourgeois regimes, is not likely to be proof against the weight of tradition and the power of the international investor-class to isolate and punish any nation that starts down the road to Socialism. Socialists as well as Communists overestimated the loyalty of Mitterrand to the program he endorsed from 1972 to 1977.

It is not too harsh a judgment to conclude that Mitterrand was simply using the Socialists and the Communists to further his ambition to win the presidency. Once elected, he started his turn toward the center by giving important roles to Delors and Attali. By 1984 he was no longer a Socialist, but that did not matter to him, since he had four more years as president, free of any commitment to the Socialist Party, to prepare his candidacy for re-election in 1988. Since the Socialists also very much enjoyed the perquisites of power, most of them chose to follow him without criticism along the new Mitterrand road to a "united France," capitalist and competitive, with 10 percent unemployment, and on into a united Europe, capitalist and competitive under the hegemony of the German mark. This is clearly not what the Socialists had in mind when they elected Mitterrand their first secretary in 1971.

Some will say it could not have been otherwise. Capitalism, they will say, has too strong a grip on all the levers of power, material and spiritual, to be challenged successfully in Europe at this stage of history.

Many, like Fabius, celebrate Mitterrand's abandonment of Socialist goals and stake their claims to play leading roles in France at the end of the twentieth century and the beginning of the twenty-first century on the terrain of capitalism, promising to improve it with reforms and more democracy. In his book, *C'est an allant vers la mer* (1990), Fabius attributes to the Socialist Party a "silent" turn to social democracy during the period 1983–84. If this took place, indeed it was "silent" and undebated at any public congress or conference. The French Socialist Party never held a debate such as that of the German Socialists at Bad Godesberg, which led to a conscious abandonment by the Germans of traditional Socialist goals pursuant to a vote after debate. In France, Socialists have never formally repudiated Jean Jaurès, who taught that a Socialist Party should be the representative of the world of workers in the institutions of the Republic.

What took place in France under Mitterrand was the turning in government policy to "rigor" and "modernization" of industry with massive layoffs of workers. Fabius accepted this radical reorientation and helped to implement it as minister of industry and then as prime minister (1984–86). In his book he recognized that he had earlier joined in the project of the Socialist Party leading to the elections of 1981 for a "rupture with capitalism." By 1990 he was writing that the "silent" change to social democracy in the 1980's had been a good thing. He now calls on the Socialists to make of their party a "great modern social democratic party."[26] His formula is: The market to the extent possible, the plan to the extent necessary. He is champion of a mixed economy, which he defines as the coexistence of a predominant private sector and an important public sector; it is the market economy corrected by the intervention of public authority and some counter powers, salaried workers, unions, consumer organizations, and associations for the protection of the environment.[27]

He recognizes that such an economy is a "generator of exclusions ever more numerous" with no end in sight. Nevertheless, the intervention of the state must not prevent these "exclusions" from taking place:

The economic role of our state in this end of the twentieth century consists, on the one hand, of helping French enterprises make the changes of the new technological revolution by reducing the uncertainties in costs and risks of the mutation; and, on the other hand, of conferring on the economic system more rationality in organization and justice.[28]

"More rationality in organization" is the phrase used to refer to organization with a view to winning a place in capitalist world markets, leading to a maximization of profits for private investors. This is necessary to ensure the needed flow of new investment, since capital is to be given its freedom to go where it is best rewarded with security and profits. "Justice" is undefined, except that it does not exclude the dismissal of workers where such is the demand of "more rationality." Fabius sees without flinching that subordination of the economy to the laws of the world market leaves France with the prospect of permanent high unemployment. No capitalist country can guarantee to its workers the elementary right to work for a livelihood, the basis of self-esteem and of opportunity to develop and utilize the unique gifts of men and women. Social democracy, as defined by Fabius, accommodates to this fundamental inhumanity in liberal capitalism. If Fabius is correct in his assertion that the Socialist Party of France has accomplished silently its own "Bad Godesberg" to become a social democratic party, it would represent a profound change in the French left. For many years in France there has been a procapitalist party, clearly to the right of the Socialist Party, which calls itself the Social Democratic Party (PDS). If this is the terrain Fabius now wants the Socialist Party to occupy, a name change would seem to be in order.

If Fabius has his way and the Socialist Party openly declares itself to have changed its ideology to social democracy, this may prove to be one of the more lasting effects of the Mitterrand years on French politics. It would mean that the Socialist Party, greatly influenced by Mitterrand's own move to the center as he prepared for his campaign to be re-elected with or without the party, had decided to forget the teaching of Jaurès and meekly follow the opportunist Mitterrand, not really one of their own, into a new political identity. The political spectrum in France would never again be quite what it was from the founding of the SFIO to the election of Mitterrand.

NOTES

1.   Jean-François Lyotard, *Toward the Postmodern* (Atlantic Highlands, N.J.: Humanities Press, 1993), 87–114.

2.   Parti Socialiste, *Changer la vie* et *Le Programme commun de la gauche* (Paris: Flammarion, 1972), 273.

3.   Alain Savary, *En toute liberté* (Paris: Hachette, 1985), 11.

4.   Alain Savary reported that some "qualified observers" were of the opinion that such a meeting took place; Savary, *En toute liberté*, 79. After Savary's resignation as minister of education in 1984 following the collapse of the effort at school reform, he published *En toute liberté*.

5.   Pierre Favier and Michel Martin-Roland, *La décennie Mitterrand*, Vol. 2 (Paris: Editions du Seuil, 1991), 99.

6.   Ibid., 99.

7.   Savary, *En toute liberté*, 108.

8.   Ibid., 122.

9.   Ibid., 127.

10.   Favier and Martin-Roland, *La décennie Mitterrand*, Vol. 2, 103.

11.   François Furet and Mona Ozouf, *Dictionnaire critique de la Révolution française* (Paris: Flammarion, 1988.)

12.   Excerpts from the text of the speech appear in Savary, *En toute liberté*, 113–16.

13.   Favier and Martin-Roland, *La décennie Mitterrand*, Vol. 2, 106.

14.   Ibid., 106–107.

15.   Ibid., 112.

16.   Ibid., 113–14.

17.   Ibid., 127.

18.   Ibid., 138.

19.   Ibid., 140.

20.   Ibid., 142–45.

21.   Thierry Pfister, *La vie quotidienne à Matignon au temps de l'union de la gauche* (Paris: Hachette, 1985), 336.

22.   Ibid., 333–57.

23.   Alain Duhamel, *Les prétendants* (Paris: Gallimard, 1983), 193.

24.   Favier and Martin-Roland, *La décennie Mitterrand*, Vol. 2, 155.

25.   *Cahiers du communisme* (Paris) no. 9 (September 1984): 123.

26.   Laurent Fabius, *C'est en allant vers la mer* (Paris: Editions du Seuil, 1990), 154.

27.   Ibid., 53.

28.   Ibid., 55.

9

Completing the Turn With Fabius

Be a child of the times.
—Shakespeare
Antony and Cleopatra

When the composition of the new government to be headed by Prime Minister Fabius was announced on July 19, 1984, one name caused surprise. The new minister of education, replacing Alain Savary, who had resigned in anger at Mitterrand's withdrawal of the Savary project for education reform, was to be Jean-Pierre Chevènement. Fabius had offered this post to Michel Rocard, who preferred to remain minister of agriculture. Chevènement, mayor of Belfort, had approached Mitterrand indicating that he wanted to resume his national political service in a ministerial post. They agreed on the Ministry of Education, distant in its tasks from the economic ministries which would be implementing the policies Chevènement had objected to when he protested in 1982 and resigned in 1983. This appointment, which Fabius ratified, coming as it did from the president, may not have been entirely to the liking of the new prime minister.[1] Fabius had moved to the right wing of the Socialist Party, while Chevènement represented its extreme left wing. Mitterrand seized this opportunity to improve his relations with Socialists and secularizers estranged from him by his conduct of the school controversy.

As minister of finance in the governments of Pierre Mauroy, Jacques Delors had played a dominant role in the reorientation of the government toward austerity and subordination to the world market. He was undoubtedly disappointed not to be named prime minister in July 1984.[2] However, another opportunity for him was taking shape, as president of the European Commission with its headquarters in Brussels. He accepted this post as the new Fabius government was being formed.

This left the all-important post of minister of finance to be filled. It was given to Pierre Bérégovoy, who had the confidence of the financial community. Like Fabius, he had been supportive in 1981 of the policy of Keynesian stimulus through increasing buying power in the poorest sectors of the society. For a while in early 1983 he had favored France's departure from the European monetary system, accompanied by protectionist measures for French industry. But, like Mitterrand, Mauroy, and Fabius, he had been won over to the Delors view of France's economic future. The naming of Bérégovoy to the post being vacated by Delors was seen as an assurance that there was to be no backsliding into the 1981 policies (still advocated by the Communists) of giving priority to job preservation and job creation. "Modernization," "rationalization," and "competitiveness" would continue to be the justifications of policies of austerity for working people.

Georgina Dufoix was named to succeed Bérégovoy as minister of social affairs. Fate was preparing for this new minister and Health Minister Edmond Hervé, as well as for the prime minister himself, a cruel ordeal related to contaminated blood administered by health officials in 1985. In this period before testing for the H.I.V. virus was practiced in France, approximately 1,250 hemophiliacs were infected by contaminated transfusions. By 1995 some 400 of them had died from AIDS. In 1996 criminal charges against Fabius, Dufoix, and Hervé for "complicity in poisoning" were still awaiting final decision before the newly created Court of Justice of the Republic.[3]

Another woman, Huguette Bouchardeau, was named minister of the environment. Claude Cheysson remained minister of foreign affairs, Charles Hernu minister of defense, Robert Badinter minister of justice and Jack Lang minister of culture.

Gaston Defferre requested relief from the burdens of the Ministry of the Interior, which is responsible for police and security. He was transferred to the ministries of the plan and management of territory. There he would focus on regional development, including that of Provence and his own political base, Marseilles. Pierre Joxe, a young and energetic Mitterrandist who served for three years as coordinator of the 285 Socialist deputies in the National Assembly, was named minister of interior.

Three Socialists replaced the four Communist ministers withdrawn from the government by the decision of their party:

1. Paul Quilès succeeded Charles Fiterman as minister of transport.
2. Michel Delebarre, for three years an aide to Mauroy, declined the post of minister of employment, but agreed to accept appointment as minister of labor, employment and training (*Formation professionnelle*). Thus he took over posts hitherto held by two Communists, Jack Ralite and Marcel Rigout.
3. Jean Le Garrec succeeded Anicet Le Pors as minister of government employees (*Fonction publique*).

At the first meeting of the new Council of Ministers, the president expressed his regret that the Communists had declined his and Fabius's invitations to continue in the government. This could not be laid to any projected change in orientation, he said, because the new government headed by Fabius would be carrying out the same policies developed while Mauroy was prime minister. There was a certain cruel truth in those remarks. Both the president and the new prime minister were at pains to assure the country that the departure of the Communists did not signal any change of direction.

The change of direction, as explained in earlier chapters, had indeed taken place under Mauroy with Communist acquiescence. Many times over the next months and years, Communist criticism of government policies would be answered by reminders that the PCF had been a "party of the government" when such policies were adopted. From Communists the frequently heard rejoinder in this debate was self-criticism for having given the Mitterrand-Mauroy government formal support for too long. Within a year or two this self-condemnation had become a feature of Communist analysis of the Mitterrand experience. It was joined to the already established self-criticism of the party's slowness to denounce Stalinism after the revelations of 1956. The PCF, with the aid of these two forthright repudiations of its own policies in earlier periods, strives in the 1990s to maintain an important presence in Europe as a party that is neither Stalinist nor social democratic.[4]

The president had lanced the festering boil of school reform by announcing he would call for a "referendum on the referendum," that is, a referendum on an amendment of the Constitution to permit a referendum on school reform to be held under a broadened Article 11. To amend the Constitution in this way, it was necessary to have prior approval of the Senate as well as of the National Assembly. Though it was quickly evident that the majority in the Senate would oppose this Mitterrand solution, it was necessary to go through the motions of presenting it. To hasten the process, the proposal was sent first to the Senate, where Charles Pasqua, who had previously led the Senate in proposing on its own initiative a referendum on school reform, now had the task of explaining why this new, preliminary referendum on the amendment was unacceptable. He used slanderous rhetoric to discredit the president's proposal, referring to it as a trick of "prestidigitation." The president, he said, had been constrained to withdraw his project of *liberticide* (the killing of freedom) concerning private schools. That is the reason Mitterrand now wished to organize, at whatever cost, a referendum tailored to his own design by which he expected to refurbish his personal image and increase his powers. The Senate, Pasqua concluded, will not underwrite this abuse of the referendum procedure.[5]

In heated debate the two sides accused each other of "maneuvers." There was evidence to be cited against both. It had become a parliamentary charade with the outcome never in doubt. The Senate rejected the president's proposal along party lines. The National Assembly, where the Socialists had the most votes, approved it. This sent the measure back to the Senate, which again voted it down, allowing the proposal to be buried. It had served its purpose. Mitterrand told several people he never expected it to pass.[6]

Therefore, there was to be no referendum on the school question. Was there to be any legislation at all? Chevènement, the new minister of education, showed he had accepted Mitterrand's commitment to do nothing without the consent of the Church. (It seems likely this was a condition laid down in the discussions between him and the president before his appointment as minister was recommended to Fabius.) Chevènement believed both sides wanted a resolution. He resumed negotiations with the Church and private school representatives, Father Guiberteau and Pierre Daniel. They accepted his project, which renewed the provisions of the Debré law and of the Guermier law dealing with teachers. There would be no single, unified corps of teachers, all subject to state licensing requirements. The private schools would continue to set their own standards for teacher selection.

Claims of the private schools on local governments for financial aid lost some ground in that the Church agreed to return to the Debré-law regime, giving up the gains it seemed to be promised by the Guermier law of 1977. These promised increases had proved illusory in communes governed by the Socialists or Communists. Private schools, including Church schools, would continue to receive financial aid under the Debré regime of "contracts" negotiated with the state, that is, with the Ministry of Education.

Chevènement succeeded in persuading the Socialist deputies who had earlier defied Savary and Mitterrand that it had come down finally to this new project or nothing at all. It meant that some public funds for education would continue to go to Church schools and that there was to be no "unified and secular" national system of education. It was a hard pill to swallow, this sacrifice on the altar of national unity of an ancient and much cherished Socialist goal. With Mitterrand having the last word, there seemed to be no alternative.

The National Assembly passed the Chevènement proposal. The Senate amended it to restore the abandoned provisions of the Guermier law. This sent the measure back to the National Assembly, where the Socialist majority, with discipline restored, removed the Senate amendments and on December 20, 1984, passed it as Chevènement had proposed. It was an inglorious conclusion to three and a half years of work and debate.

This outcome did not mean the government intended to neglect the quality of education in the public schools. On the contrary, the new prime minister made this a major focus in his general strategy to modernize French industry and prepare it for competition on the world market. He announced in January 1985 a goal of training all students in the use of computers, "*l'informatique pour tous.*" This involved budgeting money for the purchase of 100,000 computers to be placed in public schools. As minister of education, Chevènement insisted this be balanced by a revival of emphasis on the basics of reading, writing and arithmetic. He was not favorably impressed by reforms in teaching methodology advocated by progressive elements in the teachers unions. Edmond Maire reproached the minister for his simplistic, backward-looking ideas. However, many experienced teachers welcomed this insistence on keeping hold of the basics as the new reliance on computers entered the classroom. This debate, in which Chevènement succeeded in restoring an environment of respect for old-fashioned intellectual discipline, showed one of the reasons he had accepted the unpleasant task of concluding the fiasco created by the impasse on financing of private schools.

Mitterrand and Fabius had completed the turn away from any rupture with capitalism.[7] The twenty months of the Fabius government, from July 1984 to the legislative elections of March 1986, were a dreary, day-to-day struggle to strengthen the French economy by encouraging managers to do what was necessary to reduce their costs and increase their efficiency. This meant more layoffs and unemployment, with frequent expressions of sympathy from the government and explanations that French industry would be enabled in this way to prosper, outstrip its foreign competitors, and ultimately reverse the rising unemployment curve. With Bérégovoy at Finance and the "modernizer" Fabius as prime minister, economic policy was hardly distinguishable from what it had been under Raymond Barre and Giscard d'Estaing. The president, with his sights set on the presidential election, stressed that he was determined to show the country that his regime, elected as the standard bearer of the left, could, after all, provide a continuity of "good government," thus creating the conditions necessary to a true democratic system of free elections. He was pleased to be changing the nation's idea of what "the left" meant in French politics: "Instead of conquering power once or twice in a half century, thrown up by brief movements of crisis, the left will appear as the permanent guarantee of a good government of the country."[8]

The president's idea of the French left had evolved to something very close to the definition given it by Michel Rocard. During a television interview in the United States, Rocard had reassuringly characterized his Socialist Party of 1984 as not much different from the left wing of the American Democratic Party. From Rocard this was praise, not criticism, and it summed up the Mitterrand "revolution." The conclusion is inescapable that Mitterrand, with full support from Fabius and the First Secretary of the Socialist Party Jospin, was quietly burying 100 years of tradition shaped by the beloved Jaurès, Jules Guesde, Jean Longuet, and many others.

Given the very difficult trials facing Mitterrand and Fabius in 1983-86, it is not surprising that rank-and-file Socialists withheld public criticism of the president as this fundamental reorientation of the Socialist Party took place in consequence of policies adopted by the Mitterrand governments. Representatives of the right were not so considerate. In an interview for the economic journal *L'Expansion*, Jean Boissonnat asked the president whether Socialism retained in his eyes the same definition it had had before his election. Mitterrand replied:

Yes, socialism is the search for a true political, economic and social democracy, more liberty, responsibility and knowledge for each and everyone; the mastery or control by the nation of the great means of production; a just partition of profits; national solidarity without failure; the end of class privileges.[9]

It is a pity Boissonnat did not ask Mitterrand what had been done to put an end to the class privileges of the bourgeoisie. But that is not the kind of question to be raised by the editor-in-chief of *L'Expansion*. In fact, the readers of *L'Expansion* and the bourgeoisie in general in France, Britain, and the United States, were finding that "socialism" à la Mitterrand was a divine surprise. Under his leadership, capitalism was safe, not at all menaced by the high-sounding words with which he glibly answered questions as to his continuing fidelity to Socialism.

Mitterrand's phrase, "the mastery or control by the nation of the great means of production," had a Socialist sound. Yet what did it mean in the light of his policies as president? The nationalizations of 1981, added to those of the liberation era following the German occupation (e.g., Renault Automobile), created a mixed economy in which all firms, whether privately or publicly owned, were expected to meet the requirement of producing a profit (*rentabilité*). After abandoning the 1981 attempt to practice "Keynesianism in one country," Mitterrand, accepting the recommendations of Delors, steadily moved toward France's inclusion in the capitalist competition of the European common market. "Mastery by the nation" meant nothing other than using the powers of the government to assist French companies to reduce their costs of production so as to improve their profitability in international capitalist markets.

Typically, the failing nationalized companies benefited from infusions of new capital drawn from public revenue. They received loans from the nationalized banks on favorable terms. Mitterrand insisted on the necessity of reducing the burden of assessments for taxes and social security, *prélèvements*, borne by all French companies. Part of this burden was henceforth to be shifted to society at large, thereby improving the profit potential of companies by reducing an important item in their costs of production.

The bulk of this revenue lost to the state in the budget for 1985 was recovered by increasing taxes on gasoline and fuel oil and by increasing the rates paid by the general public for services from the state-owned telephone company. The value of the dollar relative to the French franc had risen sharply, causing all oil products to increase in price in France, since they are imported. Mitterrand surprisingly called this increase in the cost of fuel a piece of good fortune, because the increase in the tax on fuels more or less matched the rate of increase in the base price of fuel, determined by the market. Thus it could be claimed that the tax portion in the greatly increased amount per liter paid by the customer was no greater a percentage of the final price than it had been in previous years.[10]

Wage raises to keep up with inflation were to be braked, over opposition from all the labor unions, by abandoning the cost of living adjustment, the hard-won indexation of automatic wage raises on the rise in prices. In the future, wage levels would be fought out on terms more favorable to the employers. Unemployment was high (more that 10 percent by 1984) and rising every year.

The potency of the Western European capitalist market to shape policies in participating nations like France was being demonstrated. Since job security was a handicap in capitalist competition, Mitterrand governments strove to increase the freedom (called "flexibility ") of employers to reassign and lay off workers, against opposition from the labor unions. Mitterrand's "mastery by the nation of the means of production" was used by the government to strengthen the hand of employers against workers. This was justified as an unfortunate necessity created by the realities of competition in the common market. Tears were shed in public speeches with expressions of hope and confidence that ultimately there would be good jobs for everybody.

Many analysts who write in the tradition of free-market capitalism have found realism and wisdom in Mitterrand's accommodation to the pressures brought to bear on France by the international investment community. Jeffrey Sachs, professor at Harvard's Kennedy School, collaborated with Charles Wyplosz in an *Economic Policy* article published in 1986, "The Economic Consequences of President Mitterrand." They gave Mitterrand high marks for ordering the Socialist "turn-around " in 1982–83 and drew general conclusions unfavorable for the working class: Unemployment is now inevitable, especially where labor unions are strong; and unemployment is essential to making the market economy "work" in a highly developed country like France.[11]

It is becoming clear that the technological revolution, which seems to carry such promise of increased efficiency of production, also carries the threat of permanent exclusion of millions from work. The Mitterrand governments proved unable to deal with this problem. If the parties of the right under the presidency of Jacques Chirac, elected to succeed Mitterrand in 1995, are no more successful, the stage will have been set for a return of the left to power. That will be the moment for a germinal France to live up to its promise, which it failed to do under Mitterrand.

NOTES

1.   Jacques Attali, *Verbatim: Chronique des années 1981–1986*, Vol. 1 (Paris: Fayard, 1993), 672.

2.   Pierre Favier and Michel Martin-Roland, *La décennie Mitterrand*, Vol. 2 (Paris: Editions du Seuil, 1991), 158; Attali, *Verbatim*, 670–71.

3.   *Le Monde* (Paris), September 22, 1994; *L'Express* (Paris), June 22, 1995.

4.   Robert Hue, *Communisme: La mutation* (Paris: Editions Stock, 1995). Hue was elected national secretary of the Communist Party of France in 1994.

5.   Favier and Martin-Roland, *La décennie Mitterrand*, Vol. 2, 181.

6.   Attali, *Verbatim*, 668; Favier and Martin-Roland, *La décennie Mitterrand*, Vol. 2, 182.

7.   Patrick McCarthy writes: "As a left-wing party the PS was unable to escape the fate of the Western European left in general. Certain historical options have been closed but surviving the depression, helping modernize the French economy and encouraging solidarity will stand as the hallmarks of the Socialists in power." Patrick McCarthy (ed.), *The French Socialists in Power, 1981–1986* (New York: Greenwood Press, 1987), 195.

8.   Interview in *Liberation* (Paris), May 10, 1984.

9.   "Mitterrand parle," *L'Expansion* (Paris) No. 249 (16 November-6 December, 1984), 65.

10.   Favier and Martin-Roland, *La décennie Mitterrand*, Vol. 2, 186.

11.   Jeffrey Sachs and Charles Wyplosz, "The Economic Consequences of President Mitterrand," *Economic Policy*, Vol. 2 (April 1986), 296–300.

Glossary of Acronyms

CAI: Center of Institutional Action. An organization in the 1960s of the democratic and Socialist left.

CERES: Center for Socialist Studies and Research. A principal revolutionary faction within the SFIO.

CFDT: French Democratic Confederation of Labor. The major national labor union confederation close to the Socialist Party.

CGT: General Confederation of Labor. An important national labor union confederation close to the Communist Party.

CIR: Convention of Republican Institutions. A political group formed in the 1960s out of the CAI, headed by François Mitterrand.

CNAL: National Committee of Lay Action. Group organized to promote the secularization of education.

CNEC: National Catholic Education Commission.

CNPF: National Council of French Employers.

COMINTERN: The Communist International. The Third International, established by Lenin and the Bolsheviks.

DST: French Counter-Intelligence Service.

EIP: Public Interest Establishment. A grouping of public and private schools in a particular region, proposed in 1982.

EMS: European monetary system. System established in the 1970s by several Western European governments to attempt to narrow exchange fluctuations among their currencies.

ENA: National School of Administration. Prestigious graduate school for training candidates for careers in government and business.

ENS: Superior Normal School. Prestigious school of higher education in Paris with special focus on philosophy and literature.

FEN: National Education Federation.

FGDS: Federation of the Democratic and Socialist Left. The electoral alliance Mitterrand created for his presidential candidacy in 1965.

IGF: Tax on Large Fortunes. Tax on real and personal property of the wealthier classes; one was enacted in 1981.

MNPGD: National Movement of Prisoners of War and Deportees. A movement created during World War II to promote the interests of French prisoners of war in which Mitterrand played a leading role.

MRG: Radical Party of the Left. The left wing of the (centrist) Radical Party.

MRP: Popular Republican Movement. A political party representing liberal Catholic views.

PCF: French Communist Party, formed after a split in the SFIO at the Congress of Tours in 1920.

PS: Socialist Party, the name adopted by the SFIO in 1970.

PSA: Autonomous Socialist Party. A party formed by about one-fourth of the members of the SFIO when the party split in 1958.

PSU: Socialist Unity Party. Strongly anti-capitalist party formed in 1960 by some leftist members of SFIO and others. Merged into the renewed Socialist Party in 1971.

RPF: Rally of the French People. A Gaullist party created in 1947.

RPR: Rally for the Republic. Name taken by the Gaullist party after reorganization in 1976 under the leadership of Jacques Chirac.

SFIO: French Section of the Worker Interna tional. Founded in 1905 from a fusion of several Socialist groups, it was thereafter France's principal Socialist party. In 1970, its name was changed to Socialist Party.

SME: European monetary system. See EMS.

SMIC: Minimum Interprofessional Salary of Growth. Minimum wage in France, fixed by legislation.

TVA: Value Added Tax. A kind of sales tax.

UDF: Union for French Democracy. Created in 1976 by supporters of Giscard d'Estaing. Aimed to occupy centrist position, but is frequently allied with the RPR.

UDSR: Democratic and Socialist Union of the Resistance. A centrist political group founded by René Pleven in 1944–45. Mitterrand joined it in 1947.

UNAPEL: National Union of Associations of Parents of Students in Free Schools. Association of private-school pupils' parents.

UNEF: National Union of Students of France.

Selected Bibliography

Attali, Jacques. *Verbatim: Chronique des années 1981–1986*, Vol.1. Paris: Fayard, 1993.

Becker, Lucille F. *Louis Aragon*. New York: Twayne Publishers, 1971.

Cadiot, Jean-Michel. *Mitterrand et les communistes*. Paris: Ramsay, 1994.

Courtois, Stéphane, and Marc Lazar, *Histoire du Parti communiste français*. Paris: Presses Universitaires de France, 1995.

Daix, Pierre. *Aragon*. Paris: Flammarion, 1994.

Debray, Régis. *Loués soient nos seigneurs*. Paris: Gallimard, 1996.

Duhamel, Alain. *Les prétendants*. Paris: Gallimard, 1983.

Duras, Marguerite. *The War: A Memoir*. Translated from French by Barbara Bray. New York: Pantheon Books, 1986.

Fabius, Laurent. *C'est en allant vers la mer*. Paris: Editions du Seuil, 1990.

Favier, Pierre and Michel Martin-Roland, *La décennie Mitterrand*, 3 vols. Paris: Editions du Seuil, 1990 (Vol. 1), 1991 (Vol. 2), and 1996 (Vol. 3).

Friend, Julius W. *Seven Years in France: François Mitterrand and the Unintended Revolution, 1981–1988*. Boulder, Colo.: Westview Press, 1989.

Furet, François. *Le passé d'une illusion*. Paris: Robert Laffont/Calmann Lévy, 1995.

Giesbert, Franz-Olivier. *François Mitterrand ou la tentation de l'histoire*. Paris: Editions du Seuil, 1977.

———. *Le Président*. Paris: Editions du Seuil, 1990.

Laughland, John. *The Death of Politics: France Under Mitterrand*. London: Michael Joseph, 1994.

Martelli, Roger. *Communisme français: Histoire sincère du PCF 1920–1984*. Paris: Messidor, Editions Sociales, 1984.

Mauroy, Pierre. *A gauche*. Paris: Albin Michel, 1985.

McCarthy, Patrick (ed.). *The French Socialists in Power, 1981–1986*. New York: Greenwood Press, 1987.

Mitterrand, Danielle. *En toutes libertés*. Paris: Ramsey, 1996.

Mitterrand, François. *Ma part de vérité*. Paris: Fayard, 1969.

———. *L'abeille et l'architecte*. Paris: Flammarion, 1978.

———. *Ici et maintenant*. Paris: Fayard, 1980.

————. *Mémoires interrompus*. Paris: Editions Odile Jacob, 1996.

Nay, Catherine. *Le noir et le rouge*. Paris: Bernard Grasset, 1984.

————. *Les sept Mitterrand*. Paris: Bernard Grasset, 1988.

Péan, Pierre. *Une jeunesse française: François Mitterrand, 1934–1947*. Paris: Fayard, 1994.

Pfister, Thierry. *La vie quotidienne à Matignon au temps de l'union de la gauche*. Paris: Hachette, 1985.

Roucaute, Yves. *Histoires socialistes de la Commune de Paris à nos jours*. Paris: Editions Ledrappier, 1987.

Savary, Alain. *En toute liberté*. Paris: Hachette, 1985.

Starr, Peter. *Logics of Failed Revolt: French Theory After May '68*. Stanford, Calif.: Stanford University Press, 1995.

Index

Aragon, Louis: Breton, André, relationship with, 44–51; central committee of PCF, member of, 53; Khrushchev's denunciation of Stalin, reaction to, 53–54; Matisse, Henri, tribute to, 52; military decorations, 44; mobilization in 1914, 44; Nazi–Soviet pact, reaction to, 51; PCF, membership in, 45–46; poet of the Resistance, 52; portrait of Stalin by Picasso, 53; the Prague Spring, role in, 55; socialist realism, support for, 50; Soviet Union, attitude toward, 47, 49–50, 53–55; surrealism, birth of, 44–45; Thorez, Maurice, support from, 53; Triolet, Elsa, relationship with, 49–53. Works: *Les beaux quartiers*, 51; *Les cloches de Bâle*, 48; *Front rouge*, 47; *Histoire parallèle de l'URSS et des Etats-Unis*, 54; *Le mouvement perpétuel*, 45; *Le paysan de Paris*, 45; *La peinture au défi*, 46; *Le roman inachevé*, 49, 53–54; *La semaine sainte*, 54

Attali, Jacques: Fabius, Laurent, support for, 147; the other policy, opposition to, 116; special counselor, 77. Works: *Verbatim*, 116

Auroux, Jean: Labor code, reform of, 94–95; minister of labor, 94

Badinter, Robert, 154, 180

Bérégovoy, Pierre: on Mitterrand's campaign staff, 72; chief of staff, 77; minister of finance, 153–54; minister of social affairs, 108; the other policy, support for, 112

Blum, Léon, 43

Breton, André, 44–51

CERES (Center for Socialist Studies and Research): Congress of Epernay, 37–40; Congress of Nantes, 68–69; Congress of Valence, 82–83; Union of the Left, support for, 62–63

Chevènement, Jean-Pierre: Congress of Epernay, 37–40; Congress of Metz, 71; freeze of investment, condemnation of, 97; minister of education, 153, 155–56; minister of industry and research, 108; radicalization of policy, support for, 99–100; resignation in protest, 113–14; rigor, opposition to, 103, 112, 122–23; Union of the Left, support for, 55–58, 62–63

CIR (Convention of Republican Institutions), 25, 30, 31, 33, 40

Communist Party of France: accord with Socialist Party, 78–79; Argenteuil in 1966, 55–56; Champigny manifesto, 57; common program, promotion of, 61–63; decentralization, support of, 89; founding at Congress of Tours,

About the Author

JOSEPH P. MORRAY is a retired teacher, lawyer, and writer. After completing studies at the United States Naval Academy, Harvard Law School, and the University of Paris, he began an academic career at the University of California at Berkeley. Morray gave this up to go with his family to Cuba to teach at the University of Havana and write a book on the Cuban Revolution. He also taught at the University of Chile. In his eight books, he has explored modern attempts at socialist revolutions in Latin America, Siberia, Algeria, and France.

ISBN 0-275-95735-7

90000>

EAN

9 780275 957353

HARDCOVER BAR CODE